Date Due

Bayfield			
DEC 27			
MAY 1 9			
FEB 9 - 1980			
EB 1 9 1980			
ZUR Feb91			
DEC 1 6 '97			

THE RENAISSANCE OF CANADIAN HISTORY

A BIOGRAPHY OF A.L. BURT

A.L. Burt in his study

LEWIS H. THOMAS

The Renaissance of Canadian History

A BIOGRAPHY OF A.L. BURT

UNIVERSITY OF TORONTO PRESS
TORONTO AND BUFFALO

© University of Toronto Press 1975
Toronto and Buffalo
Printed in Canada

The author wishes to thank
the editor of
The University of Minnesota Alumni News
for permission to reproduce the
photograph of Professor Burt

Library of Congress Cataloging in Publication Data
Thomas, Lewis Herbert, 1917–
    The renaissance of Canadian history.
    'A.L. Burt: a bibliography': p.
    Includes index.
    1. Burt, Alfred LeRoy, 1888–1971. I. Title.
    F1024.6.B8T47   971.06'07'2024 [B]   74-79988
    ISBN 0-8020-5304-1

For

FORREST

MARY

JOHN ARTHUR

and

JOAN

Contents

Foreword

Every biography is a part of history large or small depending on the person, and if it is to live, it should be recorded like the whole story of mankind, without fear, favour, or affection. That would have been the view of the late A.L. Burt, the subject of this book, to whom I owed much as a teacher of history and for whom I had such affection as a lifelong friend. Admittedly, I am a partial witness, disqualified from contributing to Professor Thomas' text, but perhaps I may add a few words of prologue, to say how much I have enjoyed reading it and how grateful I am to him for having written it.

There must be few biographies which reveal a man's acts and ideas so directly as this one. This is due in part to the letters referred to in the preface, written by Burt to his talented helpmate, Dorothy Burt, and carefully conserved by the family. Those written in 1918–19 relate to his overseas service with the First Canadian Tanks Battalion and the Khaki University. Beginning in 1921 they cover the years of Burt's absence from home every summer to do research in the Public Archives in Ottawa. His initiative in using the latent wealth of the Archives set a pattern for many other Canadian historians and gave leadership to a revision of Canada's early history through a return to original sources. After many summers of painstaking perusal of a mass of unorganized documentary material, dull in part and dusty, but containing the very substance of authentic history in the hands of a man who could fit the pieces into a broad picture, this phase of Burt's historical labours came to a fruitful end in the publication in 1933 of *The Old Province of Quebec*. His mastery of the period was confirmed.

In effect, Burt's venture into the Archives became a 'movement,' the significance of which for Canadian history is evident from the names of those who joined in. From the letters, one can identify as mutually helpful friends and members of the estival coterie, the following (among them several Canadian Rhodes scholars who had shared Burt's experience at Oxford): G.B. Brebner, G.W. Brown, George Glazebrook, D.C. Harvey, Harold A. Innes, W.P.M. Kennedy, W.A. Mackintosh, Chester Martin, Duncan McArthur, J.L. McDougall, A.S. Morton, Chester New, George M. Smith, Frank Underhill, and G.E. Wilson.

Lester B. Pearson, a history don at the time, jokingly said of Burt's long hours with the documents, 'Professor Burt was planning to copy all of the National Archives and then set fire to the building, so that he would have a complete monopoly.'

I knew 'A.L.' Burt first and best as a gifted and enthusiastic teacher in the University of Alberta at a time when life on that young campus was interrupted by World War I.

In 1917, fresh from an officers' training course at Sarcee Camp, he put us through our daily drill in Convocation Hall before he left to serve with a newly formed universities' Tanks Battalion. It amused us that his deep professorial voice, produced with chin tucked in, used to break under his energetic commands into a falsetto squeak.

Upon the return of peace, he came back from the Khaki University to resume his teaching and advocacy of history as a discipline and to head the Department himself until 1930 when he left for an even longer career at the University of Minnesota.

Consequently, I thought of Burt first as a Canadian historian (as he was by birth and practice) but recognized that his years at Oxford had given him a bent for the story of the British Empire as it developed into the Commonwealth. It is significant that his first published book (1913) was entitled *Imperial Architects* and his last and largest work (1956) *The Evolution of the British Empire and Commonwealth from the American Revolution*. Relations of both Canada and the Commonwealth with the United States became an inevitable addition to his themes and writings.

Professor Thomas exposes a third dimension to Burt's interests, a deep concern with contemporary international problems, which developed from his preoccupation with the League of Nations. His views were much in demand and he was glad to share them in public lectures and professional journals. In this phase, he was preoccupied with the interdependence of all mankind and alarmed by the fate which might overtake our civilization if we could not unite to solve our common problems. He foresaw the coming of World War II and warned that: 'Our civilization will go too, and it may be nearer the end than we think... '; 'The one gigantic problem which threatens to drag us down is the problem of establishing justice and order in place of chaos which reigns in the world of international affairs....' He asked: 'Is it possible to set up an international government?'

One could interject that the question is still pertinent, but the problems to be solved by united action are now expressed in such studies as *The Limits to Growth* in terms of over-population, exhaustion of natural resources, destruction of our natural habitat, and so on – but it is time to encourage you to turn to the preface and to the full story which Professor Thomas tells so well.

7 MARCH 1974   ROLAND MICHENER

Preface

The objective of this work is to present an impression of the thought and career of an historian well known in his day in Canada and the United States, Alfred LeRoy Burt (1888–1971), who taught at the University of Alberta from 1913 to 1930 and at the University of Minnesota from 1930 to 1957. As such, it is hoped that it will be regarded as a useful contribution to the intellectual history of Canada, for historians have always occupied a prominent but as yet largely unrecognized role in that history. In the definition of the Canadian identity, historians have occupied a strategic position as the interpreters and custodians of the collective memory of Canadians.

Burt was not the founder of a school of historical interpretation, but he was a key figure in the renaissance period of Canadian historical scholarship which spans the second and third decades of the twentieth century. His *Old Province of Quebec*, published in 1933, was the first fruit of the intensive cultivation of the primary sources assembled over the years in the Public Archives of Canada by the Dominion archivists Douglas Brymner and Arthur Doughty. In his teaching at Alberta and Minnesota, Burt was also a formative influence on the thinking of successive generations of students.

Extensive extracts from Burt's letters to his wife and from his public lectures and articles have been reproduced in this study. The letters to Mrs Burt were written twice a week whenever he was away from home, and hence have a diary-like quality. Each letter begins with a reference to family matters or other concerns not germane to this inquiry. The total collection has been carefully perused, and references to public affairs, contacts with professional colleagues, and reading and research activities have been included in the extracts.

The project originated with a suggestion by Mrs Joan Jenness of Ottawa, Professor Burt's youngest daughter, who has presented the correspondence to the Public Archives of Canada.

I am greatly indebted to Mrs Jenness for encouragement and advice, for renewing an association which began when I was a student of her father in Minneapolis, and for demonstrating that she maintains the tradition of warm-hearted hospitality which her parents extended to me and to many other students at the University of Minnesota.

Mrs Forrest Johnson and Mrs Mary Leinbach, Professor Burt's other two daughters, read the manuscript and made helpful suggestions. Among those who supplied valuable information or criticism were Professor Herbert Heaton of Minneapolis, a former chairman, and Miss Louise Olsen of Sioux Falls, South Dakota, a former secretary, of the Department of History, University of Minnesota, my colleague Professor L.G. Thomas of the University of Alberta, Professor Carl Berger of the University of Toronto, Professor Roger Graham of Queen's University, the archives staff of the University of Minnesota Libraries, and Mr Frank Strowbridge, former sales manager of Gage Educational Publishing Limited of Toronto. Mr James Parker, Archivist of the University of Alberta, arranged for access to the records in his custody and contributed personal information on the Burt family relationships. I am indebted to Miss Jean Wilson of the University of Toronto Press for expert editorial assistance. The secretarial staff of the Department of History, University of Alberta, aided in the typing. My wife's proofreading and preparation of the index is gratefully acknowledged. I am also grateful to the Right Honourable Roland Michener for his perceptive foreword.

This book has been published with the assistance of a grant from the Humanities Research Council of Canada, using funds provided by the Canada Council, and with the assistance of the Publications Fund of the University of Toronto Press.

LHT

THE RENAISSANCE OF CANADIAN HISTORY

A BIOGRAPHY OF A.L. BURT

1

Family Roots and
Educational Experiences

The year was 1913 and the University of Alberta in Edmonton was beginning its sixth session in September, housed in its first two buildings, Athabasca Hall and Assiniboia Hall, overlooking the tree-clad banks of the North Saskatchewan River, with a student enrolment of 425 and a teaching staff of twenty-five in the Faculty of Arts and Sciences. The campus must have seemed graceless and crude to the new lecturer in history, Alfred LeRoy Burt, familiar with the ordered solidity of an eastern Canadian university and the mellow perfection of an Oxford college. Only the impressive campus plan in the President's office revealed the vision of a well-landscaped symmetry of buildings, towers, and quadrangles.

But everything was new in Alberta in that year, and the province, organized only eight years previously, had no settled traditions and no firmly established organizations of power and patterns of life. Large-scale immigration was still continuing; thousands of pioneer homesteaders were engrossed in 'proving up' their lands. As in the other prairie provinces, there had been a frenzied speculation in town lots which had collapsed earlier that year, but the promise of uninterrupted economic progress was guaranteed by the finest-ever wheat harvest, the petroleum discoveries south of Calgary, and flourishing lumber, coal, natural gas, livestock, and fur production. Over forty-seven hundred miles of railways were under construction.

Edmonton had a population of about 60,000 in 1913 and, like other prairie cities, seemed to be in the vanguard of urban growth in Canada.

The population was youthful, energetic, optimistic, sociable; and proud of its freedom from the restraining habits, traditions, and attitudes of the custom-hardened East. A perceptive English observer was struck by the heterogeneity of the place at this time:

On the pavement, rough railway men, miners, and odd customers of every kind jostle well-dressed women and smart business men. It is just as much a curious mixture as the buildings. Imposing looking banks, small wooden shacks, and virgin bush, one next to the other, are still to be seen on some of the main streets of this wonderful city. ... Edmonton strikes me as a pleasanter place to live in than most provincial towns in England. It is certainly every bit as civilized, with its broad asphalted streets, large churches, banks, shops, and excellent tram service.[1]

Across the river from the university campus, the Lieutenant Governor had moved into a handsome residence which, with the imposing Legislative Building still under construction, symbolized the emergence of the capital city and province from the primitive stage of frontier development. It was an exciting setting for a new university and, to young academics, a stimulating environment for personal achievement.

A profound transformation could also be detected in the nation itself at this time. Although the eastern provinces had long passed the stage of pioneer agricultural settlement, it was only in these first years of the new century that industrialization and urbanization could be regarded as significant facts of life in Canada. Factory production, extensive new transcontinental railway construction, trade union organization, town-planning activity, women's rights agitation, and the Canadian Club movement were some of the visible portents of a new era in Canadian history. Less tangible but no less revolutionary was the burgeoning consciousness of national identity and national destiny, which was particularly noticeable in the West.

The literary event of 1913 was the completion of the 22-volume historical work *Canada and Its Provinces*, the largest co-operative effort ever undertaken by Canada's leading Anglophone and Francophone intellectuals. Among the contributors were a number of university teachers, but by no means the majority, for Canadian history was still of peripheral interest in university departments of history and there was still no national organization of professional historians.

There were additional contributions to Canadian literature in the same year by Charles G.D. Roberts, Sir Gilbert Parker, Stephen Leacock, Arthur Stringer, Sir George W. Ross, Marjorie Pickthall, Beckles Willson,

Hector Garneau, Arnold Haultain, Colonel William Wood, J.S. Ewart, N.E. Dionne, the Honourable Thomas Chapais, Isaac Cowie, Lawrence J. Burpee, and others. Among works singled out by the editor of the *Canadian Annual Review* as 'the chief Canadian books of the year' was one by the young lecturer in history at Edmonton, entitled *Imperial Architects*. 'This book,' the editor of the *Review* wrote, 'fills its own place in the greatly growing roll of Canadian publications ... It deals with the problem of Imperial construction, with the growth of the Empire, with the schemes of closer union – Defence, Tariffs, Federation, Imperial Council, etc.'[2] Even more important than this tribute was the brief but favourable reaction in the *Review of Historical Publications Relating to Canada*, whose stern application of high standards had challenged so much shallow scholarship. 'It is to be hoped,' wrote the reviewer, 'that Mr Burt will deal later with proposals subsequent to 1887,' the terminal point of the study.[3]

Alfred LeRoy Burt was born on 28 November 1888, at Listowel, a town of about 2600 inhabitants, in the northern part of Perth County, Ontario. The area had a population of mixed origin – English, Scottish, German, and Irish. His father, Christian Kimpel Burt, was a drygoods merchant in Listowel, in partnership with his half-brother John Croft Burt. Their father, Johann Bört (his children spelt it Burt), was born in Oberant Ehringer, Württemberg, Germany, and had migrated as a young man to Canada in 1846, where he settled on a farm at Gowanstown in Wallace Township. He was twice married, and his second wife, A.L. Burt's grandmother, Salome Kimpel, was also of south German origin. A.L. Burt's father married Sarah Large, a girl of Irish extraction, the daughter of a furniture factory owner. She was a determined young woman who worked in her father's factory to finance her studies in music and art at Hamilton Ladies' College. A gifted pianist, she nourished in her son a lifelong love of music and gave him the training which permitted him to find inspiration and relaxation at the keyboard of the piano.

Like many other distinguished Canadians of his generation, Burt's earliest education was in a small-town school. He attended the elementary school in Listowel, but about 1898 the family moved to Toronto, where in due course C.K. Burt became head buyer in the Canadian firm of Tip Top Tailors. A.L. and his brother Arthur attended city schools, and in 1906 he graduated from Humberside Collegiate, winning the first Edward Blake scholarship in mathematics and science. That year Burt enrolled in Victoria College at the University of Toronto, but after a year in science he switched to the honours course in modern history. His courses included Roman history, medieval and modern history, English and Canadian constitutional history, economics, and German and English literature. A student of George M. Wrong, he became a member of the History Club which Wrong had founded in 1904 to promote informal contacts between staff and students, of the type which Burt was to organize later at the University of Alberta. Other extracurricular activities included piano performances, tennis, and the presidency of Victoria's largest student organization, the Union Literary Society. One contemporary remembered him as 'a poet with a gift for thought and the firm technique of a mature mind.'[4] A handwritten notebook of his efforts in the composition of verse survives in his personal papers.

Tragedy touched the Burt family when the younger son, Arthur, was drowned in a swimming accident during his first year at university. A.L. thus became an only child, bearing that emotional burden as the supporter of the parents' hopes which the only child alone can comprehend. At this time his mother's influence was particularly intense, and she encouraged him to compete for the most coveted prize available to Canadians, the Rhodes Scholarship. In 1910 he was the unanimous choice of the University of Toronto's selection committee from among the graduates of that year. A press notice of this event deserves quotation:

'In view of the oft-heard condemnation of musical study and athletics as being a waste of time and energy and as distracting with disastrous results the minds of young people from more practical things, it is interesting to record the fact that Mr. Alfred LeRoy Burt, the brilliant young graduate of the Ontario Provincial University, to whom has fallen the honor of being selected as Rhodes Scholar from the institution, is both a trained athlete and an accomplished musician. Since a mere child he has been an enthusiastic student of music, and he acted as accompanist for the Alexandra Choir of Toronto, a chorus of 400 voices, for over a year. When Gipsy Smith was in Toronto last May at Massey Hall, Mr. Burt was the pianist. He often appears in concerts, and his playing has been spoken of very highly by competent critics. He has had a number of flattering offers to enter upon a musical career, but prefers the studious life of a scholar. In athletics he has always taken a prominent part, being one of the bright particular stars of the university gymnasium and an active worker in committee and on the field and ice. Lawn tennis is his forte, however, he having been in the finals several times, but losing the championship by narrow margins....[5]

It is probable that his university experience was already leading Burt beyond the normal thought pattern of middle-class Victorian Ontario and the narrower tenets of his parents' Methodist faith. But he remained a loyal and affectionate son, and he never abandoned the best qualities of the family tradition – a strong commitment to high principles and to the disciplined life.

In winning the Rhodes Scholarship for Ontario, Burt joined the highly select group of young Canadians who had received this award since 1904 under the terms of Cecil Rhodes' will. In the mind of the founder, a period of study at Oxford would have the great advantage to young colonists, irrespective of race or religion, 'for giving breadth to their views, for their instruction in life and manners, and for instilling into their minds the advantage to the Colonies as well as to the United Kingdom of the retention of the unity of the Empire.'[6] Though the passing years have destroyed Rhodes' hope of Empire unity, it was a goal supported by many English-speaking Canadians at the time, for they did not regard it as incompatible with their growing sense of nationality.[7] Burt shared Rhodes' ideal only in the sense that he was to adopt a practical-minded view of the desirability of a multinational political association of which the Empire was the sole example before World War I.

The university authorities assigned Burt to Corpus Christi College, one of the smallest in Oxford, founded in 1517. It had been his first choice, and had an excellent scholarly reputation. The register for the Michaelmas term in 1912 records seventy students in residence, including four Rhodes scholars, Burt being the only Canadian. His tutor at Corpus Christi was a Fellow of the College, Robert B. Mowat (1883–1941), a young Scot who began as a specialist in medieval English history and subsequently produced numerous works on European diplomacy and on the history of Britain. In later years Mowat devoted much time to popular exposition of the themes of the League of Nations and the contributions which the English-speaking peoples could make to the problems of political organization. Two older scholars whose lectures Burt attended were H.A.L. Fisher (1865–1940), Fellow of New College, and H.E. Egerton (1855–1927), of Magdalen. The former was the leading English-speaking authority on the French revolutionary period and also on modern Europe; both were fields which engrossed Burt's attention for many years. Egerton was the first Beit Professor of Colonial History at Oxford, a chair established by Alfred Beit, close friend and associate of Cecil Rhodes. He was best known for his *Short History of British Colonial Policy*, and for a study of federations and unions in the Empire which was used in the Oxford syllabus in modern history. Years later Burt recalled his work with Egerton in the following terms:

On proceeding to Oxford, I was surprised to find that one of the special subjects offered by the School of Modern History was a rather intensive study of a short period of Canadian history. I did not choose it. My tutor chose it for me, and I still remember a smothered feeling of resentment at the thought of having to learn about the history of my own country from a man who had never lived in it. That feeling, of course, was an unconscious reaction of nationalism. But I was soon grateful to my tutor for sending me to sit at the feet of that ripe scholar, the late Professor Egerton, who introduced me to the source materials of Canadian history. He also made me look at the history of other parts of the British Empire ....[8]

Burt's extracurricular activities included piano music, voice training, and tennis. His associations with other Canadians at Oxford were close, particularly with three other 1910 Rhodes scholars. There was D.C. Harvey[9] from Prince Edward Island, a Dalhousie graduate. Then there was John E. Read from Nova Scotia, who was educated at Dalhousie and Columbia universities. J.T. Thorson of Manitoba, like Read, was specializing in law while Harvey and Burt were enrolled in modern history. Read has written of Burt that 'of all my friends, there is none who had greater gifts for friendship,'[10] a tribute which is echoed by many of Burt's professional colleagues and students. He and Read spent six weeks in the summer of 1911 travelling in Italy, each with £25 in his pocket. 'Florence,' Read recalls, 'gave us both an insight into the march of civilization which we have never lost.' On another occasion Burt and Thorson spent a holiday together on the Isle of Wight. His most intimate English acquaintance was Arthur Forrest, from Bath, who was later killed in the Gallipoli campaign, and after whom he named his first child, his daughter Forrest Burt.

Burt's continued enthusiasm for music is substantiated by the article 'The Relation of Music to the Other Arts,' which appeared in the college's *Pelican Record* in 1913. It is a sophisticated and analytical discussion of the nature of music and its historical development.

The other arts [he concluded] speak to us in terms of this world, and appeal to us indirectly through what we have seen with our physical or intellectual eye. Music's appeal is direct; it speaks to us not in terms of this world; it tells us what we have never seen or heard. The soul may be lifted up by a noble poem or exalted by a masterpiece of painting or sculpture, but it can never rise beyond a certain height, and there it stays. Under the spell of music, however, it seems to be freed from the chains of earth and to soar ever upward. ... as music ... discards the principle of imitation for the great principle of creation; as it possesses a mysterious power over the soul unknown to any of the other arts; as it is the purest expression of beauty; is not this, the youngest art, at the same time, the noblest art?[11]

Oxford University prizes, wrote one don in 1912, 'tempt the more ambitious'; they were not numerous, 'and are the reward of exceptional ability.'[12] The Alfred Beit Prize, established in 1905, was awarded annually for an essay on some subject connected with the advantages of 'Imperial Citizenship,' or with colonial history. The subject for 1913 was 'Proposals in the direction of a closer union of the Empire before the opening of the Colonial Conference of 1887.'[13] Burt competed for this prize, and he and Lewis Bernstein Namier of Balliol College (who was to become one of the most influential historians of the present century in Britain) were co-winners. Burt also won the Robert Herbert Memorial Prize, established in memory of a former Under-Secretary of State for the Colonies, awarded on the result of the competition for the Beit Prize.

Burt's essay was published in Oxford with an introduction by Egerton, under the title *Imperial Architects*. The work deals with an aspect of Anglo-American intellectual history. Although the relationship between the self-governing colonies and Britain had been a major preoccupation of Canadian and British historians and political thinkers for a generation, the subject had been treated hitherto primarily in terms of the events of the struggle for responsible government, or as a subject for partisan debate on imperial unity. Burt's book was essentially a dispassionate analysis of the philosophy of imperial relationships, although it is clear that the author sympathized with the ideal of a multinational political structure to promote commonly accepted objectives. The first third of the study is concerned with the schemes of American and British political thinkers for the maintenance of the unity of the Empire prior to the American Revolution. The balance of the work deals with the revival of British interest in the Empire, from its hesitant beginnings in the second quarter of the nineteenth century to its full-blown expression in the Imperial Federation League of 1884 and the Colonial Conference of 1887. 'The opening of the first Colonial Conference,' Burt wrote in his concluding paragraph, 'closed the door on *ideal* Imperialism and ushered in *practical* Imperialism. The era of ideal Imperialism was very fruitful of paper plans. The age of practical Imperialism is not less concerned with the ideal, but more engaged in its fulfilment – the attempt to build a far greater political structure than the world has yet seen.'[14] For a twenty-five-year-old student, the publication of this essay was a remarkable achievement, displaying the maturity of his mind and his firm grasp of the essentials of historical analysis.

Apart from the stimulus of the Beit Prize, one can assume that there was another reason for Burt's interest in this subject. The question of Canada's relations with Britain was vigorously debated in his native land in the pre-war years. Imperial preference and imperial defence were issues of practical politics, and the usually strident utterances of the proponents and critics of the idea of imperial unity were widely discussed. In this situation, Burt viewed the role of the historian as one who contributes to public enlightenment by relating current ideas to their earlier manifestations and to their implications for contemporary society. He undoubtedly was influenced by the widespread view in English-speaking Canada that the country was emerging to nationhood under the British monarchy, and that she should cultivate an association with Britain based on the principle of equality. Burt had no strong emotional commitment to the ideology of imperialism, a fact which probably explains his early conversion to the League of Nations ideal during the war years. Nevertheless it is interesting to note that he returned to the theme of empire in his last book, *The Evolution of the British Empire and Commonwealth from the American Revolution*, published in 1956. The subject, he wrote in his foreword, 'began to intrigue me forty-five years ago, when I was a student of the late Professor Egerton and lived in daily contact with other students drawn to Oxford from all over the empire.'[15] Nearly half a century had passed since the composition of his first work, but despite the revolutionary changes in British imperial relationships in the intervening years, one can justify his inclusion of the earlier work in the 'Suggestions for Further Reading' in the 1956 book. From first to last, he remained the moderate and pragmatic observer, who rejects both English-Canadian and French-Canadian isolationist nationalism.

As his Oxford career neared its close, having won his BA degree in the autumn of 1912, Burt naturally began to look for a teaching appointment in Canada. He wrote to the President of the University of Alberta, Henry Marshall Tory. 'An appointment in Edmonton would be very acceptable to me,' he stated, 'for outside of Toronto I have not so many friends and relatives in any place as Edmonton.'[16] Tory replied that there was no opening; but the situation had changed by the time Burt returned to Toronto and in August he was offered and had accepted a position as lecturer in history at Alberta. He certainly met the criterion of Tory's appointment policy, derived from President Remsen of Johns Hopkins University who, Tory noted, 'realized that it would be difficult to get distinguished men to come to a new institution because such men would ...

be settled in ... but that the choice must be for young men of promise who, if not great at the moment, had the possibility of becoming great in the future.'[17]

As with all new institutions, the character of the University of Alberta was being shaped by the ideas and personality of its first president, who held the position for twenty years.[18] Born on a pioneer farm near Guysborough, Nova Scotia, his childhood circumstances were not markedly different from those of the young lecturer in history whom he appointed in 1913. Moreover, like A.L. Burt, he had a mother of singular intelligence and force of character who encouraged her sons to educate themselves for careers in the mainstream of Canadian life. By dint of hard work Tory had accumulated funds to attend McGill University, and after a brief career as an ordained minister of the Methodist Church he was appointed to the teaching staff at McGill. During the following seventeen years his abundant energy and initiative won him a position of prominence as a teacher and administrator. In 1907 he accepted the invitation of the Premier of Alberta, the Honourable A.C. Rutherford, to become the president of the new provincial university.

Tory was singularly well suited by long experience and convictions to head the University of Alberta in its formative years. He had already expressed his devotion to the principle of extending high standards of university education throughout Canada, particularly in the West; he was (despite the official policy of his own church) equally firm in his opposition to denominational colleges and to the proliferation of institutions which would be unable to offer the benefits of a true university. Moreover, in his view the scholar should not lead an ivory tower existence. 'The fact is,' he wrote on one occasion, 'one can hardly take an abstract idea like the truth and separate it out as unrelated to life, and say it is the only thing worth while.'[19] This philosophical principle was particularly important for a state-supported institution of higher learning in a democratic society. In his first convocation address in October 1908, Tory expounded this doctrine:

The modern state university has sprung from a demand on the part of the people themselves for intellectual recognition, a recognition which only a century ago was denied them. The result is that such institutions must be conducted in such a way as to relate them as closely as possible to the life of the people. ... This should be the concern of all educated men, it should never be forgotten.

He must have been thinking of his own youth, as he continued:

It is the glory of our Canadian institutions that they have directed from the homes of those we are accustomed to call the common people, a steady stream of men into positions of responsibility among us. Without that which the university has to offer this would never have been possible.[20]

But Tory's adherence to this principle did not mean that exclusive priority was to be given to applied science and professional education. When the first term opened, the Faculty of Arts and Science consisted of a staff of five (including the President, who taught mathematics and physics) comprising professors of classics, English, modern languages, and civil engineering. In later years new faculties appeared, offering a variety of professional studies, and the humanities were overshadowed; their prestige, but not the quality of instruction, was impaired. The program of the Extension Department, created in 1912 to serve the rural area and smaller urban centres, to which Burt was to contribute, nevertheless stressed the humanistic as well as the practical interests of the pioneer population.

Of classroom teaching in Alberta, the first professor of classics wrote: 'The plan which we followed from the start was to fix our standard of instruction on an equality with that of the older institutions of the country.'[21] The principle of appointment reinforced this standard – no one was to be given professorial rank who had not been trained in at least two universities.[22]

The first few years of Tory's presidency were not easy: there were financial stringencies and pressures from ambitious towns to decentralize the university by locating some faculties in other centres; the effort to establish a rival university in Calgary; the feeling in some quarters that the creation of a university was premature; the uncertainty created by Rutherford's resignation as Premier in 1910; the suspicion in the minds of some of the members of the Senate that Tory would be unduly influenced by McGill traditions. By the time Burt joined the staff, however, most of these issues had been resolved by the determination and diplomatic skills of the President and the prospects for steady expansion seemed highly favourable.

The history department which Burt joined in 1913 consisted of Gordon Stanley Fife and the President, who in the early years, when time permitted, lectured on British and Canadian political and constitutional history; occasionally his lectures were given by Dr J.M. MacEchran, head of the Department of Philosophy and Psychology. Fife, a Rhodes Scholar of 1908 and a native of Peterborough, had attended Queen's University. He was appointed to the university in 1911 as the first lecturer in history and English. When Burt joined the staff, six courses in history were listed in the calendar. In his first year he taught European history.

In 1914, following the end of the spring term, Burt proceeded over-seas to pursue post-graduate studies at the ancient University of Freiburg, in the beautiful upper Rhine region near the Black Forest. Here he took a course on 'The French Revolution and the Wars of Liberation.' The French Revolution was his major historical interest at this time. He also wished to make a first-hand assessment of the situation in Germany, for the growing tensions in Anglo-German relations had produced wide-spread concern in Canada and other parts of the Empire. Discussions with German students were revealing. He would have been interned in Ger-many had he not been tipped off by a friend who had received his army call-up. Hastening to the border, Burt found it closed, but being fluent in the language he was able to discover another exit point and a man who could be induced to accompany him with a wheelbarrow to transport his books. He crossed into France in the nick of time. Fife, who was also travelling in Germany that summer, had a comparable experience.

During the academic year 1914–15 at Alberta the teaching of political economy became one of Burt's responsibilities, and the department was renamed history and political economy. He offered general history (an introductory course), European history from the Renaissance to 1648, and a general introduction to political economy; one suspects that his University of Toronto courses in this latter subject and Alberta's financial position during the war years dictated this combination of disciplines, which continued until 1920, when the two departments were separated.

Burt and Fife lived in apartments on the third floor of Athabasca Hall, and near the beginning of Burt's second year they organized the History Club on the University of Toronto model, which still flourishes today as the oldest undergraduate society on the campus. The two young bachelors took turns entertaining the Club, whose membership over the years has included many Albertans who have subsequently distinguished themselves in various careers.

Before the beginning of Burt's third term in Edmonton, an event occurred which was to have a profound influence not only on his personal happiness but also on the success of his academic career. This was his marriage, on 18 August 1915, to Dorothy Duff, a Master of Science in biology from McGill, who had been appointed to the University staff the previous year. Her grandfather, a Scottish Congregational minister, had migrated with his family to the Eastern Townships in 1856. Dorothy's father became a well-known hardware merchant and subsequently a chartered accountant in Montreal, where he lived for sixty-four years. Charming, firm-minded, and comely, Dorothy Duff had been a brilliant student in high school and university. The fact of her appointment to the university, even though it was in a junior capacity, was indicative of her intellectual qualities, for this was an era when few Canadian women were given university appointments. The fact that Burt could regard his wife as his intellectual equal was a stabilizing element in their marriage. This circumstance is implicit in the language and content of his letters, which provide clear and ample evidence of his philosophy and of his attitude to public affairs and to the study and teaching of history. Throughout their life together he relied on her as a severe and constructive critic of his prose style.

Burt's teaching assignment appears to have been heavier in 1915–16, probably because of Fife's enlistment in the spring of 1915 in the Third Universities Company. Not long after, Fife was transferred to the Princess Patricia's Canadian Light Infantry and a year later he was dead, killed in the Battle of Mount Sorrel, not far from Ypres, one of the many potential intellectual leaders of which the nation was robbed by World War I. During the 1916–17 term, Burt was promoted to assistant professor of history and economics, and it was in this year that he offered, in addition to courses in British and European history, the lecture course in Canadian political and constitutional history, which had first been listed by the department in 1914.

The following year the first honours courses were introduced, and Burt gave a seminar in seventeenth-century English constitutional history. His first students were Aileen Dunham, Lillian Cobb, and Alan Harvey. The former two subsequently had distinguished academic careers in the United States, and the last was an Alberta Rhodes scholar. The course was based on S.R. Gardiner's works, and each student prepared a half-hour paper every week, to be read and discussed. Professor Cobb[23] recalls:

How hard he worked, and how hard he worked us! On January 28, 1918 word got around that Mr. Burt would probably not meet his 9:00 o'clock class, because his first child had been born that morning. None the less he met us. Once, when we thought we couldn't stand the pressure, we drew lots as to which of us would ask him for a day off. He seemed very surprised, but said readily: "I had planned for a day off at the end of the course. You may take it now if you wish." We did!

'It was ... the major inspiration which later led me to graduate school and a life-time career in History,' Professor Dunham declares.[24] Burt's students were frequently entertained in his home, where his wife's domestic skills and personal interest in the young people complemented her husband's efforts to overcome institutional impersonality in faculty-student relations. Since the History Club was an all-male preserve, Mrs Burt had organized the Bluestocking Club for women students. These initiatives were among the enduring influences which the Burts had on those students who took up academic careers.

Invited in 1917 to contribute an article to the monthly edition of *The Gateway*, a student publication, Burt wrote 'Is Life Worth Living?,'[25] a concise statement of his approach to university education. Referring to the bitter experience of war, the disillusionment with old forms of religion, and the obvious incompetence of governments, he urged his readers to avoid 'misplaced beliefs' and to lead society by giving 'a truer meaning to life' than that provided by materialistic standards.

The University [he wrote] aims to teach its students two things – to do something and to be something. It turns out young lawyers, doctors, teachers and engineers inspired to do their best in their chosen professions. But that is not all. The University imparts another training, another inspiration – to be something ... to have a large mind and a strong character. This is the product of no single university course, but of the whole atmosphere of the institution – lectures, laboratories, reading and companionship in all. ... This is the vision, the light that dawns upon the University student....

This declaration expressed the essential elements in Burt's philosophy of life and of higher education.

2

The Tank Battalion

The first year of the war did not have much effect on the university, but from 1915–16 on the reverse was true. Before the war ended enrolment declined, many students interrupted their studies to enlist, and nearly half the members of the faculty had joined the army. Both staff and students, including Burt, participated in the Canadian Officers Training Corps program on the campus, and in the summer at Sarcee Camp near Calgary; in 1916 he was commissioned as a lieutenant in the active militia but was rejected for the infantry because of flat feet when he tried to enlist the following year. In 1917 the University of Alberta contributed a company to the Western Universities Battalion, and medical students joined the 12th Field Ambulance. Late in the year the President left the campus to organize the work of the Khaki University in the United Kingdom. Having completed basic officer training, Burt was able to join the First Canadian Tank Battalion when it was established early in 1918, with the rank of lieutenant.

The First Tank Battalion was exclusively recruited from Canadian universities,[1] presumably because the military authorities assumed that young men of proven intelligence would quickly master this new and complicated form of weaponry. The two officers in the Alberta contingent were lieutenants Burt and George H. Steer, a Queen's graduate and barrister in Edmonton. Since there were no tanks in Canada, training in the use of this new instrument of war had to be postponed until the troops arrived in England. The Alberta contingent of seventeen men left Edmonton in the last week of April 1918, and arrived in Ottawa on the 30th.[2]

Despite the fact that the great German spring offensive of 1918, which began on 21 March, was scoring notable successes against the British and French forces and reached the Marne River only 37 miles from Paris by 30 May, no sense of urgency seems to have been conveyed to the men of the Battalion. Training in the theory of this most difficult of tactical arms was delayed until well after the unit arrived in England.

Burt's first day in Ottawa is described in one of his regular twice-a-week letters to his wife:

Ottawa, April 30, 1918

...We had a pleasant train journey. ... At Winnipeg ... D.C. Harvey of Wesley College, a friend of Oxford days who taught you remember at McGill for a year, came to the station and cheered my soul by his chronic grousing.

...Dinner was to have been ready in the station here on our arrival 7:52, but the train was late and the chef gone. Coventry (Lieut.) (Oxford and Toronto. Biology) met us and said the Russell House had a good cafeteria. So there I marched the men and persuaded the man in charge to accept my coupons on the G.T.R. for 18 meals, to the surprise of Coventry who feared I should have to pay. ... 139 men and some officers are already here. The Toronto Company which I hear is over strength is not yet arrived. There is a whole batch of Laval students under a man named Bourassa, no relative or any affinity of the infamous. ... The general talk is that we will be away in a fortnight. We report tomorrow morning to assist in giving the men some elementary drill. It is now 10:30 and we have been unsuccessfully trying to see the o.c. [Major Macfarlane] since breakfast. He must be, like you, a great friend of his bed.

We expect to get two or 3 days leave at most, if we can get that; I am writing mother I am trying to get it next weekend.

Now I must off to see if we can get a glimpse of the o.c. who I hear has distinguished himself in France and is not yet 30, a fine fellow.

Burt's reference to Bourassa is typical of contemporary English-Canadian reaction to the Nationalist leader. In later years Burt was to write perceptively on the reasons for French-Canadian opposition to conscription, but not sympathetically of Bourassa. What he regarded as extreme nationalism in all its manifestations was repellent to him. The following three weeks were occupied with drilling and meetings with his parents and friends, including Vincent Massey, a contemporary at Toronto and Oxford, then secretary of the Dominion War Cabinet. The highlight was the arrival of Mrs Burt and Forrest, who came to Ottawa for a few days' visit. From the Women's Patriotic League of Listowel he received handmade accessories for his outfit. For reading matter on the voyage, his kit held *The Thoughts of Marcus Aurelius* and Palgrave's *Golden Treasury*.

During the first week of June the Battalion boarded ship in Montreal and arrived in England a little over two weeks later. Although the danger of German submarine attack was almost non-existent by this time, the usual precautions were still in force. The following letter summarizes the events of the voyage.

Rolling on the billows

June 20, 1918

At last our long voyage is just about to close unless a submarine intercepts us very shortly and there is some real danger yet. We have all worn our life belts all the way across, and in obedience to orders have slept in all our clothes during the last few nights. It was really very comfortable.

The days on board have passed very lazily. They were so much alike one might almost question if there was such a thing as time. Each morning I rose at 7 a.m. bathed, dressed and had a short walk on deck till breakfast at 7:45. The next event in the day was P.T. at 10:30–11:30 and it has been great fun balancing on one leg when the ship was rolling well. There were only two other regular events in the day, lunch at 12:30 noon and dinner at 6 p.m. The lacunae were filled in by learning and practicing the semaphore system of signalling, (I have also learned but not yet used the Morse Code.), a very little bridge, a little more reading and shuffleboard, still more conversation, even more musing and a great deal more of sleep. All through I have never been as lazy in my whole life before. The total result I feel to be distinctly good.

I have not played much bridge because practically everybody plays for money and then I hate it. I have only played twice for money, each time unsuspectingly losing and gaining 80¢ and 25¢ respectively. I do not anticipate playing much more.

My reading has been more patchy than this letter is and will be, for I never knew when I sat down with a book what I would be doing in fifteen minutes – still reading, playing shuffleboard, talking, idly dreaming or soundly sleeping. Under such conditions I finished Morley and Kipling's Tales and have read much of Marcus Aurelius. In the past I have several times approached M.A. but somehow it never went as I expected, but now – I suppose because of the new manner of life I have undertaken for a short while – I find myself revelling in it. It is not a book to be swallowed in big gulps, but to be chewed slowly in small morsels; I know nothing like it. Of course the stoic philosophy in its entirety is not acceptable to me. I refer particularly to its fatalism. But the rest of it is strong meat to the soul. It teaches me that whatever my environment may be, yet I have full control over myself – that while the body lasts the spirit should not fail – that no matter what may come it matters not, for I may be self-contained, serene and even happy. ... I was quite amused the other day when Capt. Gerrie of the Y.M.C.A., said to me "I never see you but you are wearing the smile that won't come off." I think you might like the stoic Emperor now though like myself you might not have relished him very much not long ago. I am greatly anticipating in the days to come the ever fresh moral treat I carry in my pocket. I will send you some of the passages that appeal particularly.

Conversations on board have been delightful. ... With quite a number of our own officers too I have had many good serious chats. Their company is going far to offset my dislike for military life.

As for the externals of our journey, it has been much pleasanter than I anticipated. After the first two nights on board, and we sailed within 24 hours of when I last saw you – Steer and I have had the cabin all to ourselves. The other two officers were badly bitten and chased out by bed bugs which have left us un-molested. The weather has been nearly perfect. I have had a strong sunburn which took the skin off my manly brow – so genial was the sun. The boat is so steady and the sea so very calm that although some of the men below were seasick the officers were all immune. Our convoy was a good-sized one and the camouflage paint made it difficult to tell whether the ships were floating nightmares or cubist or futurist illusions. More interesting even is the sight of destroyers scurrying hither and thither. We of course had boat drill every day and wore our life belts constantly. The last few nights a few have tried to whisper wild rumours but we have not seen any submarines. A cloud has been cast over us today by the disappearance of one of our officers. I understand he was invalided home from the front suffering from shell shock and when last seen was in very low spirits. A court of inquiry is now sitting upon the case.

We have a good idea of where we will land but naturally may not tell and our letters may be held some time after we land. Our further destination is unknown. All we know is that we will be in quarantine for about a fortnight after landing as is usual with troops reaching England. ...

The Alberta boys are all as usual. I see quite a bit of them visiting them usually at every meal time except breakfast. Old Bill Sykes has taken to playing whist with great gusto. Fife[3] has very much improved and Archie McGillivray is into every fun that is going. Marsden[4] is now called nothing but Bishop and is I think a most wholesome influence. I like all the boys much better even than when we pulled out of Edmonton.

Burt's letters from the training camp in England are in essence a per-

sonalized diary of the Canadian tank training program, which lasted for four months. Since no comparable accounts seem to exist, they are a unique historical record. For about six weeks the Battalion was housed at a segregation camp at Frensham Pond, near Aldershot and Farnham, Surrey, putting in time until they could move to Bovington Camp in Dorset for tank training. The time was spent in squad drill, sports activities, swimming, and listening to lectures on map reading, motor mechanics, and infantry attack tactics. There was time for some long walks about the country, and for reading. Marcus Aurelius was a familiar companion. Those who knew Burt later as a teacher and friend can imagine him savouring some such passage of the philosopher-emperor's as the following:

Suppose that men kill thee, cut thee in pieces, curse thee. What then can these things do to prevent thy mind from remaining pure, wise, sober, just? For instance, if a man should stand by a limpid pure spring, and curse it, the spring never ceases sending up potable water; and if he should cast clay into it or filth, it will speedily disperse them and wash them out, and will not be at all polluted. How then shalt thou possess a perpetual fountain and not a mere well? By forming thyself hourly to freedom conjoined with benevolence, simplicity and modesty.

'I have found an equilibrium of spirit such as I did not know a few years ago,' he wrote to his wife.[5] But all was not serious. Describing a picnic under the trees with Edmonton men, with Steer producing cakes of chocolate from his trunk, Burt remarked, 'Now you will think from this that I am no stoic but an Epicurean which I hope you *know* is not true.'[6]

A short leave in London permitted Burt to attend a performance of J.M. Barrie's *Dear Brutus* at Wyndham's Theatre, and to visit R.B. Mowat, his Oxford tutor, who was working in the Intelligence Department of the Admiralty, and who promised to try to find another one of his students as a temporary replacement in the Alberta history department. One evening was spent reading about the Montague Report on the Government of India, 'which interests me very much.'

...If carried out, as seems most likely, it will effect one of the greatest reforms and be one of the greatest experiments in government in modern times. The report, though very lengthy, has a simple, short principle, the careful extension of responsible government in India until ultimately after a long period the government will be on a par with that of the Dominions.[7]

Around mid-July the Battalion moved to its permanent training quarters, the Imperial Tank Training Camp (Bovington Camp) near Wareham, Dorset – on the edge of the heathland beloved of Thomas Hardy. Bovington was a great improvement over Frensham Camp, where eating at the mess involved a half-mile walk and 'where we never got enough to eat and what we got was seldom properly cooked and invariably gritty with sand and dirt.' 'I learn,' Burt continued, 'that our experiences at Frensham – which was not so terribly bad but seems so by comparison, will have been the most uncomfortable in our whole army life. ... They say life in France for us will be better than here – at least so far as food goes ... The W[oman's] A[uxiliary] A[rmy] C[orps] are settled here and are responsible for the good cooking.'[8]

The episodes of the training program are best described in the following extracts from Burt's letters home:

July 20, 1918

Until yesterday we had easy work i.e. the officers in the same group as myself. But yesterday we found we had done with the snap courses and that laborious days had begun. We have barely an hour for lunch, which is less than it seems, as we have to march back to our quarters, doff our overalls – scrub up and after lunch dress again for toil and march back. We were plunged into the intricate theory and working of large engines and find it confusing but even more interesting. The preliminaries over – we are now in the beasts themselves, but I fear the awful censor would frown dark blots if I ventured into any descriptions. When this particular course is over we switch on to gunnery on which Steer was put first. Each lasts a few weeks. It feels good to be really at work after we have been pottering about for so long at squad drill, etc. I find that study after the day's work will not be too strenuous for the pleasure of life, and I anticipate many enjoyable hours reading....

July 28, 1918

Thursday we began to drive our awful beast in the open. (It is called a bus in ordinary language among us) – each taking his turn. We are divided up in groups of five. It is not bad fun, but it is inconceivably dirty. We have to do all the work [of] cleaning and keeping it greased, oiled, etc. I have never been so dirty in my life before. I am sure you would have difficulty in recognising me returning from work. I lack only the tin dinner pail. My overalls are already black and shiny – the oil has come through, staining my underwear, and my hands! They are like a mechanic's, and in spite of any soap, promise never to be really clean again till the war is over. Friday afternoon we had an intersting time. Our instructor told us to get out and have a smoke, then he got busy dickering with the works. After a while he emerged and told us to start the bus. Of course it would not work, and we had to puzzle out the various troubles and straighten them. But we succeeded in the end. I will be able to *run* our motor [car] after the war. Yesterday morning we spent the whole time cleaning – from 8:30 to 12:15 working like Trojans. When noon came we were all played out and glad to have a half holiday....

August 11, 1918

This week finished up one section of our work. Wed[nesday] night and Thursday we were examined on our driving. Clames and I were best of our class of 10. Friday we were examined in the shops on the engine, etc., and I came out all right. Yesterday we spent an extra day on the new engine.

Steer returned from Lulworth Cove Friday night, having finished his gunnery. I have a week yet, on repairs in the shops and then turn on gunnery....

Wednesday orders came out that we must each select a batman from our tank crews. ... My new man is a young French Canadian – Barrette – a law student from Laval. ... He is a tremendously clever boy and possesses wisdom as well as knowledge. I have many good chats with him. Last evening I spent most of the time discussing the French Canadians and the Roman Catholic Church with him. He is very liberal in his views. Of course he is hardly French Canadian. His mother is from Paris and his father's mother was also and he has been in France a number of times.

A Quebecer with such views was a rare bird at a time when the conscription controversy was raging, and Burt recognized that he was hardly representative of Canadian opinion.

August 25, 1918

Friday was another day full of surprises but of a different kind. We were shooting "classification" *i.e.* to be classified as shots good or bad. To my astonishment I led the class with 188 out of 200. The next was 178 by Capt. Gardiner – an attached officer. Then Clames got 163. We three were thus made Marksmen. Five were first class *i.e.* between 130 and 160, and four 2nd class shots *i.e.* between 100 and 130. 80% is necessary for markman. I cannot tell you how it happened. The major was quite bucked with my performance. That night was mess night. Several big officers down from London were our guests and the concert in the messroom lasted till after 10 p.m. It was excellent – there were no piano solos to ruin it. The old general, who was the chief guest, moved the Col. to relax the rule against pipes after dinner, which made many of us happy. These concerts are always in the mess room itself – which is the dining room hut – not the ante-room, a hut which is our sitting room.

A few days later there were several examinations, including one on the use and care of the machine-gun. About the middle of September Burt and his party marched about five miles from Bovington Camp to Lulworth Camp near the south coast, for the first of several sessions of tank combat training. The countryside here is beautiful, particularly near the chalk cliffs of Lulworth Cove. 'The country here,' he wrote, 'is very rolling, the hills high and cut away in steep cliffs to the sea. The hills look like great green velvet masses.'[9] They remained here for about a week before returning to Bovington Camp, and he described their activities as follows:

September 18, 1918

...Monday morning we did a little practice laying guns on targets. That is from a moving tank. A lecture or so filled up, with some messing about, the first day. Yesterday we began the actual firing of the six pounder. The shell and cartridge together must be about 18" long. The bore of the gun is $2^1/4$". It has a great bark and flash. But curiously the noise inside the tank is very small compared with the noise outside. The flash reaches about 10 feet out of the muzzle and sometimes there is a back flash in the tank when loading rapidly. The actual projectile weighs six pounds and explodes on contact. Yesterday I was unfortunate. By my third shot I had found the range and hit the target. But the tank was away around and there was danger of sending a round into the cove so I was commanded to select a new target. But it needs three shots to get a target and I had only two left. So my average error was 11 yds. 10 yds. is necessary for a 1st class shot and this morning my name was read out among those who must do better. So I set to and in this morning's practice had an average error of 2 yds. which is not very easy to beat. I had imagined I would be afraid of the gun but I like it. They will not let us wear anything in our ears and it is well. The noise is not very much.

By 25 September they were back at Bovington Camp. The training program during the whole period in England was not so exhausting that Burt was unable to find time for a considerable amount of reading, of both history and fiction. The works of Thomas Hardy and George Meredith were his favourite novels, although he also devoured *Jane Eyre*, *Don Quixote*, and some of Kipling. Studies by A. Fournier on Napoleon and F.V.A. Aulard on the French Revolution were among the books he ordered from Blackwell's: 'I prefer to spend my spare money in that way than in bridge or poker debts and wine treats, as quite a number do.'[10] William O'Brien's life of Parnell he found 'a very biased work, but interesting reading.'[11] Guglielmo Ferrero's *The Greatness and Decline of Rome* was 'enlightened as great history should be with general observations of a pointed nature.'[12] But although cards failed to attract, and books were a solace, he was not unsociable, supervising the construction of a tennis court and always in demand as a pianist. Steer and Marsden were his close friends and they spent much time together.

The next three weeks were spent at Bovington Camp.

September 25, 1918

Life is very sweet especially at afternoon tea when I have my rapidly diminishing store of honey with perhaps a couple of friends. I have been thinking of late how foolish many of us – selfish indeed and myself quite so – really are. We have plenty to eat and yet we encourage those at home to spend on parcels of foodstuffs amounts foolish in comparison to the quantity sent. Really we are greedy spoiled children and nothing else – like boys at boarding schools who are all stomach. So please do not spoil me and instead of wasting your good money on sending me superfluities spend it on something you yourself need – or something nice for Forrest. I am just beginning to realise the terrible extent to which you have spoiled me...

October 2, 1918

...Monday morning I began a fortnight's course on reconnaissance which promises to be quite interesting. It is chiefly a study of ground so that we may be able to visualize ground from a map, and recognising its different qualities know how to use it. We have some lectures but more practical work. For example we drew an enlargement of a square on a map of this locality. Took it out yesterday morning and examined the ground, inserting everything in pencil on the map. Then in the afternoon we finished it all in india ink. This morning we had some lectures and again this afternoon we spent examining a small section of country on either side of a road for a 'road traverse' which must be finished and handed in Friday morning. I wish I had your artistic eye and deft hand here to give me a little help. The tennis court is all finished now but the marking of the court, the erection of the net and of the big net around the court. Yesterday after tea we had a lecture by the General of this camp telling us he wanted an improvement in discipline etc. of which he said there was a noticeable falling off among officers and men. Indeed it is very true and natural when there are no regular parades, and all – officers, N.C.O.'s and men are off at schools all day. So saluting grows lax and men slouch around etc....

October 6, 1918

...I am quite busy. The reconnaissance course is no snap. I have been working overtime every day. Thursday after dinner I went back and worked the whole evening, Friday after tea again, and then yesterday afternoon and to-day also. We are busy finishing up a panoramic sketch and a river reconnaissance. I find I am no great artist for my maps get only fair average marks – a necessary humiliation to my pride. We have this week still on the course. The company goes off to Sherford Tuesday for a week's tank manoeuvres and then to Lulworth for a week's gunnery. As I am on this course I stay here and when finished go to Lulworth. Steer returns at that time and most likely we will go together. In my last letter I mentioned a reduction of establishment. The result is not finally settled and will not be published for some time so please don't mention this abroad....

It is beastly hard to write, for everybody is now talking and several will discuss the war with me. There is a widespread general expectation. One of our section commanders returned from the front last night and says we have the Germans on the run and will keep it up. To my mind everything hinges on Turkey. As the allies practically demand her extinction she will fight on as long as she can. Then Austria will be open to the south and she likewise will collapse. Germany still has 4 million men on the west front and could fight on – but a losing battle. The German people will then see the futility of their much vaunted military government, and the latter to stave off revolution will conclude peace and yield somewhat (or appear to) to the people's demands. The point is how long can Turkey resist – not long I think, for her sole source of supplies of munitions and large source of foodstuffs are cut off unless the Germans made a sudden eruption to the south and seize the Constantinople railway. Thus the war may end this year quite precipitately, but if not will be brought to a close in a great spring campaign. This conclusion seems generally held among the men here and in France....

Burt's observations are shrewd, for the Allies were able to advance only very slowly in Belgium and France, and the German armies were never destroyed in battle.

October 13, 1918

...My course on reconnaissance finished yesterday. By strenuous labour I managed to get a first again. Two tied at 90. I averaged 84. There were about three of around there. It was very interesting. Thursday morning, Friday all day, and yesterday we spent upon a problem of finding a course for tanks over a couple of miles, and establishing necessary posts for them – of course drawing a careful map for the whole. I may send home some books wrapped up in one or two of my splashes. The comment on my panoramic sketch is most amusing....

By this time, the question of the abdication of the Kaiser had become a subject of public discussion in Germany and various rumours were circulating. If Wilhelm II had abdicated promptly in favour of his grandson's installation as a constitutional ruler, the monarchy might have survived World War I. President Wilson's first communications with the German government culminated in a Note which was reported in the London *Times* on 16 October 1918. This stated that Germany must change her constitution to eliminate arbitrary power, that the Allied military advisers must determine the conditions of an armistice, and that any armistice must safeguard Allied military supremacy.

October 16, 1918

...I received in a letter from father a P.O. order to buy myself a chamois vest for my birthday – so you need not be afraid of my taking pneumonia, consumption, or anything like that if I should go to France this winter. By the way, a wire came to the orderly room here this evening stating that the Kaiser has abdicated in favour of his grandson. If that be true peace is very much nearer by that stroke. Pres. Wilson's reply was very pleasing. Steer and I have had a few great arguments over the matter. He inclined to believe and I to distrust the *bona fide* of Germany in her recognition of Wilson's 14 points. But the Kaiser's going is most significant.

October 20, 1918

...Saturday morning [at Lulworth Cove] I was with a party loading ammunition and cleaning M.G.'s (machine guns). ... Today I expected to be on a fatigue party in charge of men digging trenches for the royal 'show' [for King George V] but the lot fell to others. It was cold and rainy so I spent the morning by the fire in the hut reading a little but most of the time chatting with the major and a few other officers. This afternoon from lunch to tea I went for a long walk over the cliffs and exploring a cave. I climbed over 500 ft. and had a great view. At the end of my climb I found a secluded nook commanding one of the loveliest valleys running down to the sea that I have ever seen. The wind was high and it was spitting rain more or less, but it was a beautiful afternoon. The leaves are falling fairly fast now....

Our plans are changed. We leave here Oct. 28 for a week's manoeuvres at Sherford Bridge. We go to France Nov. 18 as a unit. The intervening fortnight we spend at Bovington. I hope to get some leave then....

Early in November the unit had a few days' leave, which Burt spent in Bradford, Yorkshire with Mrs Burt's uncle, Professor Archibald Duff, a distinguished Old Testament scholar at the University of Leeds. Here he received the news of the armistice. Writing on 10 November, he commented:

...The great news is crowding in these tremendous hours. Last night we learned of the Kaiser's abdication. Amidst the general joy and sense of relief I cannot help feeling sad and somewhat shamefaced that though I am in khaki I have not served in France and in all probability will not be able to. Though I have satisfied my conscience I feel something lacking – I suppose a sort of consciousness of public opinion. I now want to tear off the khaki lest I be mistaken for one of those who suffered in France. ... I had intended getting my picture taken when I next got leave – but now I think not – I don't want to have it taken in my uniform.

In the normal course of events the armistice would have been the termination of Burt's military career, and there were rumours that the Battalion was to be shipped back to Canada within a week or two and discharged on arrival. But the demobilization arrangements were obviously confused, since at the same time an education officer had been appointed and a survey of the educational qualifications and interests of the men had been made, which indicated the possibility that the unit would be remaining in Britain for some time. Then, on 24 November, Burt received a letter from President Tory, in London, asking him to transfer to the Khaki University.[13] On 20 November he wrote home as follows:

Sunday night the few of us interested in Education discussed plans for work in the B[attalion] here. We expected the Col. but he did not appear. So the plan that I should go up with him to London did not materialize. But I decided to go, paying my own way. I left at 9 a.m. and arrived 1:30 p.m. and found Dr. Tory in his new quarters, the old Alberta Government offices – very luxurious indeed. He had just received my letter – but it was in a pile of mail he had not yet read. When I told him my application to be transferred had gone to Argyll House (Canadian Headquarters) he said he would see it was put through at once as he needed me in the worst way. He was very busy so I did not remain long. ... I then proceeded to the old headquarters of the Khaki University to see what could be done immediately in the line of books and courses for our unit. I had a very pleasant time with Capt. Cameron[14] – collected quite a mass of literature of the K.U. and arranged for a parcel of text books to be sent up at once....

I do not know what to think or say. It is clearly my duty as well as my interest to stay here and work in the K.U. As I cannot fight in France it is the next best thing to do....

November 24, 1918

Yesterday afternoon Dr. Tory came down for the weekend as Col. Mills' guest.

(Col. Mills is an extremely able and most charming man). A Khaki College Canadian Tanks is being founded here where the unit expects to remain for some months until the general demobilisation after the signature of peace. He departed this afternoon just before tea, having made quite an impression – I like him more and more and apparently he reciprocates. ... He thinks a lot of you. He was surprised I had not already reported in London and is impatient my transfer is not through yet. He says he must have me right away and so has arranged with Col. Mills that I be sent to London at once, if necessary on leave till the transfer is through. So off I go tomorrow or the day after. ... Dr. Tory is in a further difficult position because the Alberta Govt. offices are only loaned to him. He has to go to France immediately and needs a good Alberta province man to take charge of his office during that time and selects me particularly because Miss MacAdams,[15] who is likely to cause trouble has, he says, a very high opinion of me. Then he wants me to go in and out of London organizing the work in different centres and later – if the bulk of the Canadian army is to be kept in France, I may have to go through [sic]. I almost tremble at the responsibilities he is thrusting upon me but at the same time am inspired by the opportunity of greater work. I am astounded at the confidence he places in me.

Burt spent the next seven months in London occupied with the affairs of the Khaki University, and was to justify Tory's confidence in his knowledge, administrative abilities, and good judgment.

3

The Khaki University

Apart from the enlistment of University of Alberta students and staff in the armed forces, the most important contribution which the university made to the nation during the war years was in releasing its President from his normal duties to serve overseas as head of the Khaki University of Canada. The organizational principles for this institution had been formulated by President Tory in the summer of 1917 at the request of the Canadian YMCA.[1] The YMCA and the Chaplaincy Service had been providing reading matter and sponsoring informal lectures for the troops, and these were so well received that the idea of providing an organized educational service had emerged. Tory was selected to survey the situation in France and England and propose a specific scheme. He arrived in England in July and his report was published in September. This recommended that the service should have personnel support and sponsorship by the army authorities, with the YMCA providing financial assistance; the universities of Canada were to co-operate by establishing an advisory board and by recognizing university level work undertaken by the men. In the end, the program covered the whole spectrum of educational interests – elementary school subjects, instruction in agriculture, commerce, applied science, theology, and regular courses in British universities. The work began in a limited way in the autumn of 1917, but was stepped up in 1918 following Tory's return at the beginning of the year as Director of Educational Services, with the rank of Hon. Colonel. Area study centres were established in fourteen locations in England, and

Battalion schools were created for illiterate soldiers and others wherever servicemen were stationed.

The administrative aspects of this project were formidable, and frequently contentious, involving the differing views and personalities of army officers, YMCA officials, the chaplains, and university authorities in England. By the time of the armistice, Tory was overburdened with organizational details – hence his desire to obtain Burt as his personal assistant in the central office in London. The following letters describe Burt's initiation in this activity.

November 27, 1918

Well, here I am presiding in Dr. Tory's offices while he is spending the day at Whitley Camp. Monday my transfer did not arrive, so Col. Mills as agreed sent me to this institution "on command" i.e. temporarily attached for duty till my transfer was actually through. ... He [Dr. Tory] was much relieved to see me and sent me up to Bedford Square to straighten out the history courses – which were just going to press in the calendar of the K.U. It was lucky I did not wait for the train Tuesday morning for the courses were a bad jumble and it took me the morning to straighten them out and make sure the necessary books were available. The afternoon I spent trying to find a place to lay my head. ... I had just time to call on Frank [Underhill][2] for 5 m[inutes] and arrive at the Central Hall Westminster where Dr. Tory was lecturing under the auspices of the R[oyal] Col[onial] Inst[itute]. ... At the lecture (Dr. Tory spoke very well) I was much struck by Sir Charles Lucas[3] who presided. He looked a frail and very unfashionable old gentleman but betrayed himself in his words as president to be a remarkably incisive intellect and an attractive master of style. Mrs. Tory of course was there looking as well as ever. After the lecture Dr. and Mrs. Tory, Lt. Col. (Dean) Adams,[4] Marsden and the future Mrs. [Marsden] and your humble husband drove up here in Dr. Tory's official car and indulged in an unofficial cup of tea. I met Col. Adams only yesterday morning – submitting my report to him – and find him a most charming person. ... I had a few words with Dr. Tory in which I received orders to take charge of this office during his absence and to take any action immediately necessary that might arise in his mail or with the advent of callers. It is really a roving commission to sit in a chair before a large desk in a large beautifully furnished room with two ticking stenographers in two rooms, one on each side. He tells me he is going to keep me quite close to him until the New Year anyway....

...there was another incident today. You see these are still nominally the Alberta Gov[ernment] Offices – the K.U. name is not advertised on doors or windows at all. So benighted or prospective Alberta people are liable to drop in.

One such appeared this afternoon finding me ensconsed in the erstwhile chair of the Agent-General for Alberta, and I was faced with the necessity of behaving as much as possible like the original occupant. (Keep this quiet – this is one reason I am here – to save trouble and a possible awkward situation). He was a poor devil of 55 or so who was doubly steeped in sin, and so caught in the mesh of the devil. To wit. His first wife refused to go to Canada to live with him so he sought, found and bound a more amenable partner, and slept in prison 15 mos. as a bigamist. His second sin was to dabble in Calgary oil stocks. In fact he is a real live stock promoter over here. Now for the mesh. He is contracted to return to Canada but is having difficulty with the immigration officials. I looked tremendously wise – as you know I can – and gave him a little advice from the abundant fountains of my wisdom. He threatens to return in a week if his problem is not solved.

December 1, 1918

My work in London keeps me very busy. I am doing all sorts of things from outlining courses in history – in considerable detail – for the guidance of students, and attending to benighted Albertans who need the assistance of the Agent-General of Alberta. My chief duty at the present is to fulfil the latter function (Breathe it not in Gath). Miss MacAdams has been very worried over the situation. The Agent General – Reed – was hopelessly incompetent and she is greatly relieved to know I am there to protect Albertan interests from being neglected. It is a tremendous joke. She [Miss MacAdams] insists to me that I have the proper qualities for the Agent General's function, and that I am not a political heeler [and] should have the job. Indeed she swears by all the serious gods that she is going to move it in the house when she returns.

The Khaki University plan for the admission of Canadian servicemen to British universities had not been implemented so far, and Tory directed Burt to solicit the co-operation of the university authorities. This involved him in considerable travel during the next few months. His first visit was to Oxford, which he described in the same letter:

Friday and yesterday Dr. Tory was at Seaford, leaving me in charge of the offices and any business that arose needing immediate attention. I am up here [Oxford] this weekend on his orders to see what arrangements can be made to send senior students here from January till the summer. I expected that the reactionary University authorities would do nothing, and that I would have to fall back upon arrangements with the different colleges. I am fairly sure of the latter now in any case, and have good hopes of getting something out of the university. A.L. Smith, the greatest historical tutor Oxford has had – the present head of Balliol – has been kindness itself. I spent the greater part of the time from two till 11:30 – coming back here [Corpus Christi] to dine pleasantly with the dons. He even insisted on coming out with me and going around Oxford to see a number of people who might give valuable assistance. I have a number of appointments to-day which will take up the most of my time, I expect. It is a great treat to mingle again in a scholarly atmosphere. For example last night I dined here with Schiller – the leader of the pragmatic school of philosophy, Plummer the church historian, Dr. Grundy, the ancient historian – my own tutor Mr. Mowat, and Clarke, Corpus Professor of Latin. We had a great chat in the senior common room over wine afterwards – before I rushed back to Balliol. I interviewed that old beast Tommy Case – the president of Corpus – to get permission to sleep in college. All he could say was that the war had ruined Europe. He has very few if any friends, for though he has a pleasant social manner he insults everybody. I counted myself lucky to escape in a few minutes unscathed. I had a pleasant 15 min[utes] chat with Wylie and his wife yesterday before I found the Master of Balliol in. Wylie is Oxford secretary of the Rhodes trust. They are great friends of mine. I go to tea with them to-day. At the Master's last night I met ... MacInnes – he is quite blind but has an alert mind and is a good scholar[5] – he wants to get a university post somewhere in Canada. I told him how he might manage it at Queen's and suggested B.C. as a good chance....

In a few minutes I am to go for a walk with my old tutor – then I meet Capt. Fife who has charge of imperial soldiers sent here for study by the British gov[ernment]. After lunch I have another appointment with the Master of Balliol and then I must see Barker,[6] the historian, author of Plato and Aristotle on our shelves. I hear he is keen.

In London, Burt had a modest room at the Red Court Hotel, Bedford Place. The guests were sprightly, and their activities would have been a continuous distraction to a less serious-minded person.

December 8, 1918

...This is really a very comfortable hotel. ... In the drawing room is a very good Bechstein piano. Many of the guests are kind and flattering and insist on my playing for them every evening. Some of them are extremely nice people – a few are not – particularly a creature called Mrs. Bland. She has a soldier husband who is here this weekend. It would be well if he were here always. She gets on my puritanical nerves. I sit at a table with three American [privates] – one a grad[uate] of Yale. I don't mind their consuming every dinner with the aid of a fork firmly grasped in the right hand, but their kind friendliness has a difficult job sometimes to make up for their perpetually talking shop. ... But the nice people are considerable....

Later on, Burt frequently took his meals with Hugh McLaughlin,[7] for whom he had arranged accommodation at the Red Court. McLaughlin, a Toronto graduate and student-at-law, had also been with the Tanks, and was now secretary of the London College of Khaki University.

On 9 December Burt was named head of the Khaki University's Department of History, and thus became a member of Tory's Advisory Council.[8] Early in January 1919, he visited Glasgow and Edinburgh universities. His departure from London and trip north is described in a letter of 8 January, written in Edinburgh:

Monday I had a severely busy day. I was getting Dr. Tory off to Seaford in the morning and had to "shoo" off a lot of people to get the necessary business done. The rest of the day I was rushed with correspondence and students at British Universities –which is largely in my hands – and later with making arrangements for my trip up here. In the morning Killam[9] walked in. It was good to see him again. Directly after going to France in July he was taken away from the artillery and attached to the intelligence corps, spending most of his time questioning German prisoners. He came across several of his old friends. He has come to take charge of Mathematics. ... I left 11:30 p.m. from Euston for Glasgow. It was impossible to get a berth but I secured a whole seat for myself on which I had a good sleep. I arrived 9:30 a.m., had breakfast and a bath and interviewed Sir Donald MacAlister head of the univ[ersity], and the registrar, and after lunch the head of the Royal Technical College. Everything was plain sailing. I arrived here a little after 5 p.m. and visited every hotel on Princes St. until I found a bed in a room with another officer. I met a South African officer with whom I chatted till 9 p.m. and then read till midnight. Then I slept – till quarter to ten. I hastily shaved and dressed and rushed off to the Univ[ersity] (it was too late to get breakfast) and thence to the residence of Sir Richard Lodge, prof. of history and dean of the faculty of Arts, with whom I had a very pleasant interview and then back to the university. ... I expect to spend tomorrow and perhaps the next day at Cambridge. We are getting excellent arrangements here also....

I like Dr. Tory better every day, and I think he likes and trusts me, so the future looks good. I have suggested to him that MacGibbon (economics) who was in the Tanks and is now with the k.u. of c. would be an acquisition for Alberta. He seems to think so too, and we may see Mac. in Edmonton next fall.[10] He is a very keen studious fellow who has written some good things, esp[ecially] a book on the Railroad problem of Canada.

On 12 January Burt noted that the Khaki University 'is going not badly though military authorities do not make the way easier.'

...I am off early to Cambridge to make arrangements there for students who may never go. Friday after we had been told to go ahead we received a letter from an authority at Argyll House (Can. H.Q.'s) which threw a heavy shower of cold water on our scheme for studying at British Universities. But we expect it still to go through. The college camp for matriculants, 1st and 2nd year Univ[ersity] students is starting at Bramshott the latter part of this week. Killam is going there to take charge of mathematics and I perhaps in history – such is the uncertainty of life.

By mid-January this issue was resolved:

January 19, 1919
The question of sending men to British Universities has been finally settled. We can select 100 from France and England each and I have the matter in hand. The actual selection rests in the hand of a committee composed of Dr. Tory, Dean Adams, Maj. Gill[11] and myself – any three can act. I am secretary of the works – which kept me busy all yesterday afternoon and which will keep me busy most likely until next June. I may have to do a couple of days teaching each week in Bramshott into the bargain.

By 25 January Burt was able to write that the worst of his organizational work was nearly over, and that he might go to Ripon to teach, along with Killam. However, in the end Frank Underhill, who had enlisted in 1915 from the University of Saskatchewan history department, was assigned to this position. Burt remained in the London office, where he wrote as follows on 19 February:

...Since Sunday I have had my nose to the grindstone – in the office all day except for 20 min. or so for lunch round the corner. The great pressure of work just at present – the men are swarming from France to attend universities here – has entailed extra long hours. To-day I was up to my ears in work from 9:20 a.m. till nearly 7 p.m. My correspondence for three days had been almost neglected but to-day I caught up a great deal and expect tomorrow morning to get up to date. Many men are simply shipped over from France with imperfect papers by ignorant c.o.'s for education. The poor men are quite at sea, know nothing of British educational institutions and would sit all day asking advice. Then there are constantly other distractions, Dr. Tory asking me this and that, and now and again I have to abandon everything else to help him bring forth a report or an article. It is almost a turmoil I live in, and when I get home I will do nothing but breathe constant sighs of relief that it is all done.

The pressure of work here continued for another three or four weeks. His letter 2 March detailed further activities:

The Khaki University is thriving mightily in spite of many difficulties internal and external. Sometimes I am tempted to get mad with some people who are actuated by petty jealousies and animosities....

Canada's Khaki University was a unique educational venture which attracted much public interest. Tory was in constant demand as a speaker and writer of articles on the subject, as Burt noted in the following letter of 25 March 1919:

I am really in a villainous temper for I have a filthy cold and my head feels exactly like a block of wood. Colds, however, are very fashionable around here now – due I believe to very unseasonable cold weather. Col. Tory is not immune. He was down only from lunch till tea. He had promised an article for the Empire Review and forgot about it till the last moment. I saw he was in no state to manage it so I took over the task. ... It was quite amusing – Dr. Harrison head of MacDonald College walked in in the midst of it, and the last time he saw me I was wrestling with a similar task – last December – when Dr. Tory on the eve of his departure for France remembered he had promised Galsworthy an article for his paper. Don't mention this business of article writing outside, for Dr. Tory is supposed to be the writer and signs them....

The record of servicemen in the universities proved highly satisfactory. 'Several of our students at British Universities,' Burt wrote, 'are covering themselves with glory – heading class lists, being drawn by professors into special research, etc.'[12] He must have found this result of his efforts a compensation for laborious days, uncomfortable train travel, and above all the homesickness and restlessness to which he refers in almost every letter to Mrs Burt. By the end of June his work, and that of the Khaki University, was over, and he was able to leave for home. President Tory and his associates had the satisfaction of having created a service which contributed to the development of similar work among the armed forces of New Zealand, Australia, the United States, and Great Britain, to the maintenance of morale during the confused process of demobilization, and to the encouragement of many young Canadians to complete educational programs at home which they might not have undertaken without the stimulus of this opportunity.[13]

4

London Days

Burt's months in London with the Khaki University coincided with the period of the Peace Treaty negotiations and with a year of marked political and industrial unrest in the United Kingdom. These public issues were very much in his mind, and the constant references in his letters reveal much of his political and social philosophy at this time. He found relaxation and stimulation in visits with English and Canadian friends with similar interests. Other evenings were spent in extensive reading.

The Britain of 1919 had changed greatly from that of post-Edwardian times when Burt had studied at Oxford. The war and its aftermath had deepened class conflicts in the country and had produced a ferment of reformist and revolutionary attitudes which were beyond the capacity of the coalition government to comprehend. No consistent and comprehensive program was developed by Lloyd George's ministry to cope with labour unrest, and the conflict between corporate economic interests and those who sought a greater degree of social and economic equality. The general election of 1918 was conducted by the government on the basis of such conflicting slogans as 'A Country Fit for Heroes to Live In,' 'Hang the Kaiser,' make Germany bear 'the Whole Cost of the War,' and 'the Menace of Bolshevism.' The curious mixture of Conservatives and unprogressive Liberals who comprised Lloyd George's cabinet was incapable of devising an industrial policy which would be fair to the working class. The Labour party achieved its greatest electoral success to date, with over 2 million supporters, 22 per cent of the total votes cast. Its campaign was based for the first time on a program, *Labour and the New Social Order*, compiled by the Fabian, Sidney Webb. But although it became the largest opposition party, its parliamentary performance was indifferent.

In many industrial centres labour resorted to direct action. There were alarming strikes in the Clyde area where the engineers and shipworkers demanded a 40-hour week. Even policemen were sufficiently dissatisfied that strikes or threats of strikes occurred, and in Liverpool the government called in the troops. More formidable was the threat of a strike by the coal miners. The government threatened the use of troops, then appointed a royal commission and promised to implement their recommendations, but subsequently repudiated this promise. The railwaymen were also restive and resorted to strike action later in 1919. The Red Scare, which so alarmed the Establishment, coupled with the resentment of the workers over inadequate housing, meagre and poor food, the high cost of heating, and low wages, produced an explosive mixture.

Burt's assessments of economic and political conditions in Britain at this time are to be found in the following letters, which indicate that his observations were radicalizing him to a marked degree.

January 29, 1919

Conditions in England are now and will be quite serious, for labour unrest is deep and widespread. Some fear a real revolution shortly. The general feeling seems to be that there must be a very radical change in the whole scheme of things in the immediate future. If this is not accomplished by regular means it will in all probability be brought about by force, but I do not think accompanied by violence. The old system of the distribution of wealth and the conditions of labour are doomed, and if statesmanship is exercised no one will be injured really and the working world will be regenerated. The toiler must labour fewer hours and under more liberal conditions. He will not be ruled autocratically as he has been by his employer, but must have some governing say in the environment and manner of his work. The wages system is only a makeshift and strikes and rises in wages are no solution because the level of prices fluctuates. Some solution by which 'real' wages are substituted for 'nominal' wages must be found (nominal – money wages, real – what they are worth in purchasing power) by establishing a fixed relation between a set and recognised standard of living and the remuneration necessary to sustain it. This is a most difficult problem and will be followed by another – the readjustment of this equation from time to time. Then there is also the problem of accumulated wealth – inherited fortunes and large incomes. A readjustment here would give our old society a new lease of life. Ideally inheritance and bequest should be abolished, but there are many practical difficulties. They could be limited much more than they are at present. Profits and large incomes must be taxed very much more heavily than at present. Indeed confiscation may be necessary to a certain extent. The present distribution of wealth is too uneven. Land of course in England is a crying problem. The owners of land in the future must regard themselves less as absolute owners and more as trustees for the nation. Do you think I am a Bolshevik? Really however such a revolution peacefully carried out will alone save English and other societies sooner or later from Russian Bolshevism....

March 9, 1919

...I am experiencing a curious conflict. On the one hand I sympathize heartily with the pressing desire of the working class for the elevation of their standard of living. It is unjust that such a large portion of mankind should have such a disproportionately small amount of pleasure. There should be more compensation for their work being a task. Moreover the existing distribution of wealth is unjust. The disproportion is greater than the difference of merit. But on the other hand a fear battles with this sympathy. In the past you see again and again in an ever recurring cycle, liberty awakening, struggling painfully, conquering, misusing its victory, descend into license and end in dissolution, out of which in turn a new power arises creating order. Is it not the same as ever? The present is only a little point in the continuous stream of time. The rising of the lower classes under the inspiration of a more or less developed socialism is largely materialistic – a search for happiness in a readjustment of material things and conditions. Will their reign, which is inevitable, not be unfavourable to the finer things which are not practical in the vulgar sense – which are a nobler adornment of real life than the luxury of worldly goods? I fear for the ideal, the intellectual. The vast machine of the modern world is ever more complicated till it is almost impossible to regulate it consciously, and yet this is becoming every more necessary with the appearance within – here and there – of new formidable forces which if not controlled and adjusted in harmony with the whole, will surely wreck it. So I fear the coming dissolution but have no forshadowing of the power that is to emerge from it. Do you call me a pessimist? I hope not, for in spite of it all life is worth living, for it is like a work of art that may be improved....

Thus, like most intellectuals, Burt was uncomfortable in a society dominated by materialist values, whether the domination was a product of middle class aquisitive capitalism, or of proletarian welfare statism. Nor has the dilemma been resolved in their minds during the last half century.

To Burt, at this time, parliamentary institutions seemed incapable of dealing with the contemporary economic crisis and with increasingly complex forces in modern industrial society; party politics and the existing political structure had become irrelevant. On both sides of the Atlantic before and during the war years there was much theorizing by critics of the democratic state as it existed at this time – the chief targets of criticism being the party system, unbridled individualism, and majority rule. Various remedies for the complaints were advocated, and some liberal-minded thinkers preached the virtues of the pluralist state, where interest groups would have greater autonomy. In his home province the leader of the United Farmers of Alberta, Henry Wise Wood, under the pressure of agrarian discontent, was articulating his idea of group government, which shortly thereafter was to destroy the system of bipartisan politics in the province.[1] Burt expressed his own views in the following terms:

March 23, 1919

...The greatest need of the day is for organizing genius and the greatest problems are no longer political but economic. Government is of necessity coming to regard its greatest problems to be those of the production and distribution of wealth. To this end the existing form of government, a relic of the past, patched and remade in parts, is far from being able to cope with the situation. Our house of commons is a relic of days long ago when the districts represented by the members were each distinct, more or less self-sufficient units of society. The basis was geographical, the town and the country each with its corporate existence. But with generations have appeared new and more vigorous and vocal units which quite overshadow these old moribund ones. The new units are those bound by common economic interests and the most pressing present day problems arise out of the relation between these units. A great industrial parliament, in which the professions as well as the trades and business would be represented as such, would square very much more closely with existing needs. In fact what we want is an industrial parliament to replace our moth-eaten political parliament. But we are the slaves of our forefathers because inertia is as important a factor in human life as in physical. The task ahead is a stupendous one. In the past our economic life resembled a machine which regulated itself automtatically in some respects very well – particularly in determining what goods and how much of each would be produced. With countless competing producers this was the natural result of each seeking his own gain. But this is no longer possible. The labour world has organized with sufficient strength to throw the machine out of gear and now we face the appalling task of adjusting and regulating this stupendous machine in full consciousness. How it can be done the Lord only knows. Whenever I have had too much dinner I fear the result will be failure and chaos. It would be easier if there were not so many prejudices current in society. Miss Bowers nearly made me say "damn" to her face. She was very loquacious and disdainful of the lower class – they were getting good wages and as they did not know how to spend their money, should not have any more – their whole moral standard was infinitely lower than that of the middle and upper classes. She was aghast when I asked her what was going to happen to her dear England if it were true that the vast majority of the nation were such as she depicted them. I was nearly rude enough to ask her how she would like to have to keep a family on the mere existence a "tommy's" wife has been getting through the war. I am sure she thinks I am a Bolshevist...

For a time he had high hopes of Lloyd George, but soon became disenchanted. He was initially pleased by the Prime Minister's attack on Lord Northcliffe, who was advocating harsh peace terms for Germany. Northcliffe was the first press lord to substitute interestingly presented news for long reports of political speeches and weighty editorials, and this was what the working and lower middle classes wanted, although only slightly over half of English households subscribed to a daily newspaper of any type.[2]

April 20, 1919

...Lloyd George's attack [on 16 April] on the Northcliffe press is the thunderclap which promises the present freeing of a surcharged atmosphere. Northcliffe deserved it and more. The syndicated press which he personifies is a standing menace, for it creates public opinion and deceives the public into believing they thought it out themselves. But more than this. Ll[oy]d G[eorge] has been wandering into a far country with unnatural companions. His present government is a pasteboard structure in no way representing the people or their needs of today. The people are radical and in their hearts are crying for radical reforms – a peaceful revolution. I think his blow from the shoulder means that at last he has seen it and is going to slough off the present unnatural government of worn out or incapable or unknown politicians, to organize a strong national government that will build strong from the foundations. England needs to pass through changes as great as France in 1789. He will do it....

Beginning in 1919, the British worker was caught between the millstones of rising prices and lagging wage increases, combined with a severe housing shortage, which aroused Burt's humanitarian sympathies:

June 29, 1919

...The next chief interest of the hour is the Labour Conference where they voted for direct action i.e. strikes to force the government into a policy of 'hands off Russia.' Many are alarmed at this threat of using unconstitutional methods to gain political ends. Some of the papers are not kind to the Labour World. They do not

see that every large effective measure of reform in England since Catholic Eman-
cipation 1829 has been carried as a result of the use or threat of force. It is nothing
new. That is the madness of it. Another thing they fail to see is that the present
government which was based on grand election promises has been comparatively
marking time. The Government is responsible for much. If the people were crazy
enough to transform the election into an orgy of vengeance, the elected of the
people should have realized the situation of the country and set about bravely to
effect some very necessary reforms. But the world is going to the Dogs. The
complexity of society and government has completely outgrown the development
of human ability to manage it and we are like to come a cropper as a result. ... Of
course capital is necessary but the holding of it in large blocks by private individuals for selfish ends is not necessary. ... Violent revolution and seizure would be bad,
so would full compensation (such as for land and mines) for it would only
transform not remove the evil. The best way I think is by progressive taxation –
leaving some fruits to individual enterprise but taking more and more for the
state. Death duties should be heavier and if direct heirs fail, property in case of
intestacy should revert to the state. But this is only the dull machinery. We need a
new spirit of service for the state. We have, due to the form of our political
development, over-emphasized rights at the expense of duties. We need to em-
phasize that duties are proportional to ability....

This humanist position was in part a product of his own spiritual quest
as a young man, and in part a disenchantment with contemporary
institutionalized Christianity. Reporting a conversation with London
friends, a disillusioned clergyman and his wife, he declared:

... The Church has suffered by the best men leaving it. Up to a certain point this is
cowardice. But a time may be reached when this ceases to be – when the balance of
good lies outside and it ceases to be worth while remaining in to save it.[3]

This was a common reaction of many British and Canadian intellectuals at
the time, as the experience of James S. Woodsworth and others indicates.
On 29 June Burt returned to the topic:

In a few conversations of late I have poured out my scorn upon the Churches –
shipwrecks of the past because they could not navigate modern strange waters. I
have analyzed the church of today and extracted the following formula 2 parts
spiritual – 1 part gregarious instinct, all in a solution of perverse self-deceit. But
poisons may do good sometimes. It would be folly to shake the faith of those who
lack the vigour or ability (excuses valid almost solely in middle or old age) to find a

better. I think Christianity as we have known it is rapidly dissolving and that before we reach old age it will play a very much smaller part in the great game of life than since its foundation.

Yet despite his strictures, Burt was not unaware of new life stirring in the Church. Commenting on an address by Dr William Temple, he described him as 'one of the greatest forces in the new and rising generation of the Church of England' – an accurate prediction.[4] It is clear that throughout his life he was never a sterile sceptic; rather, religion in its philosophical dimension was always a vital element in his thinking. Half a century later, Malcolm Muggeridge was to express himself in almost identical terms:

For me the only great joy is understanding. This means being attuned to God, to the moral purpose of the universe, to the destiny of the human race that I belong to, to the things that are good – this is joy, and it is of course experience.[5]

On the position of women in society, Burt had shed most of the vestiges of Victorian middle class ideology, if indeed he ever possessed them prior to his marriage. Writing on Christmas Day 1918, he commented:

Your letter of the 19th raised the question ... of the economic position of woman. I agree with you that the conditions that have subsisted are not good or right, and also that the solution is difficult, for making a home and raising a family is something hard to combine with making money to keep the family. Some say that the solution lies along the line of paying someone, a nurse, etc. to look after the children. But this may be good for some. It certainly does not suit me, for I think it eliminates one of the most beautiful things in life. Certainly I agree that no woman on marrying should be obliged to give up her career and that every woman as every man should be trained for a career, also that it might often be wiser for the woman to be the wage earner and the man the home maker. Though I think the reverse condition will always be much commoner....

As an historian, Burt had a special interest in the momentous decisions which were being made in Paris during 1919. He had approved Wilson's 4 July (1918) speech at Mount Vernon, where the President had summarized allied war aims: 'What we seek is the reign of law, based on the consent of the governed and sustained by the organized opinion of mankind.'[6] On 16 March 1919, Burt wrote as follows:

The chief interests here are Paris and the investigation into the coal mining industry. Feeling here is not at all like that of the Bulletin editorial you sent or your diatribe against Wilson and the Americans. All here look to him to hasten the coming of peace and its establishment upon the justest foundation. For here at closer range people see the terrible difficulties that may easily arise from the clash of national interests and aspirations within the ranks of the allies. An independent disinterested arbiter is necessary. England is tremendously unfortunate and handicapped in that several of her colonies are receiving considerable additions of territory. ... More than any other man perhaps, Wilson is possessed of the general confidence.

A week later he returned to the same theme:

...People here are now beginning to worry a bit over Paris and the European situation since the turning over of Hungary to the Bolshevists. The whole mess is simply the result of what comparatively few people have been able to see – the almost impossibility of making the interests of the different states to coincide even for an appreciable time. The present trouble is a healthy shock to the empty headed fools who have thought it would be easy to straighten out the world's problems in a short while at Paris, and a partial awakening to the fact that larger politics are so tangled and involved by geographical conditions and the mixing of races, that in undoing one wrong you only make another. ... Compromise is necessary. It is also perhaps a shock to the faith in a league of nations. I fear few in America, France or England would be willing to fight to straighten out the Roumanian boundary of Hungary, and very naturally. You cannot make a new heaven and a new earth in one day. National characteristics grow, they are not made and remade. It is a question of time, time, time!

A conversation with family friends of Mrs Burt living in Finchley aroused his unspoken ire ('Rest assured I was very polite'), and prompted these observations:

April 6, 1919

...Imperialism – the instinct of one nation to dominate over others – is inherent in all peoples. Sometimes it breaks out here and sometimes there. All have been guilty. Moreover nations differ so vitally in character and interest that the mass of one race cannot understand that of another to which it may be opposed or even connected by alliance. People cannot see this – they think other people must be like themselves and when they find they are not, they put the difference down to wickedness. The clash of interests and ambitions at Paris today finds a very close parallel in the Congress of Vienna – the same desires for increased territory and punishment of the victim – the same deadlock due to conflict of interests and desires. In fact in some ways the situation is worse. There is perhaps as great if not greater eagerness for vengeance as in 1815. But it would require the return of the Kaiser and a terrible renewal of the war to present the same justification.[7]

Burt saw very clearly that the dynamic nature of modern society precluded 'permanent' solutions in international affairs, and that constant adjustments of the peace settlements of 1919 would be necessary in the future. 'There are fundamental clashes of desires and interests and imagined interests,' he wrote, 'which cannot be definitely solved.'

You can solve them one way, but you only create by that solution new and difficult problems. ... Paris will give us peace in our time I hope, but not for all time.[8]

Unfortunately, British, Canadian, and French political leaders in the twenties made the maintenance of the status quo the chief article of their political faith, with disastrous results for mankind.

Burt was not affected by the growing hysteria over Communism.

April 30, 1919

...The Russian situation is very suspicious. The newspapers are unanimously loud in their condemnation of Bolshevism. They announce the Bolshevist power tottering to its fall, but at the same time we retire before it – withdrawing from Odessa and planning to evacuate Archangel and the Murmansk coast. There is a vigorous life in Russia which is too sustained to be explained by the tirades of the press. Coleman's brother told me a friend of his had travelled, after living a while under the supposedly bloodthirsty Bolshevists, from Moscow to Vladivostock and had been treated only with courtesy. Indeed there is internal war but of a particular type – a war on all who are not engaged in any labour which may be directly or indirectly useful to society but who are living "independently" that is upon their money – really parasites. ... Of course in some ignorant minds the cry is simply against capital and is interpreted as heralding the destruction of society. Capital however is fundamental – the real question is the ownership and control of it. This in the past has been too much in the hands of individuals and too little in those of the state or society....

About the time he penned these lines the Winnipeg General Strike began. The strike had overtones of revolutionary rhetoric, but in reality was a struggle for jobs and a peaceful readjustment in the relations of labour and capital. But to the Canadian economic élite and to the political establishment it was Bolshevism, and they reacted by suppressing civil liberties and smashing the strike, but not its objectives, which were to be almost universally accepted in the years to come.

As the date of the publication of the Treaty of Versailles drew near (9 May 1919), Burt described the state of opinion in Britain.

May 4, 1919

...Every interest here seems in breathless suspense awaiting the publication of the peace terms and the action of Germany. I think I detect the growth of a juster frame of mind though some still make a parade of ridiculous demands. No adequate reparation can be made for war. The greatest danger is that too much will be taken, to the material injury of Germany, which will reflect injuriously upon us, to the creation of a spirit of revenge, and to our own moral injury. I am afraid that the present settlement will be relatively less just than that of France a century ago. But behind Germany lies an extremely complicated Europe with unalterably conflicting rights. ... The acts of nations are almost entirely pure selfishness. For the most part they try to clothe them with motives of broad justice and right. But it is more self deception than general deception. Because each is different in character and interests each is bound to suspect the others. England is very unfortunate. She cannot help herself in appearing as the head of an Empire that has gained more territory than all the rest put together. ... Yet as time goes on and the bonds of alliance relax there will appear peoples on the continent to accuse England of being always Napoleon's "perfidious Albion" – pretending to fight for the justice of Europe but really reaping a great harvest overseas.

His final words on the subject, as he prepared to depart for Canada, were prophetic: 'Well, the peace is signed at last – a rotten peace that will cause much trouble unless it is soon mended by the League of Nations.'[9]

Burt's reading during his sojourn in London was almost exclusively in the field of French history, particularly in the period of the French Revolution and Napoleon, for which he purchased numerous multi-volume works.[10] These included Albert Sorel ('He is most penetrating and brilliant – an extremely difficult matter in a sustained work'),[11] Lavisse and Rambaud, Vandal, Chateaubriand, Lanfrey ('written 50 years ago and yet perhaps the best life of Napoleon by a Frenchman'), Taine, P.P. Segur ('It is good to read partial accounts if they are well written – and of course one reads both sides'), Thiers, and Gustav Le Bon. The latter's *Psychology of Revolution* he found 'very suggestive.'

The working of psychology, especially mass psychology, has not been sufficiently recognized by writers of history. ... We need more of this method of approach. The mere study of documents is insufficient. The historian of the future must know more of the principles underlying the working of the human mind and human conduct.

Of the various biographies of Napoleon he wrote: 'The extreme difficulty of forming a tempered judgment about Napoleon is due to the old conflict of state or political morality with personal and individual morality, complicated by the clash between liberty on the one hand and prosperity, order and glory on the other.' This intensive study program perfected his reading knowledge of French and heightened his enthusiasm for European history during the period 1789–1815.

Why should I not tackle this period [he wrote on 20 April] which attracts me so, and for a few years devote the most of my time to it? It has the supreme value over other periods of presenting a highly concentrated history of all Europe in a few years. There is a tremendous mass of printed material available.

This inclination received the encouragement of Professor George Wrong, who was visiting Britain at this time on Khaki University business.[12]

Burt's views on historiography are expressed in a letter of 9 March 1919, prompted by his reading of Sorel:

...He takes long views of history and connects up distant but similar effects by unearthing deep and permanent causes. That grander style of history appeals to me more and more. The present American tendency – it was common also in Germany before the war – of digging in one little corner should be left for the painstaking but unenlightened toiler – the kind that denies the existence of any inspiration except perspiration. Big minds should essay big tasks. These of course demand much more knowledge and require much wider and more reading. But the rewards are infinitely greater. ... This, the synthetic view, appeals greatly to me. ... So the ambition is growing upon me to know more and more of history in the wider sense, and to postpone to a riper period the distillation of this knowledge into published work....

April 30, 1919

...We in America are at times impatient with these beastly European peoples who apparently intentionally misunderstand each other and hate each other so cause perpetual strife. But the same mental attitude so strongly condemned is just as strongly entrenched at home. What is the outlook of this old world! We talk so loudly about education doing so much. We prescribe it as a panacea for all ills. But the people supposedly the most educated – taking things largely – are no better. I suspect that we have made a great mistake in prescribing so beatifically without examining the quality of our medicine. It is a material education that we have developed and we are trusting blindly in a great God to bring all right, forgetting that the real and true God is in our minds and spirits. Education today could take many a good lesson from classic times, from Greece, Rome and the Renaissance, when character and mind in the broadest manner were prominent ideals. We have got lost in the mechanism of life, the nobility and beauty of life have faded from our vision. It is our duty to restore these as much as possible...

As is the case with most thoughtful graduates of Oxford and Cambridge, Burt felt that these communities of teachers and students most clearly approached his ideal, and he coveted something of their spirit and organization for the University of Alberta.[13] A conversation with one of his former Oxford lecturers who had been in intelligence work during the war is revealing.

May 4, 1919

...We discussed the new tendency so stimulated by the war for the government to call in trained minds for advice and assistance. He says they gave them quite a free hand. One thing very interesting was the value of the broadly trained mind as against the highly specialized trained man. They were able to approach and solve almost any problem that came up and were not cramped in their view by a narrow training. All said and done, I think the Oxford don the best of his type. He knows so much of so many things and does not make a parade of it. The atmosphere is exactly as Dr. Parkin[14] once described it to me – one of intellectual luxury, and it was a great treat to breathe it once more...

Though there was little hope that the University of Alberta, or any Canadian university for that matter, could be reconstructed on Oxford lines, Burt returned home in a positive frame of mind, committed to doing his best for the students and the institution as a whole.[15] He also brought home from his London experience and reflections an intense interest and concern for international relations, which remained a dominant concern in his subsequent academic career.

5

Scholar and Commentator

When Burt returned to Edmonton, the Department of History and Political Economy consisted of himself, Professor D.A. MacGibbon, and Morden H. Long. Long, a graduate of McMaster and a Rhodes Scholar of 1908, had been teaching at a high school in Edmonton before his appointment as lecturer in the history department in 1918.[1] Between the two historians a warm friendship developed. There was a sharp upturn in university enrolment in 1919–20, with nearly five hundred more students than the 618 who were on campus the previous year. History registrations reflected this over-all increase, and Burt taught three courses – British history beginning in the Tudor period, Canadian political and constitutional history, and an honours seminar on Europe from 1789 to 1815. During the year the honours program was revised to include seven or eight courses in history and a reading knowledge of French or German. Burt's course on Canadian history required four texts: Sir Charles Lucas's history of Canada from the discoveries to 1763, Egerton's *Canada Under British Rule*, Lord Durham's Report, and W.P.M. Kennedy's *Documents of the Canadian Constitution, 1759–1915*.

In the following year the departments of history and economics were separated, and Burt was promoted to associate professor. Tory remained the nominal head of the department. Burt offered four courses – two covering the entire period of British history, the Canadian undergraduate course, and an honours seminar on British history from 1603 to 1660. There were no graduate students – a university library of only 17,000 volumes was patently inadequate for this purpose.

In March 1921, Burt contributed a brief article to the student magazine, *The Gateway*, entitled 'Thoughts on the Russian Revolution.'[2] This article was a typical example of an activity which became a distinguishing feature of his career – to challenge students in other disciplines and the lay public with the practical value of historical knowledge and with the opportunities which historical study can provide in developing the faculty of judgment. This strongly-felt obligation to public service conjoined his personal inclinations with one of the basic principles upon which Henry Marshall Tory had established the provincial university. Throughtout the twenties Burt accepted speaking engagements in every corner of the province, and he was the chief contributor, outside the faculty of agriculture, of articles in *The Press Bulletin*, published by the Department of Extension. These articles dealt with such topics as the League of Nations, international affairs, and French-English relations in Canada.

The article on the Russian Revolution revealed his insight, sense of proportion, and commitment to the value of the historical approach to contemporary issues, which had been deepened by his wartime experiences in London. Writing at a time when 'the Red Scare' was still a powerful influence on public opinion in Canada and the United States, he urged his young readers to adopt a more objective and historically informed attitude.

The Russian Revolution [he wrote] is an epoch, perhaps the greatest, in modern history. ... Those who possess treasure and are possessed by fears see the red doom of our civilization stalking westward, while those who are burdened with little property or fear acclaim the rising of a new day.

But it was the phenomenon of revolution, and particularly the characteristics of the French Revolution, which would enable the observer to view the events of the Russian Revolution in proper perspective.

The great paradox of the French Revolution was the intimate conjunction of an ethereal idealism with a crass materialism. It exalted the best and debased the worst in men.

There was the same intellectual ferment and unrest, he noted, in the last half-century of Russian history as in France in the eighteenth century, the same rooted antipathy to monarchial absolutism, the same reliance on government to create new men and a new society, the same aspirations of an ignorant and oppressed peasantry, the same outbreak of mob violence, the same messianic zeal in exporting the revolution to neighbouring countries.

The Bolsheviks with the soviets are the Jacobins with their clubs. ... Their strength lies in three things; their fanaticism, their use of force, and last but not least patriotism roused by the hostility of foreign powers.
      The outcome will be different and yet the same....

The year 1921 was a major turning point in Burt's career. It was obvious that further intellectual satisfaction and professional recognition would depend on research and publication, no matter how effective and brilliant his performance as a lecturer presenting 'the synthetic view' of the broad vistas of European and British history, of which there was ample evidence in the popularity of his courses. Despite his earlier strictures against 'the mean scholar who sorts out and arranges neatly the small details of a dark corner,'[3] he had come to realize that work of this type had its value and its scholarly rewards. The best historiography, he realized, combines the two elements. Wide acquaintance with historical forces and movements is vital in the selection and elucidation of a theme chosen for laborious, detailed investigation. At the same time, Burt never abandoned his enthusiasm for the broad perspectives of history, and this was expressed in the form of popular articles and public addresses, of which his article on the Russian Revolution was a typical example.

Since research in the primary sources of British and European history was impractical because of the inadequacies of the university library and the expense of overseas travel, he directed his attention to the investigation of a Canadian theme, 'the dual nationality of Canada, where public questions have so often been seen out of focus because viewed with only one eye – French or English.'[4] It was a congenial subject, since it possessed the philosophical dimension which Burt so much admired in European historical scholarship. But he was soon confronted with the limitations of the existing accounts on which his generalizations could be based. 'The inadequacy of the secondary authorities on the crucial period [of the conquest and post-conquest years] drove me to the Public Archives of Canada,' he wrote.[5]

Burt first visited the Archives after the end of the spring term in 1921, spending a month in research on the beginnings of British rule in Canada. By this time the acquisitions program of Arthur G. Doughty (1860–1936), Dominion Archivist since 1904, and of his predecessor, Douglas Brymner

(1823–1902), had built up a large body of significant source material relating to pre-Confederation Canada. But comparatively few historians had yet made use of the ore in this rich mine. Doughty had also 'worked out a system under which the Public Archives of Canada remained open all day and all night to accredited historians and research workers.'[6] This was to be a boon to Canadian historians. University teachers were not well paid, and there was no Canada Council to assist their research activities.[7] The arrangement was particularly significant in the depression years, which otherwise would have seen few if any significant publications in the field of Canadian history. With a growing family, Burt was often hard put to make ends meet during the 1920s, and his visits to Ottawa were in the plain living and high thinking tradition.

May 21, 1921

When I scribbled my last I had just secured but not got possession of my room. It was then being decorated. By evening I got in. It is much like a student's room in the U. of A. except that it has running water. My meals I get at a boarding house 'round the corner where hosts of clerks eat three times a day. The substance is much better than the style. The respectability of the place is guaranteed by 15 Y.M.C.A. lodgers who board there. I have added eggs and bacon to my usual breakfast. The terms are most reasonable as they would need to be after the way my money has disappeared. I ... pay $5. a week for my room. The board is $7. per week.

I plunged into the Archives yesterday afternoon at 2 p.m. and stayed till after 5. I was back after dinner for another three hours. Today I worked morning and afternoon. ... At the Archives I met an interesting French Canadian [Gustave Lanctot] who was just ahead of me and overlapped me at Oxford.[8] He has a post here – I believe second in command to Dr. Doughty the Archivist. He is writing books on the French Régime and spends his days and nights at the Archives. Though the hours are 9–12:30 and 2–5, I can work all night and Sunday too. I merely have to be sure I get enough books out in those hours. Your father and I are going round tomorrow morning and Lanctot is going to show us the whole place.

Before leaving Edmonton I made a list of the Archives Publications in the Alberta Library and have characteristically lost it. I enclose a full list of their publications. Would it be too much trouble to give it to Miss Calhoun or to Cameron[9] with a request to note on it what we have not got and return it to me as soon as possible? Some things are scarce and a few days may determine whether we secure or miss some of the lacking volumes. Dr. Doughty has promised to do what he can.

May 26, 1921

...Working away in the Archives this morning I was also accosted. Looking up I saw a strange face. It was that of Chester New, an old Toronto man who took his graduate work in Chicago with a year abroad. [10] He has been known to me and I to him for some time through MacGibbon and Long, after both of whom he warmly inquired. He has been some years collecting material for a Life of Lord Durham and will now be sitting across the table from me every day. We lighten our labours by little breaks discussing phases of Canadian history. I am pleased he has turned up, for I like him.

My task is mountainous. I have been writing for over nine hours today securing facts for only one detailed incident. Walker, a magistrate of Montreal and one of the English minority that followed the Conquerors into Canada, was assaulted in his own home by some carefully disguised soldiers in December 1764. There is no end of letters, writs, positions and legal examinations. The affair was never sifted out at the time and is still referred to as a mystery by modern writers. It caused Murray's recall, however, and is intimately linked up with the strained relations of English and French immediately after the Conquest. The last thing I copied tonight was a long document inspired by Walker. It is a thorough going indictment of Governor Murray and his whole Government, charging him with ruling tyranically and setting race against race. Of course it is violently biased. Tomorrow morning I dig into Murray's reply paragraph by paragraph.

...I do not expect to get much reading done for I can work nights and Sundays at the Archives, and I must make the most of having come so far for such a short time.

...I have a pleasant walk of about 10 minutes from here to the Archives....[11]

May 29, 1921

...It is very pleasant now sitting across the table with New. We have frequent minute chats and having a great deal in common, these little breaks are not vain conversation. He commends my purpose in digging through the sources of Canadian history....

I am really getting a lot of valuable material. It is slow work – I shall not be able to finish collecting the material for General murray's period of Government which is only to 1766. I think I will be able to clear up much that has been doubtful.

The next letter records the formation of the League of Nations Society in Canada, an event of considerable importance because Burt became deeply involved in the work of the Society in Alberta throughout the decade. It also led to his friendship with Sir Robert Borden, Sir George Foster, and the officers of the national organization in Ottawa.

May 31, 1921

I have just returned from an organization meeting of the League of Nations Society for Canada, which passed off very well. I will enclose a clipping in the morning if there is an account in the paper. I there met Dr. Tory who has just reached Ottawa from Toronto....

...I had a delightful chat with Mr. Adams, a most charming Scot. He says the abolition of the Conservation Commission, of which they were a part, was a piece of party politics. It was an important body with a number of highly paid specialists who aroused the jealousy of lesser-paid civil servants in the regular departments and also of the politicians who had little control over the Commission. We had also a good chat on Architecture in Canada....

The Conservation Commission had been created in 1909 with Clifford Sifton as chairman. It held its first meeting in 1910 and inaugurated a far-reaching program of scientific investigations on natural resources conservation, land use, industrial development, water pollution, and other matters, working in close co-operation with experts from the municipal, provincial, and federal governments and the universities. It issued recommendations for government action and published voluminous reports. Sifton resigned as chairman in 1918, and the Meighen ministry abolished the Commission early in 1921, despite the protests of the supporters of the Commission's work.

May 31, 1921 (continued)

Harvey from Winnipeg appeared yesterday in the Archives and we have now a pleasant trio. Of course I know and like Harvey of old. I am getting to know New better and begin to feel as if here were a good old friend. It adds delight to the work.

...I am collecting some good stuff which I think will enable me to produce a good article this winter on the beginnings of my problem right after the conquest....

June 3, 1921

It is true I have been sticking very close – but it is necessary if my short stay here is to allow me to utilise the material I collect without letting it lie suspended in mid-air for a year or so. I am limiting myself to Murray's Government. He succeeded to the command on Wolfe's death and became Governor on the conclusion of Peace. Three years later he was recalled. Those three years from the peace to his recall 1763–66 are about the most critical in Canadian history. He sought to win the hearts of the French to British rule, and at the same time saw rise up against him the bitter opposition of the few hundred British merchants in Canada. The latter in their desires to crush the French and treat them as a subject people planted the seeds of the conscious racial strife. Their relations with Murray are at present only vaguely known. I am tracing the origin of this clash and have discovered some valuable material which will enable me to clear up much that has been in doubt. To me Murray is standing out more and more as a real statesman and I have unearthed one very clear cause of quarrel which has hitherto been unnoticed and have been able to fix a pretty close date for its origin. But I would not be able to produce these results in an article until I had examined all the available material. This I can do I believe in my stay here – but only by spending every available hour upon it. I have gone through about 15 huge folio volumes of correspondence already. I have to plan it so that I will have several days at the end searching for loose strands that I have missed by the way. The bulk of the material I am examining is neither calendared, i.e. summarised roughly in the printed archive reports, nor indexed, i.e. having a table of contents for each volume. Thus I have to go through it all letter by letter. I should be able to produce a good article for the Canadian Historical Review. It is now 11:20 and I am fairly weary having worked there every evening this week but Tuesday....

June 18, 1921

...Yesterday noon New took me to lunch at the University Club where we had a good meal and a delightful chat with several others. So my noon hour was prolonged guiltily into the afternoon and we three stopped early for a chat and a stroll back to the city together. ... I returned to the Archives [this morning] to find that Underhill had been looking for me and that I had been demanded on the telephone. New insisted on my lunching with him again to meet Underhill that we might arrange a date for returning together....

June 21, 1921

...Yesterday I worked in the Archives till 1:30 when I went to dinner, read a little, wrote a note to Toronto and then met the trio at the University Club. We took the car to Rockliffe – walked round a little lake, found a pretty nook looking out over it, and indulged in light historical conversation. We all know each other pretty well and are very congenial, and so we had a most delightful time. The three of us in the Archives have really had a great time imparting our discoveries and view to each other and having many a laugh. On our return Harvey went off to have supper with his brother-in-law whose guest he is in Ottawa. He is a Deputy Minister. Frank Underhill entertained New and myself to supper in a pleasant Japanese restaurant. ... This morning we went through the Mint. Frank was to have come but did not appear. It is a great place. They melt the metal and purify it in crucibles heated by oil, then they pour it out into ingots an inch or two wide, a couple of feet long and as thick as your finger. These they put through tremendous rollers which roll it out into long ribbons just the thickness of the coin. From these the coin is punched. They are then softened by heating and being suddenly plunged into cold water. Then they are stamped by the dies. Finally they are all weighed and sounded carefully (except the coppers and 5¢ pieces) one by one. The balance for weighing is remarkable. We saw 25¢ pieces going through. The scales are manufactured in the mint in England and are as delicate as the finest chemical scales. They work automatically 3 sec. for each piece. The light, heavy, and exact weight coins are automatically separated. They all have to be sounded by hand. If there is a blister or crack they ring like lead.

June 23, 1921

...Tonight I am going back to the Archives in a last mad rush to finish. I fear I cannot get off tomorrow night. I have much material and am determined on one article at least. I have solved one mystery (the Walker affair) I think very neatly and fully, and have my judgment confirmed by a conversation with Wm. Smith the secretary of the Archives, who is a keen student of Canadian history.

William Smith (1859–1932) was educated at the University of Toronto and in 1913 was appointed to the Archives staff as deputy keeper of the public records. He was the author of three historical works of which the best known is his *History of the Post Office in British North America*. Burt developed a great admiration and affection for him, and Smith became his closest friend on the Archives staff.

Returning to Edmonton, Burt completed his first article for the *Canadian Historial Review* during the summer, which was published the following year under the title, 'The Mystery of Walker's Ear.' In this year (1921) he was promoted to full professor and, although Tory retained his connection for one more term, Burt became, in effect, the head of the department in 1921. In addition to carrying a full teaching load, he gave himself unstintingly to the life of the university as musical director of the choir for the Sunday morning services in Convocation Hall, as one of the lecturers for the Philosophical Society on the topic of international relations and the League of Nations, and as a member of the national subcommittee of the League of Nations Society for promoting its work in Canadian universities.[12]

Burt did not visit Ottawa in 1922, and during the 1922–3 academic year he was much involved in League of Nations Society activity. In an Armistice Day address, and in a speech delivered at one of the Sunday services in Convocation Hall in the spring of 1923, he presented cogent reviews of the functions and problems of the League and of actions taken during its brief existence which had solved a number of acute problems. These addresses,[13] the editor of *The Gateway* noted, 'are attracting much attention in the city,' and corrected impressions conveyed in the daily press.

The nature of the League [Burt declared] is often misunderstood. It is neither a superstate nor a powerless body. The Covenant is simply an agreement whereby the various member states forego some of their fullest freedom in the future for the good of themselves and the welfare of the world at large....

The difficulties of the League have been tremendous – enough to destroy it, were it not the sole hope of a shipwrecked world. It was born into an atmosphere surcharged with national hate and mistrust, an atmosphere arising out of the war and the peace settlement....

...More and more we are coming to see how faulty was the settlement of Europe effected at Versailles.

Burt stressed that naïve optimism and negative pessimism were equally inappropriate in estimating the prospects of an institution which 'represents the world as no other body ever has.' There was evidence, he thought, that universality of membership would ultimately be achieved.

But there is a grave danger. In these democratic days the breath of life of all government is public opinion. What is true of ordinary government is equally true of the League of Nations. Only in so far as it has the backing of a continuous and intelligent public opinion throughout the world can it hope to succeed. Here then lies a tremendous moral responsibility upon everyone of us. We must work out our salvation through the League; it will not work our salvation for us. If we fail to shoulder this great responsibility, we will stumble along the same old way which we all know leads to disaster.

In addition to his public addresses, Burt published two articles in the Extension Department's *Press Bulletin*,[14] reiterating this argument. In these and subsequent articles and addresses during the 1920s Burt was performing the function which today is almost monopolized by the newspaper columnist. The recent emergence of this class of journalist has overshadowed the former influence of the editor and of the few academics who assumed the role of commentators on national and international affairs.

Devotion to the interests of the League of Nations Society was expressed in travels around the province, and in the spring of 1924 the Extension Department published a booklet which he had prepared, *A Short History of the League of Nations*, which was suitable for use in schools or in discussion groups. Burt received an appreciative letter from Sir Robert Borden:

I have just read your "Short History of the League of Nations" and I hasten to send my warm congratulations. It is admirable in every way. ... You are entitled to the sincere thanks of all those who take an interest in the purpose of the League and who have some confidence in its usefulness.[15]

Burt viewed the League of Nations as a constructive force in the modern world, and he did not hesitate to stress its achievements in resolving potentially dangerous disputes. But he was quite aware of its limitations and did not believe that mankind had moved into a new era of perpetual peace. The pursuit of national interests and the emotional power of mob psychology were realities which he analyzed in an article entitled 'The Horoscope of Mars,' published in 1923 in *Queen's Quarterly* – in which his talents as a commentator on international affairs were never better displayed. The theme was the nature of war in the modern world – its endemic character, its effects on civilization, and the prospects for its elimination. The 'dark half of the horoscope of Mars' was evident, he argued, in deeply rooted characteristics of the society of sovereign states. There was the hard fact that the devices of arbitration, international conferences, and international law had not triumphed over resort to force, where vital interests were at stake. History was replete with examples of a great power or group of powers intervening to settle disputes, and would have to be accepted unless an international organization existed to prevent war. The principle of the sovereignty of the state was still operative, with the consequent 'unwillingness of states to curtail their full freedom of action.' The divergence of national interests might be mitigated to some extent, but differences based on ethnic and geographic factors were permanent. It was usually impossible 'to fix a frontier which does not violate some fundamental principle, racial, economic or military,' and compromise arrangements often became obsolete.

There were other threats to peace, among them mob psychology, which 'may be even more powerful in the future.' 'In proportion as governments are controlled by the mass of the people, it is possible that foreign relations will be guided less by cold calculation than by hot

passion, by mob impulse.' Still another consideration ignored by inter-
nationalists was 'the danger that any system of perpetual peace will lead to
the establishment of a static world' – a comfortable arrangement for the
beneficiaries of the status quo, but a grievous vexation to the discon-
tented. 'We have not yet learned to solve,' he pointed out, 'the gigantic
problem of harmonizing the vital element of growth with an artificial
system of order.' 'The pacifist ideal opens out the prospect of justice
sacrificed on the altar of peace.' Finally, on the dark side of the horoscope,
was the fact that war was 'an age-old instinct.'

It is a human institution older than private property and more ancient than
marriage. As its roots are deeper, is it not probable that it will outlive the sacred
right of private property and the honourable state of marriage?

Despite the pessimistic prognostication which it was possible to make,
with abundant historical evidence to support it, there was also the 'bright
half of the horoscope of Mars,' which was struggling for predominance.
The increasing destructiveness of modern weapons, the involvement of a
nation's whole population in a war effort, the increasing cost of arma-
ments, the danger of national bankruptcy, all suggested that 'war has been
approaching the point where it must swallow up civilization, or be
abolished by it.' Moreover, Burt argued, increasing economic interdependence provided a powerful self-interested motive for avoiding war.
Reinforcing this influence was the growth of international voluntary
organizations representing the common interests of scientists, scholars,
and trade unionists. Humanitarian activity and concern was also growing.

In so far as our feeling and our thought are focussed upon the problems of human
suffering and human betterment, we are evolving an ideal that takes precedence
over the limited and lower ideal of national welfare.

These influences were affecting men's ideas. The thought of war as a
glorious thing 'has been buried deep in the mud of Flander's fields.' The
sense of international morality that was beginning to grow and the increasing acceptance of the concept of a divided sovereignty were hopeful
signs. 'A final solution may not be attainable, yet something can be accomplished,' Burt claimed. Progress could be made by reducing trade barriers
and by revising school curricula to curb national prejudice, to demonstrate the relation between the evolution of warfare and the rest of life,
and to stress humanitarian ideals.

6

The Old Province of Quebec

The spring of 1923 found Burt again at the Public Archives, for nearly two months of continuing research on the theme which he had begun to investigate in 1921 and which in following years was to result in seven significantly original articles in the *Canadian Historical Review* and the *Transactions of the Royal Society of Canada*. The culmination of this effort came in 1933 in *The Old Province of Quebec*, which his distinguished student, Dr Hilda Neatby, a noted specialist in this field, has described as 'a work so thorough and detailed that it is still without a rival as the standard work of reference for the period.'[1] 'Had I known how many years it would take,' the author noted in his foreword, 'I might not have begun it. But I could not leave off once I had started.'[2]

As before, his letters to Mrs Burt gave a detailed running commentary on his activities and relationships in Ottawa.

June 18, 1923

Here I am at the above address [the YMCA] for the present. It is not exactly what I would desire in every respect, but it is good, and I have saved the time and trouble in looking for a room in a private boarding house....

This morning I met Dr. Tory right after breakfast, and with him attended the annual meeting of the League of Nations Society, which sat both morning and afternoon. Sir Robert Borden presided in the morning and Sir George Foster in the afternoon session. The meeting gave a great reception to the account of our doings in Edmonton, and requested Dr. Tory to prepare a detailed account to be laid before the Executive Committee, for they said that a knowledge of the work we had done and were doing would be of great value to the rest of Canada. Sir Robert Borden took me to lunch in the Rideau Club and put me up there for a week; in the afternoon he had my name added to the list of the General Committee for Canada....

Beside the people mentioned the only other person whom I have met so far is McArthur, Morison's[3] successor at Queen's as professor of colonial history. As he is running the Queen's summer school at the Archives, I will see more of him, and will be able after a while to give you a better impression of him.

Duncan McArthur (1885–1943) became an intimate friend whose scholarship Burt greatly admired. He had been educated at Queen's University and was a member of the staff of the Public Archives from 1907 to 1912. In this capacity he had assisted Doughty in editing *Documents Relating to the Constitutional History of Canada, 1791–1818*, one of the large volumes of primary sources being published by the Archives. He left the Archives to practice law for a number of years, and then accepted an appointment as professor of history at Queen's in 1922. In this capacity he inaugurated a summer school course in Ottawa, where his students used the collections in the Archives. Following McArthur's appointment as Deputy Minister of Education for Ontario in 1934, Queen's continued to offer the course till 1940. In addition to the widely-used school history of Canada, to which Burt refers in subsequent letters, he contributed chapters to *Canada and Its Provinces* and to the Canadian volume in the *Cambridge History of the British Empire*.

June 22, 1923

After finishing my last epistle, I went over to the House of Commons and heard Sir Lomer Gouin move the second reading of a bill on the Lake of the Woods waterways, and the Hon. Arthur Meighen deliver an incisive speech against it....

Last night I returned after supper for the first time to the Archives and got in a good evening's work. New was here as he usually is....

The Archives are busy now. McArthur has 9 or 10 students here in the Queen's summer school, George Brown[4] whom I knew in the Tanks has just turned up, and Innis[5] a new man on the economics staff at Toronto, is working here with the assistance of his wife. He is huge and youthful, his wife square and likewise – both pleasant people. But I like New best. We do not breakfast together, for we both rise at uncertain hours, but we have our lunch and supper together, and this makes the great capital city seem much less formidable.

June 25, 1923

Here I am again at my accustomed seat – I have a big book on the chair to get the right height for my machine, and to keep my trousers pure and undefiled from the cheap varnish on the chairs. I have just returned from supper and my accustomed rest thereafter with a pipe and book, and the place is delightfully quiet, – though uncomfortably hot, as it has been almost all the time since I arrived in this corrupt capital.

After meals I have been stretching out on my bed and spending a little while reading Chapais, Cours d'Histoire du Canada, and am at present finishing the first volume. Chapais is professor at Laval, Quebec, and, so I am told, was made Senator on the strength of this book.[6] They should have made him Premier, I find myself in such agreement with him.

I have been pounding away on my machine so much and so hard that I have split one of my fingernails, as I used to do when thumping the piano for Gypsy Smith in Massey Hall. But this means that I am finding some good stuff. For a day now I have been working through 100 pages of documents bearing on the beginnings of strife between the civil and the military authorities in Quebec, and it is very amusing. It began with an Ordinance that all persons must carry a lantern at night in the streets. All went well until one merchant disobeyed, Allsopp was his name. He was accosted by a sentinel and asked for his light. He pointed to the Moon, according to one evidence. In another document, he finally produced a paper folded up like a lantern, and said, as he took this from his pocket, that he was obeying the Ordinance, because the latter did not say that the lantern must be lit – which was true. It was amusing also to find that Quebec had speed laws in 1764. No one could gallop on horseback, or drive vehicles faster than a walk. The fine was 10/, and if this was not paid, the offender had to work four days in repairing the highways. In the same Ordinance I found a reference to the origin of sleigh bells, which I thought were wholly poetic or something like that. This Ordinance required 'at least six horse bells to be affixed to the horse harness, or the said sled or slay' – the honk of the silently approaching motor! Already I have 80 pages of notes typed as close as this neat little machine will let my Scottish-? soul do it.

I am losing some of my friends here. New is off to Toronto tonight. He has been here since early in May. Innis and his wife go at the end of this week...

Today is election day in Ontario, and the elections are a great gamble. No one seems certain of what will be the next government. The results are to be announced tonight at the Y. where they will be gathered by a private wire and put on a big bulletin board. There is to be music too – I suppose to smooth over the political discords and make people take what comes without too much bitterness of thought. Really the situation is most unfortunate. Drury[7] is the best man, but his chances are about as small as I feel some times when you get mad with me.

June 27, 1923

After writing my last to you, I went to the House of Commons, where I heard Meighen baiting Graham, the Minister of Railways, and drawing upon himself the ire of the veteran Fielding. I am told that as long as that Fox Terrier who leads the Conservative Party remains leader, the Liberals are sure to remain in power. He is so cocksure, so carping, so irritating. McArthur, New and I had a good political argument the other night, and we were all agreed that if the Conservatives got another head, the Liberals might split, the Quebec Liberals being reabsorbed into the Conservative fold, and the real Liberals joining with the Progressives to make a hopeful party. Then came the results of the Ontario elections. They put great heart into the Conservatives in the House here, for here they are a small band. I am not pleased with the results....

Though New has gone, and Innis is going tomorrow, I am at no loss for friends ... McArthur, too, is quite a jolly fellow. I see quite a bit of him and we have good fun together. Somehow or other he ever tempts me to jolly him, and we hit it off quite well. Like most other Queen's people, he is an incorrigible Liberal, and that gives us an opportunity of great argument. Another good friend is Mr. Smith, the Secretary of the Archives. He is somewhere in his "sixties," is small of stature and very dull of hearing. But he has the spirit of perpetual youth, is very large by nature and penetratingly acute in mind. He is one of the best natured men that I have ever met. Unlike most deaf people, who are morose, he has an ever bubbling sense of humour. When he laughs, which is very quietly, his eyes close and his mouth becomes like Forrie's when she is in the same mood. He is a wonderful talker, and it is a delight to listen to him, for his knowledge is stupendous. For a quarter of a century he has spent much of his time just steeping himself in Canadian history. I doubt if there is anyone else living who is so familiar with the manuscript material of our history. Even the minor characters, that flit now and then across the stage, he has traced, and he can talk of them as if they were his bosom friends. ... In the evening, when I had just got to work again, in he dropped, "Well here you are again!" No smoking is a rigid rule here, but Mr. Smith is wedded to his pipe. "If you're not busy, let's just close this door and have a smoke." He did it and we lit up, and talked and talked, and when we woke up it was 11:10. He is greatly concerned, as I am about the prospects of Canadian history.... "You know, New, McArthur and you are my hope" he said as we were walking home together. For more than two years he has been spending all his time in collecting and writing a history of Labrador. It is for the Department of Justice, which has charge of the boundary dispute between Canada and Newfoundland. ...

Then he is going to tackle a Constitutional History. I believe he is due to retire soon, so that his scribal ambitions may ere long have freer scope.

June 30, 1923

I am very glad that I did not attempt to use all the material that I gathered a couple of years ago, for the continuance of the search is throwing new light on the fragments which I gleaned two years ago. Moreover it is all soaking in, a most important thing, for the only way to write history is to steep one's self in the documents of the period. Already, however, I see an article or two that I may throw off in my nebular flight.

All this afternoon, I was going through the case of a Jew, Eleazer Levy.[8] It was so interesting that the afternoon went by before I knew it....

...I also collected quite a lot of material on the beginnings of trouble under Carleton, and have reversed my judgment on one famous case of Carleton's action. All the texts speak of the opposition on his arrival as factious, but after examining all the material, I have come to the opinion that he was wrong, indeed that he was very high-handed and unjust. I discussed the matter with Mr. Smith and he agrees with me. Perhaps I will write an article on this before I write on anything else.

So here I am glorying in the riches of this place. It is far from being dull. It is often quite exciting, searching through documents tracing something out and wondering where it will end. Will Levy get justice? I am itching to know. It is also quite amusing. Every volume brings a laugh. Complaints about "Hoggs" running about the streets of Quebec to the distress of many good citizens, the advertisement of the bone of a whale that had been "wrecked" in the Gulf, etc. are as good as Punch or Life.

...I was the guest of Mr. Biggar[9] at dinner in the dining room of the Houses of Parliament. Biggar is a cousin of the Edmonton man, and is the European representative of the Canadian Archives. Just at present he and Dr. Doughty have exchanged jobs. The restaurant is in a most glorious place – above the House of Commons. We had a table by the window, and from our chairs we could look down on the surging Ottawa and over many miles of beautiful country. After dinner, the session bells clanged everywhere through the buildings, and we rushed down to the House of Commons, to hear the debates which had just begun. Till nearly half past eleven, we listened to a debate upon the coming imperial conference. Some of it was most amusing. S.W. Jacobs (Member for the Holy Land – Montreal) wanted the Prime Minister at the conference to promise the vote to the Hindoos in Canada and press for it elsewhere. But this suggestion only let loose a storm from the Western Mountains....

July 2, 1923

The placid routine of my life goes on, my only excitement being in that routine. I find my digestion greatly assisted by a rest for half an hour after every meal – I frequent a restaurant near the Y.M.C.A. There in one of the topmost rooms I stretch me out after meals, light up my old friend, and read. At present I am busy with a book lent me by Mr. Smith – Dix Ans. It is the history of 1840 to 1850, and was written shortly after the time by one of the most modest authors of whom I have heard – Gérin-Lajoie.[10] It is a wonderfully fine piece of work, and would have been published when it was written, had not a friend, who had a poor book coming out on the same subject, requested him to hold his back so that the sale of the other work might not be hurt. So the manuscript remained locked up in a drawer for more than a generation, known only to a few. Then in 1888, it was given to the public by his widow. I would like to be able to do two things like that, but I fear that I can do neither. As it is a big volume, I expect that I will be reading it for some time, but I am not impatient to finish it – it is so good.

Burt was too modest in his estimate of his capability in comparison with Gérin-Lajoie. His *Old Province of Quebec* and *The United States, Great Britain and British North America from the Revolution to the Establishment of Peace After the War of 1812* are monumental achievements of historical scholarship, based on a painstaking examination of thousands of documents and supporting a narrative distinguished by balance, clarity, and vigour.

The rest of the time [he continued] I spend here, and every day I glean some more sheaves. Yesterday and today (it is now 4:20) I have been copying some documents from the Shelburne Papers. They are unsigned and bear no date, but they are valuable. Here is why. For a long time, ever since the American Revolution, there has been a theory, only now and then protested against, that the Quebec Act was the product of the coming of the American Revolution. In short, it is this, that the British Government, seeing the coming trouble with the American Colonies, passed the Quebec Act, which gave the French their laws and religion, with an eye to placating the French in order that they might be used, if necessary, against the English Colonists to the South. In other words, the motives behind the Act take away all the virtue that is in it. Now I have gone through practically all the correspondence right up to the passage of the Act in 1774, and find no evidence to support the American Revolutionary view. These documents which I have just copied reinforce my distrust of the old theory, which by the way Kennedy[11] repeats as if it were the gospel. They were papers of advice given to Shelburne when he was on the Board of Trade and Plantations, and outline an American policy. They were written between the conquest of Canada and the passage of the Stamp Act. They start from the thesis that further emigration to the colonies should be discouraged, for already the colonies are so populous that they constitute a danger. The problem then is how to keep them in proper dependence upon the mother country. The author would check all further spreading westward of the population in America, for it must be kept to the sea coast and not allowed to grow inland. His reasons for this are ingeniously involved. If they spread inland they will be driven by the cost of transportation to develop their own manufactures – which of course would compete with those of the mother country. They will also become more independent in spirit. If they are kept to the seaboard, they will remain dependent upon English goods and will always be under the shadow of English guns. But more is necessary than this, he said. The British Government should use the Indian as a counterpoise to the British Colonists. By preventing the colonists spreading over the Mountains, the Indians will find their hunting grounds preserved, and will be bound more closely than ever to the British interest as against the colonists who would like to despoil them. ... There is a suspicious parallel with the policy which was actually followed, and it has an unpleasant look about it. But what of the Quebec Act? Well here it is. The American Revolutionary theory cannot be correct, for if anyone was at that time actuated by the motives it presupposes, the author of these documents would have been the first among them. But he is utterly innocent of any suggestion of using the French in Canada as a counterpoise to the English to the South of them. It cannot be out of delicacy that he omits mention of it, for he talks quite freely about using the Indian – which is a thousand fold worse. I have become quite excited over the problem, and not a day passes without some discussion or argument upon it. Shortt, who has a violent prejudice against the French Canadian, believes the old theory with all the persistence of a hopeless Presbyterian, and McArthur, of whom by the way, I am very fond, follows him in this. But they cannot produce any documentary evidence in support of it....

Adam Shortt (1859–1931) to whom Burt refers in the preceding letter, was educated at Queen's University, and the universities of Glasgow and Edinburgh. He taught at Queen's from 1885 to 1908, when he was appointed a civil service commissioner. He was the leading pioneer worker in the field of Canadian economic history. He collaborated with Doughty in editing the first great co-operative work of Canadian historical scholarship, the 23-volume *Canada and Its Provinces: A History of the Canadian People and Their Institutions*. His first formal connection with the Archives was in 1907 when, in association with Doughty, he edited a volume of documents on the constitutional history of Canada. From 1918 until shortly before his death he was chairman of the board of publications of the Archives.

July 8, 1923

Yesterday, I was here steadily, though not working all the time, for I had several chats with Mr. Smith. He told me some good tales. One was about a prisoner in Newfoundland, who wrote to the government complaining of the dampness of his cell, and threatening, if they would not do something, that he would not stay. ... I have just returned to write this and a letter to Wallace,[12] and do a little more on an article I am writing. A few days ago I dropped Wallace a line suggesting that I could supply him with a short article on the beginning of the Carleton regime for the September number. He has asked for it and requested that I let him have it by the 20th at the very latest. Already I have broken the back of it, and it is so intensely interesting that I grudge the time necessary to go out for meals. I fear the article may kick up a rumpus, for there are many worshippers of Carleton and this material I have discovered presents him in a most damaging light, not only as a tyrant, but also as a shifty politician. He had a row with his council, and it was so serious that he dared not meet them for more than two months, and then he was able to do it only because events played into his hands. He fired two leaders of the Council and frightened the rest of the majority who were opposed to him into submission. But he carefully obscured all this from the home government. It is really quite a shocking affair.

July 11, 1923

Monday night I finished the article over which I was so wrought up...

Do you remember Benvenuto Cellini's wild excitement in the process of casting his bronze statue? My excitement was much the same. For several nights I had very restless sleep...

July 15, 1923

My article on Carleton has run the gauntlet. McArthur came back from Kingston Wednesday night, and when he came in the next day I gave it to him to read. He has been a great admirer of Carleton. He read it carefully, and agreed with me on the whole thing and that it was an important revelation. Then he suggested that I bring it to Shortt, wondering what would be his reaction. So we went over to the latter's office across the street and sat while he read it. He also accepted it and said it was a very fine piece of work. That night I sent it to Toronto, but I have not yet heard from Wallace. A nice touch of irony was added by a letter which Dr. Doughty, who has just returned, received from the present Lady Dorchester. (She holds the title in her own right). The burden of the letter was pious hope that the study of the Canadian Archives would only add lustre to the memory of her famous ancestor.

Burt's article, 'Sir Guy Carleton and His First Council,' was published in the December 1923 issue of the *Canadian Historical Review*, but it is not apparent that her ladyship (if she read it) found it as much of a revelation as it was to Burt's professional colleagues. His letter of 15 July resumes:

For the last two days I seem to have been more social than industrious. Thursday I must have spent an hour and a half in Dr. Shortt's office talking to him – rather being talked at, for he is a most wonderful talker – I can only with the greatest difficulty squeeze in a very little word every fifteen minutes. ... The morning [Saturday] was not over before McArthur came in and asked me to come over to see Dr. Shortt. McArthur and I had been talking about the state of Denmark and I had suggested that there was only one man in Canada to set it right – Dr. Shortt. I urged him to press the matter on him, but he preferred that I should do it. So he came for that purpose. I have been quite concerned, and I found McArthur the same, when I talked to him about it, over the state of historical study in Canada. There are a number of local societies organized for local antiquarian research, but nothing can be hoped for from them. Then last year the Landmarks Association and the Battlefields Association combined into the Canadian Historical Association. It will never be a *real* Canadian Historical Association, for it has been started on the wrong lines and the best students of Canadian history are not taking it seriously. Indeed, it threatens to prevent the formation of a real Canadian Historical Association, which would be a clearing house for ideas on the study of Canadian history. Then there is the Canadian Historical Review, run independently by the University of Toronto. This it seems to me, ought to be the organ of a real Association. But Dr. Shortt thought the time had not yet come for such action, and I am afraid he sees truly. The centre of any such association would be the Archives here, but at Toronto they have no one who knows the Archives, and the same is true of McGill. ... This means that Queen's is the only University which has taken a real interest in the Archives, and the rest will hold back or out. He suggests that the only practical thing to do now, is to get as many as possible back of the Review to use that as an organ of all students of Canadian history. The difficulty there is that the French Canadians have no contact whatever with the Toronto Review, and I fear that the Toronto people will not make a move of themselves, and of course the French will not ask to be allowed to come in on the Review. So I asked Shortt, if he would not try his hand at bringing them together. He agreed. He promised that he would speak to Wallace and try to persuade him that the Review should be a medium of expression for French Canada, and he also promised to approach the French Canadian historians to prepare them for the invitation, if he can extract it.

The Canadian Historical Association had been founded by the Historic Landmarks Association at its annual meeting in May 1922. Its first president, L.J. Burpee,[13] stated that the reorganized society would broaden the scope of its activities beyond the promotion of interest in historic sites and buildings to include 'the encouragement of historical research and of an intelligent public interest in the history of our country, as well as the co-ordination of the efforts of provincial and local historical societies,' and to bring 'into more perfect harmony the two great races that constitute the Canadian people.'[14] To this latter end English- and French-language secretaries were appointed, but the officers of the Association were predominantly English-speaking. Membership was open to laymen as well as professional historians and, contrary to Burt's deprecatory remark, a number of distinguished historians had joined. But he did not become a member until 1926, when he was elected to the Council. He apparently felt initially that the organization should be more restricted in membership and objectives, comprising only persons who were actively engaged in historical research in French and English Canada.

The *Canadian Historical Review*, established in 1920 as the successor to Wrong's *Review of Historical Publications Relating to Canada*, was published and financed by the University of Toronto. Although it reviewed publications by French-Canadian historians, it was not until 1962 that an article in French appeared in its pages. Three years after Burt wrote, it was arranged that all members of the Association would receive a subscription to the *Review*.

The letter of 15 July continues:

So we talked till it was after 1 p.m. and then I rushed back to get my hat and slip out for dinner. But when I came in to the room where I work, I found Mr. Smith entertaining Judge Latchford,[15] and I had to be introduced. I tried to slip away, but Mr. Smith said, "Just wait a minute, I'll go with you." Now it happens that Judge Latchford is an old man and has his mind packed with the greatest mass of antiquarian lore about Ottawa that is to be found in the compass of one small cranium, and Mr. Smith is very much afraid that he is going to take it all to heaven, where it will not be needed. So the conversation went on for over an hour, and on the way to town we had to make a detour to see the stone erected on the site of Col. By's house – which Judge Latchford says was never there at all. ... He [Smith] has a hundred books filled with typewritten notes on Canadian history, the work of many years. He hopes to use the material, and he will use some of it. But he is worrying, for he says that he has done a lot of digging and has left his material in perfect shape, so that another may use it. ...

In our conversation we drifted on to the troubles of 1827, and to William Lyon Mackenzie. ... Do you know the romance of the unpublished life of Mackenzie, [of which] I think I have told you some time? When the Makers of Canada Series was being compiled, a man named LeSueur[16] was set to work on the life of Mackenzie, and for a long time he worked in the home of the rebel's grandchildren with all the family papers. He got the book all ready for the press, and the first proofs were struck off. Then it was stopped. I had understood generally that the family objected and blocked the publication of the book. But last night Mr. Smith told me that it was Mackenzie King himself who was responsible. I do not blame the poor harassed prime minister, for certainly it would do him a great deal of harm if his grandfather's life were really published. It would be a gross injustice, for he would have to suffer for another man's sins.

July 18, 1923

I have been working on the regular despatches between the Governor and the Home Government and am down to 1778–79. The manuscripts were arranged so that a natural stop comes in the middle of 1781. So I should strive to reach there. But if I am to get the full meaning of all the material which I gathered I should round it out from the other sources available, and these I find are more extensive than I had imagined. So I am working hard to get over this ground, and have been hoping I might do it in the two months I had counted on spending here.

As we have already seen, Burt's work with the League of Nations Society in Alberta had brought him into contact with Sir Robert Borden during his visits to Ottawa, where Sir Robert was an active member of the national organization. Burt greatly admired Borden's qualities as a man and as a statesman. In later years in conversation with students, he would often refer to the fact that Borden's role in the evolution of dominion status had been ignored by the Liberal establishment of political scientists, journalists, and historians. It is not surprising that his *Short History of Canada for Americans,* first published in 1942, is unequivocal on this point. Borden's activity in forcing the British government to grant the dominions a voice in the conduct of the war and the peace negotiations and to support their claim to be independent members of the League is incisively presented. Likewise, in winning the right to the independent conduct of relations with foreign states in 1920, 'the British government,' he wrote, 'yielded before the insistence of the one man who, more than any other, forced the transformation from the British Empire to the British Commonwealth of Nations.'[17]

July 23, 1923

Yesterday I had a most delightful time when I went to tea with Sir Robert and Lady Borden. Somehow or other, they made me feel as if I were an old friend. I like them both immensely. Lady Borden is bubbling over with fun. Beside Dr. Doughty and myself, the only guests were a Mr. and Mrs. Blake. He is vice-consul or something like that for Australia. ...

The Bordens have a most beautiful place at the East end of the city. The house was designed by the late Stanford White, of Thaw fame,[18] and the ground runs right down to the Rideau River in the most picturesque manner. We had tea on a big tiled porch at the back of the house and from there the view is one of the most beautiful I have seen in Canada, and reminds me of many a charming little bit in England. Thirty feet in front of us, the garden ended in a low wall through which a path disappeared. Then we looked through the tops of trees of all varieties to the river and the rolling wooded country beyond. Through the tops of the trees a church spire peeped up. After tea was over, we walked down to the river – a drop of about sixty feet. We went down by lovely winding paths through a mass of wild vegetation. Once we descended over the brow of a hill, it looked as if we were miles from civilization. Only the asphalt paths betrayed the civilization all around us. Three little valleys, each with a spring and a rill down to the water's edge and the several paths wind in and out of these little dales. I was strongly reminded of the Gorge at Niagara. Sir Robert said that he had been told by a forester that the variety of the trees and shrubs there was so considerable that he really had an arboretum. Among the trees was one I had never seen before. It is the Striped Maple. The leaf is very large – about twice the size of the ordinary maple. The bark is very smooth, but two feet off it looks as if it were split all along it in very distinct white cracks. But when you put your hand on it, it is as smooth as paper; the white is a stripe in the grey colouring of the bark. From the front door, there is another beautiful view. Across the street is a park, and far beyond loom the spires of the Parliament Buildings and Library. We all had such a delightful time that it was nearly seven before we departed....

I am just finishing the official correspondence down to 1781, and then I am going to fill it out from various series of papers – the Shelburne Correspondence and the Dartmouth papers....

The present Lansdowne family I could curse with bell book and candle. The Earl of Shelburne became the first Marquis of Lansdowne, and so in Lansdowne House the Shelburne Papers reposed. While there they were copied by hand (a few only by typewriter) for the Canadian Archives. Unfortunately most of the papers are unsigned, but no note was taken of the handwriting. It would be very valuable to know what of these were written by Shelburne himself, but it is impossible to find out now, for the Lansdowne family have since sold this collection, which really ought to have been considered as belonging to the English nation, and these papers have disappeared somewhere into the black night of the United States.[19] Will you not join me in a good round curse?

It was at this point, in the mid-summer of 1923, that Burt visualized the final form of his first major historical work, *The Old Province of Quebec*, but many weary hours of labour were to intervene before that objective was attained.

August 1, 1923

Already my mind is clearing to the view that while I may strike off an odd article, my chief purpose must be to write a real history of the period after the Conquest. Another visit like this to the Archives, will probably enable me to fill out to the Constitutional Act of 1791, and I had thought of writing the History of Canada to 1791, in which I should make an entirely new estimate of Carleton. This new estimate is greatly needed, for there is a mass of detail covering the period of his stay in Canada which leads me to believe that the interpretation which has been accepted to the present is quite wrong. It is true that he saved Quebec and in doing that saved Canada in the winter 1775–76. But more and more I am coming to the view that the difficulties which surrounded him, were to a very considerable extent the result of his own actions towards the English element in Canada, and towards the lower class of the French Canadians. Despite all that has been said, he did not know them. His outlook was limited to the seigneurs and the upper clergy. But when I come to write, I think that I would prefer to bring my work down to 1806, instead of stopping at 1791. My reason is this. I am coming to the conclusion that the common division of Canadian history into periods – the Conquest – The Quebec Act – The Constitutional Act – The Act of Union – Confederation – is all wrong. It is a superficial and even artificial analysis. Digging underneath the surface I begin to see more and more clearly that there are three great periods in the history of our country; (1) The French Period; (2) The period when the English ruled the French, 1760 to 1849; (3) the period including the present time, when the English and French together rule themselves. The middle period is more and more attracting my attention, as the great protracted turning period in the fate of our country, and it divides itself into two equal halves. The first goes down to 1806. During this time the relations between the two races were on the whole fairly harmonious, and the government was carried on largely in the interests of the French. But the second half was entirely different. It was the troubled period in our life. The American civil war was a concentrated struggle, but our strife was painfully protracted. From 1806 to 1849, the government was carried on by the English, no longer in the interest of the French, but against them. For over forty years their backs were against the wall. To me it is a remarkable thing, that right on top of this prolonged fight for their existence, the French stepped out and marched hand in hand with the English from 1849....

August 4, 1923

Yesterday ... McArthur arrived back from that place [Kingston]. I had just settled down here to a good evening's work when he arrived at the door. I did not think of any more work that night. We went outside, it was a very hot night, and we stretched out on the grass, lit our pipes, looked out over to the Laurentian Hills, and talked and talked. I have discovered a document which I think hits on the head his pet theory of the Quebec Act – he is loath to admit it as yet. Well we discussed that for a while. Then the methods of writing history, the proper divisions of Canadian history – he agreed with me in my heresy which I confessed to you the other day. I also propounded my idea of a board, backed by a number of moneyed men, to encourage and supervise scholarship in Canadian history. He thought it was a great idea, and asked my permission to mention it to Burpee. I told him to tell all the world. It seems that it may be very apropos, for there has already been a step taken to commemorate the Centenary of Parkman's birth, and no definite ideas that are generally satisfactory have been broached. Scholarships had been suggested, but McArthur thinks that this is infinitely better.

Burt envisioned an organization which would provide financial assistance to scholars who would spend their summers, or a sabbatical year, in the Archives, where the results of their research could be shared with the group and their writing subjected to critical evaluation. Burt's proposal was not adopted by the Parkman centennial committee, but two years later William Smith was hoping that 'the round table idea applied to university teachers' could still be implemented.[20] The basic issue remained unresolved – how was the scholar and the artist to find support for the free expression of his insights and discoveries? Canada, having neither an hereditary aristocracy nor an overly-generous plutocracy could not provide the patronage so common in Britain and Europe. Nor were the meagre budgets of universities of much help. Burt's idea was realized in part when the Canadian government established the Canada Council in 1957, financed at the start by substantial returns from death duties on the estates of two multi-millionaires – Isaac Walton Killam and Sir James Dunn.

August 8, 1923

...In the same mail with yours, I received a letter from the Edmonton branch of the Canadian Authors Association, requesting me to give the opening address of a series of public lectures to be given in the Public Library this fall and winter. They want me to speak on Francis Parkman on September 17th. It will be a sort of centenary celebration, for he was born on September 16th 1823, I believe. Be prepared to help me write my address!...

I have made another friend here, Russell[21] from the University of Michigan. He is working here to collect material for his thesis, which is on the Western Posts under the British rule, i.e. from the conquest of Canada to the Peace of 1783, or more properly to Jay's Treaty of 1796. I have gone past much of the material he needs without paying very much attention to it, but I am familiar with the way about, and with the history of Canada at that time, so that we have quite a little to talk about on our work. He has been studying under Van Tyne,[22] who holds a unique place. He is one of the small group of outstanding American historians who have reversed the old tradition of the American Revolution. This, by the way, is one of the most interesting things in the history of scholarship. British historians have been too polite, and have in the past accepted the traditional American view of the Revolution, and have repeated it in their writings upon that period – they gave the American version. It has been left to American historians to return the compliment by investigating the period thoroughly and giving the British version. Thus today, if you want to see the American side of the quarrel, you have to read a British writer, and if you want to see the British side you have to read an American writer. Sometimes people smile at the American Historical school, but if it has done no more than this, it has thoroughly justified itself, and made one of the most important contributions in the world to the state of historical knowledge.

During the 1923–4 academic year, eight courses were offered by the history department at Alberta, Burt and Long sharing them equally. But in addition to this heavy teaching commitment, Burt also imparted to the public the results of his reflections on contemporary issues, both national and international. In an article in *The Press Bulletin* entitled 'The Need for a Wider Study of Canadian History,'[23] he wrote simply but forcefully on the value of a knowledge of the past as it pertained to the dual nationality of Canada, Canadian-American relations, the future of the British Commonwealth, and sectionalism in Canada. He believed the youthfulness of the western Canadian population to be a valuable asset, but it had a drawback in that 'the steadying influence of experience, of a knowledge, of the past' was lacking.

What experience is to the individual, history is to a people. There are some individuals who take all their many mistakes and call them experience, and they go on with their experience. They never learn....

English Canadians, he argued, often ignored some of the simplest facts of Canadian history: that the country had been French for about as long as it had been British; that for a century after the conquest the French remained the majority; that until 1849 the French, although the majority, did not control their government and consequently there was bitter racial strife – 'French Canada was fighting with its back to the wall, fighting for its life. ... This chapter of Canadian history is one which should never be forgotten, for it is packed with object lessons of tremendous import...'

Turning to relations with the United States, he stressed that every Canadian should know something of the history of that country, for there had been 'a most intimate action and reaction going on' between the two countries from the earliest times to the present. The impact of the Civil War on Canada was one of many examples of this process.

...The development of Canadian national consciousness since Confederation, insofar as it has developed, has been largely a reaction from contact with the United States. As it has been, so it will be....

The future of the Commonwealth, he believed, was uncertain, but its guiding principle of autonomous self-governing dominions had been Canada's historic contribution to an institution which was 'the combined product of Englishmen and Canadians wrestling with the almost baffling difficulties of colonial government.' Similarly, sectionalism in Canada was a continuing problem 'and the best weapon in this fight will be a knowledge of the common past.'

... If it be true, as some aver, that Canadians know less about the history of their own country than do most any other civilized people, our situation is most perilous. We may break asunder.

On 1 February 1924, Burt elaborated on one of these issues in an address to the Edmonton Board of Trade, entitled 'Canada's Dual Nationality.'[24] This required some courage in view of the bitter feelings towards French Canadians which survived in the post-war period in English-speaking Canada. It is clear that he believed that the transplanting of French culture to the New World was as much an element in the definition of the Canadian identity as the transit of British speech, customs, and law, and hence both components were worthy of patriotic pride.

... At various times in many lands [he declared], races have been assimilated. But this has occurred only when the assimilated did not possess an old and fixed civilization, or where they were in a hopeless minority and scattered. Neither of these fundamental conditions existed in Canada. The French belonged to a civilization as ancient and as established as that of the English and, far from being a small minority, they actually outnumbered [for many years] those who desired to absorb them. Nationality resembles gunpowder. The greater the pressure on it, the greater is its power....

His observations were not only apposite but also prophetic:

... We must remember that our national problems of today and tomorrow are shot through and through with this principle of dual nationality. ... We talk of the industrial development of Canada. Quebec has the greatest unexploited labour market in our country. Already several industries are slipping down from Ontario, and if this continues, may not the old spectre of racial strife arise once more clothed in a newer economic garb?...
... The balance of our constitution, between French and English rights, rests upon the supposition that the French are largely confined to Quebec. What if this ... numerical and geographic balance of our population shifts? ... Suppose this movement continues, what will happen to our constitution? Should it, can it, be erected into a 'dead hand' to keep French rights cooped up in Quebec? ... Is not a constitution an artificial creation, and nationality a law of nature? If a constitution is to survive must it not be in general accord with the underlying conditions and forces? In the days to come, Canada will most likely be brought face to face with this grave question. ... Let us make the most of this happy time, by getting to know each other better, by peering out upon the world through each other's eyes, so that when the day of trial comes, we may not fall out and rend our country as in the past, but pull together to make this a greater and better land!

The historical analysis in this address was largely confined to the period before 1867 and did not grapple with the complexities of dual nationality in the Confederation movement and in the Canadian West, but it was directed to laymen, not historians. The rejection of the 'black letter' school of narrow constitutional interpretation in favour of a philosophy which accommodated the changing characteristics of Canadian society was the most valuable feature of the address. As might be expected, it was welcomed by the small and vulnerable French-speaking community in Edmonton and was translated and published in the periodical of the Collège des Jesuites.[25] The Quebec nationalist politician, Armand Lavergne, also offered his congratulations:

Your idea of Canadian patriotism has been my life long ideal, and I believe it is only by its practical realization that we can achieve the prosperity and happiness of our beloved country.

You have done a good deed for Canada and I beg to be allowed to offer you my sincere thanks and the expression of my highest admiration.[26]

Burt was instructing his hearers on facts of Canadian history which Anglophones frequently forgot. But it was a stance unpopular in the West, where French was regarded as a foreign language. Few western-Canadian Anglophones accepted the dual nationality concept. Lavergne's letter suggests that had more English-speaking Canadians possessed Burt's insight and capacity to peer out upon the world 'through each other's eyes,' the future relations of French and English would have evolved in a very different manner during the next half century.

Burt did not return to the Archives in 1924 or 1925. Always a devoted and affectionate husband and father, he disliked the months of separation from his family, now numbering three children, Forrest, Mary, and John Arthur. The fourth and last child, Joan, was born the following year. Moreover, his salary did not permit annual visits to the Archives.[27] Under these circumstances, he had to draw on the 'capital' of the notes and copies of documents accumulated during his first two summers in Ottawa. In 1924 he produced 'The Tragedy of Chief Justice Livius' for the *Canadian Historical Review*. His reputation as an authority on the post-Conquest period was growing. He was selected by the editor of the 1926 anniversary edition of The Makers of Canada series to update and correct A.G. Bradley's *Lord Dorchester* and Jean N. McIlwraith's *Sir Frederick Haldimand*.[28] He completed this assignment in the summer of 1925 in twenty-eight pages of lengthy notes and comments, based on hitherto unused primary sources and contemporary research.

There were no changes in the history department's teaching program during the years 1923–6. During the mid-twenties there was little growth in university enrolment, the total number of students being about 1300. Professor C.S. Burgess (1870–1971) of the Department of Architecture, who taught the history of architecture in his own department, was pressed into service as a lecturer in history for several years, limiting Burt's and Long's teaching responsibilities to three courses each.

The History Club was flourishing and met regularly at the Burts' home for their sessions. Many of his former students look back to these years with nostalgia. One of them recalls the annual social meetings where Burt would play the piano for dancing, and in addition to the current popular tunes would produce sprightly improvisations.

In a small university such as Alberta during these years, it was not difficult for students to establish a personal relationship with their professors. One of them, William R. Watson, who did not have the use of his hands, had developed unusual skill in using his feet for all the purposes which the missing members provide. He describes in his reminiscences[29] Burt's kindness in making him feel at ease during his frequent visits with the Burt household. 'I later came to realize,' he wrote, 'that the greatest gift that the university can bestow is the possibility of personal contact with men such as these: widely read and with extensive intellectual interests. ... many of them have one thing in common: they invest their subjects with their characteristic personalities, and the size of the University is, quite happily, such as not to submerge their personal influence.'

Burt followed current developments in international relations closely, contributing informative articles to *The Press Bulletin* on reparations, disarmament negotiations, the Geneva Protocol, and the Locarno Pact.[30] While not minimizing the obstacles to international amity, he was hopeful that the League of Nations would soon move toward universality of membership and that an era of peace was in prospect. He was less optimistic on Canada's future, in an article entitled 'What Is Canada?'[31] Sectionalism, and any failure to recognize the dual nationality of Canada, were capable of tearing the country asunder, he declared.

... In all attempts to secure justice for any section of Canada, we dare not think of our own part alone. If it was worth fighting for, it is worth making some sacrifices for, and each must be willing gladly to face any sacrifice that seems necessary in the interests of the whole. Surely we would not sell our national birthright for a mess of provincial pottage!

Another threat was the Americanization of Canada:

...We are so overshadowed by the very greatness of the United States that we tend to have an inferiority complex. We cannot escape the tremendous contrast in development and are forever making comparisons at our own expense. This has been eating our heart away. ... To say this implies no disparagement of that great and wonderful people to the south of us. It simply means that we have not been left to be ourselves and to develop our own personality. American capital, to which we owe a great deal of our material development, has brought with it American business to such an extent that some are already troubled by the spectre of economic annexation....

...There are two forces which have long been acting upon us and will most probably continue to act – [British] imperialism and Americanism pulling us in opposite directions till we often know not where we are or what we are.

There are some who have a child-like faith that in His own good time, or perhaps before, God will mould this people into a great and good nation. He will never do it ... unless we face our difficulties frankly and surmount them bravely. If we are to make anything of this country we must remember that it is French as well as English. ... There are a few who would like to make Canada an Anglo-Saxon and a Protestant land, but such an attitude of mind, if widespread, would wreck this country in a generation. A frank and full recognition of our dual nationality must be at the very foundation of the Canadian mentality....

Our heritage is much greater than we often realize. We have the makings of a wonderful national spirit. We are compounded of two of the greatest races in the world, French and English. This need not give rise to internal strife, but rather to a richer national life...

Burt held tenaciously to this conviction over the years. Unfortunately he was too sanguine in his assessment of Anglo-Saxon attitudes, even though forty years later the Royal Commission on Bilingualism and Biculturalism reaffirmed the principle which Burt had articulated so forcefully in 1924 and 1926. Most Canadians are still unaware that the enjoyment of cultural diversity is more rewarding and more exciting than the dull homogeneity of a conformist society.

7

Constitutional Issues
Old and New

In 1926 Burt arrived in Ottawa about mid-June. Earlier in the year he had accepted an invitation from Cambridge University Press to contribute a chapter, which was to be entitled 'The Problem of Government, 1760–1774,' to their Canadian volume in a new history of the British Empire.[1] This would require him to provide a definitive narrative of the results of his examination of the earlier part of the history of the old province of Quebec. It was evident that after five years of effort he was recognized as the leading authority in this important field of Canadian history.

He roomed again at the YMCA. New, Harvey, Brown, Underhill, and Morton[2] were already in town. William Smith arranged a guest membership for him in the University Club, which enabled him to take meals and meet friends there. To his academic associations he was able to add the political, due to his friendship with the Conservative Member of Parliament for Edmonton East, A.U.G. Bury.[3]

At the general election in the autumn of 1925, no party had gained a majority of the seats. The Conservatives, led by Arthur Meighen, were the largest group. The Liberals under Prime Minister Mackenzie King had held office since 1921 on the strength of Progressive support, and were now even more dependent on it, for the Progressives, though reduced in numbers, held the balance of power. Since the beginning of the session in January the struggle for office between the two major parties had been intense; as the Progressives were not all of one mind, the government could never be sure of their support on a confidence motion, and the

Conservative opposition was relentless in pressing its attacks. It was one of the most exciting sessions in the annals of Canadian political history. It was therefore not surprising that Burt was constantly diverted from his study of the political and constitutional issues of a century and a half earlier. His comments reflect a lack of sympathy for both old parties, and a qualified approval of the Progressives, both nationally and in his adopted province.

June 16, 1926

Monday evening [June 14] instead of returning to dead men's words, I turned to hear those of some live specimens. The debate was just interesting enough to hold me until bedtime. But yesterday!!! As Bury had not seen the Archives, I thought I would make an appointment with him, and immediately after lunch sought him out at the House. He agreed to come this morning and then lunch with me. But we have not lunched here [the University Club] yet, though it is now 8:20 p.m.

Just as I was about to leave him [Bury], having refused his invitation to the gallery, I inquired if there might be anything interesting coming up in the debate. He nibbled at the line I thus threw out, so I went up into the gallery and caught a whale. Parliament waited until I had taken my seat and then Davis, Bury's roommate from Calgary, introduced his motion of want of confidence in the government.

Davis' want of confidence motion condemned the government for its failure to implement the legislation promised in the Speech from the Throne. One of the measures promised had been the ratification of the agreement with the government of Alberta for the transfer of natural resources to provincial control. The natural resources question was one of the long-standing grievances of the prairie provinces, and ever since the establishment of Saskatchewan and Alberta in 1905 federal control of public lands and all the resources associated therewith had been a lively political issue. Since all the other provinces of Canada controlled their resources, the prairie provinces regarded the situation as an unjust discrimination against them.

The air became electric and it was 12 hours before the thunderstorm had passed. There were many bright bolts and much heavy thunder. A kink in the rules of the house prevented all discussion of the real cause of the motion – the general question. From first to last, the Speaker – Lemieux – was frequently invoked to keep the various debaters in the path which was not straight and narrow, but wide and tortuous. To quote the words of the Minister of Agriculture, Motherwell, "many members ate of the forbidden fruit" and he pled to be allowed a nibble. He is a big man with shining pate and snowy goatee. His vigor of body and tongue suggest the cattle drover. When the members of the crowded opposition benches developed from verbal hectoring to bovine booing, he stopped his address and booed back at them as loud as he could bellow. Then no one could boo, for they all doubled up. Even the packed galleries rocked with laughter. The battle was so intense that the imperturbable Charlie Stewart lost his temper and foamed at the mouth in his effort to tell Meighen, without saying so, that he was a liar. Meighen never lost his equanimity. His enemies may have thought that he seemed to be rejoicing devilishly over the way he toasted the fat Premier on his fork. You could almost hear the victim sizzling. Bourassa, whose countenance recalls the Devil, and whose seductive words strengthened that impression in the beginning, grew very excited and began to scream like a mere mortal. For an hour and a half he fought for the white government against the orange opposition. When one Alberta progressive, and then a second, rose and declared against the government they had hitherto supported, it seemed as if the roof was about to fall or the floor to blow up. By dinner time, it was becoming apparent that the government was playing a waiting game – to stall off a vote until they could recall absent members to Ottawa. Outside the house, the government was busy courting the coy Progressives and browbeating the timid ones. Toward midnight the debate sank into weaːy words dropped on dull ears, till R.B. Bennett with a torrent of wild words whipped it into a frenzy. Without dropping the bitter party man, he rose to be the noble champion of his calumniated province. To the very last, the poison worked. Lucien Cannon, the Solicitor General, in parliamentary language, called Meighen a liar and the latter made him withdraw. Then the vote was called, and while the division bells rang for ten minutes to call the members, those present forgot their animus in spirited songs – jollier choruses than our undergraduates can sing. At the last moment, a dozen men marched in, two by two, past the bar of the house; and as they entered, keeping close military step they suggested policemen coming to arrest the government, for they all entered opposition seats amid strong cheering. Order was called and the atmosphere was that of a great court where a great judge was to pronounce great sentence. No one could tell what the sentence was to be – life or death – as the members rose one by one and their names were called off, first against the government and then for it. Cahan of Montreal refused to vote with his party against the government. Had he risen and three more Progressives joined the two who battled in the afternoon, the game would have been up. Why did they not? There were several reasons. One was the fear of leaping from the Liberal frying pan into the Conservative fire. The other was the $4000 sessional indemnity which would have been imperilled by an election, for King had openly shaken that big stick in the afternoon. Great was the government cheering which was deadened in the packed galleries, for the government had weathered a greater crisis than had been experienced during the session for perhaps many years....

It was nearly 3 a.m. before I tumbled into bed. I was as tired as if I had fought the whole battle myself, and I slept as soundly as if the victory or the defeat had been my own.

June 18, 1926

Since my last letter, I have had little parliamentary experience. Last night I dropped into the gallery to see an almost empty house engaged in dull committee work. Hearing that the report of the Customs probe was to be tabled this afternoon, I walked up the hill dragging Pearson[4] (Rollie's Oxford and Toronto friend) [Roland Michener] at my heels. Bury smuggled us into the member's gallery where we heard most of the report read. We did not remain long, for after setting the debate down for next Tuesday, the House went into committee on estimates – a matter as dull and uninteresting as other people's money.

Though I have been here a week, I have accomplished little at the Archives – gathered in a few peppery letters of Governor Murray. I have been on a vain search for further light upon the administration of justice during the military regime 1760–1764. Those four years attract me very much – they were the nuptials of French and English Canada. The former were much more prosperous and much happier than ever under the French rule. It is almost unique in the history of conquered territories.

The Customs Inquiry Report to which Burt refers had been prepared by a special committee of the House of Commons which was established in February to investigate charges of corruption in the Department of Customs and Excise made by the Hon. H.H. Stevens, a Conservative member from British Columbia. The committee held 115 sittings and examined over two hundred witnesses. It submitted a report on 18 June which was highly critical of the administration of that department. Consequently it provided fresh ammunition for the Conservatives, who had maintained a deafening barrage of criticism of King and his colleagues throughout the session. The debate on the report began on 22 June and lasted till Saturday morning, 26 June. During the debate the government was defeated on several procedural votes, but not on a formal want of confidence motion. Burt's letters of 23 and 25 June deal with the tense and emotion–charged proceedings in the House, which he was able to observe first hand.

June 23, 1926

I was up to the House last afternoon and night for the debate on the Customs report. It was very exciting. This afternoon I tried it again, but was bored by a very prolix speaker from Vancouver[5] who was apparently trying to tire the House.

In a few minutes I am going in to dinner, after which I shall try it again in the hope of hearing the leaders.

June 25, 1926

At the present moment I am very wide awake though not sure of myself, for I did not get to bed till 6 a.m. and I rose at 8.45. It has been the most exciting experience in my life since I scrambled out of Germany at the outbreak of war. At 7.20 last evening Bury gathered Pearson and myself under his spreading wing in a sardine crowd outside the members' gallery. 7.30 saw the doors open, and us flow tumultuously in. From 8 p.m. till 9 p.m. bills. Then Cahan, who was speaking when the House rose for dinner, resumed his arraignment of the government and continued it for over an hour. He is an old gentleman with white hair and pointed beard, powerfully built and with a commanding address. Though his shoulders are bent, they leave the impression not of weakness but of the ability to carry a tremendous load. He has neither the mental nor the verbal agility of Meighen. But if he lacks his power, yet he is more effective. Meighen commonly overshoots the mark, Cahan hits it. He won considerable sympathy by professing his personal regard for Boivin, and thus made his charges against his administration of the Customs Department more telling. D.M. Kennedy of Peace River, who has been bitterly attacked by the Conservatives on the ground that he was sitting in Collins' seat[6] and has consistently voted with the Liberals, was as dramatic as an undramatic individual seldom can be. He turned on the government and has virtually turned it out. His refusal to vote for the Woodsworth amendment which would have exculpated the government came as a startling announcement. A thrill ran through the house and its galleries – "The Government is lost." Now let me remind you that since Confederation, no government has been overthrown on the floor of the house. All but one government were lost in the elections. The one exception was Sir John A.'s administration in 1873 when it was wrecked by the Pacific Scandal and then it was not defeated on the floor of the house. It resigned because defeat seemed probable....

There were four divisions. First the Woodsworth sub-amendment was lost 117–115. Then a new sub-amendment was introduced by Fansher. It was the same as Woodsworth's except that instead of replacing the condemnation of the government in the amendment, it added something to it. At once Speaker Lemieux ruled it out of order. He had enough technical right on his side to justify it – but to me it seemed a violation of the spirit of the rule he invoked. At once Meighen appealed to the house against the speaker's ruling. It was startling to all present. So a second division was held on the ruling of the speaker and it was rejected by 118–116. So far as I am aware this is the only time such a thing has occurred in this Dominion.

Certain of defeat if the vote were then taken, the government started obstruction by putting up some of its members to kill time while the premier called a cabinet meeting. During the interval to the next division there was some obvious lobbying – right on the floor of the house. When the Premier returned to the house it was obvious that something was about to happen. It did, but not as the government hoped. A progressive moved the adjournment of the debate and a fear shivered through many of his hearers that the progressives might wish to postpone a decision. Of course the government voted solidly for adjournment so that they might continue negotiations over the weekend. But they were beaten 115–114 in the third division of the night. Again they played for time and opened their wind bags while a second cabinet meeting was held. This lasted till 5 a.m. [June 26th] and after jockeying for position by fusing the sub-amendment with the amendment so that they might advance a sub-amendment of their own, the government again supported adjournment – this time successfully, 114–113.

But the government has gained really nothing and lost a great deal. Firstly by clinging to power by their finger nails they are impairing their moral prestige in the country. Any other government in the same position would have resigned. Secondly, the government violated a pledge. The whips of the parties had solemnly agreed on a division to settle the debate last night, and the Liberals repudiated their whip's pledge by voting to adjourn. Thirdly, they have done some dirty work behind the scenes. It is generally understood that King demanded from Byng the promise of a dissolution should he be defeated, and has been refused. He has, during the fevered hours of the crisis, appointed E.M. Macdonald, who is minister of militia to the senate, and Tremblay, Lapointe's private secretary to the civil service commission.[7] There are rumours of other appointments, but these are taken as certain. These "death-bed" appointments are likely to be King's death warrant. I do not see how he can face parliament at 2 p.m. Monday, for this action must have disgusted several more Progressives who have hitherto supported him. His resignation over the week-end is the most likely denouement.

The interest was so intense that few seemed to feel sleepy – the galleries were almost full to the end. Agnes MacPhail was to have sailed from Montreal. Some wondered why she delayed until they heard that King had had the sailing postponed some hours and had promised her a special train to catch her boat. Immediately she cast her vote at 5.15 a.m. she bolted – the only one in the house.

The time killing speeches were for the greater part of the time quite amusing. Motherwell, half angry half humorously roared like a bull...

The Conservatives were in gay mood, but not too jubilant. They vented their feelings in songs, and did the others – while the division bells were ringing to gather the members – and in tearing up and throwing their order papers at each other.

I was interrupted in this by Dr. Tolmie[8] who is living at this club. He used to be minister of agriculture when Meighen was premier and now has charge of the organization of the Conservative party. He tells me that Bury has been a surprise. From being written down as a candidate who had no possible chance of election, he has risen to be a successful member and one "who stands in well with Mr. Meighen." I told him one or two pleasant things about Bury and he thanked me for them, because as he said, it was his business to get all the information he could about their own men. Now I have rambled on and on about the political crisis. But really, last night and this weekend are certain to be long remembered in Canadian history. There has been nothing like it since 15 years before I was born.

Although Burt had expected that King would resign, the latter clung to office, and without waiting for the House to pronounce its judgment on the Stevens committee report, advised Lord Byng, the Governor General, to dissolve Parliament so that his ministry could contest another general election. Lord Byng refused to accept this advice on the ground that Meighen, as leader of the largest party in the House, should have an opportunity, if he wished, to form a government and complete the work of the session. King thereupon resigned on 28 June. King, in his fit of anger with Lord Byng, took the unprecedented action of relinquishing office before a successor was chosen, thus depriving the country of a government and creating a constitutional vacuum. Byng thereupon called upon the leader of the opposition to form a government and Meighen, after much anxious consideration, agreed. Politically, it proved to be a mistake, but from a constitutional point of view it was correct.[9]

June 29th, 1926

Yesterday Pearson and I were just struggling into the Members' Gallery as the house adjourned after King had announced his resignation. After much argument in the rotunda in front of the chamber – with Bury, Gershaw, Liberal of Medicine Hat, and Tobin, I carried Bury off to the Archives, where Doughty graciously placed himself at our disposal till 6 p.m., unfolding all the treasures of that wonderful place....

This afternoon Pearson and I went up to the house again and saw that the members had all exchanged seats and heard Drayton make his speech on behalf of Meighen. When Rinfret, F.[rench] Liberal, resumed the debate on the customs report, we departed.

The Liberals have been very steeped in both strategy and tactics. They were expecting a defeat and wanted it to come on a matter of principle, on which they could appeal to the country. They had their chance a fortnight ago and they threw it away by forbidding any discussion of the natural resources. Now they have retired under a cloud – a vote of censure [the 29 June vote condemning the administration of the Department of Customs and Excise]. And their tactics have been in keeping. Their speakers have been very inferior to those of their opponents. They contradicted themselves and each other and they were not honest. King himself was the worst offender. Neither French nor English have much good to say of him now. Indeed you everywhere hear talk of a successor. Dunning and Lapointe are the two most mentioned, and Dunning seems to have the advantage. As Lanctot said just before I left dinner, "We would rather have Dunning, for we fear that Lapointe would sacrifice us to get English votes."

For one thing every Alberta man must condemn King. By prohibiting the discussion of our resources problem until our legislature would agree to the Bourassa amendment,[10] he prevented his English-speaking followers from understanding the real nature of that clause and Lapointe purposely deceived them. I wondered why he yielded to Bourassa's influence when he must have known that Archbishop O'Leary was opposed to the amendment. But now, looking back, I think I see his reason, – that it was not the power and insistence of the French members – but a political parachute to ease his inevitable descent.

One nasty thing may happen. The investigation into the customs administration which Inspector Duncan[11] carried on and formed the basis of the recent parliamentary investigation uncovered a hole of abominable immorality, worse than that of Sodom and her sister city. The stench was so nauseating, they had to put the lid on. Part of Duncan's report was officially stated to be too indecent to print. It was open to members to examine, however, and it turned even Agnes McPhail and Woodsworth against the government yesterday morning.[12] I don't much care what the policy of the Conservatives is. We had to have a change, and if the new government does not cleanse the Augean stable, they will have to go too.

Here I am running on at weary length about the politics of this country. But it is one of the crises in our political history and we may never see the like again. The progressive movement is performing the great function for which it was inaugurated – the purification of our politics. They have induced an energetic competition between the old parties to elevate our political morality.

These comments demonstrate how difficult it was for the Progressives to continue supporting the King government.

My work at the Archives [he continued in the same letter] has gone slowly. Parliament's storm is not alone to blame. I have been caught in a tangle in the very beginning of my chapter. The explanation hitherto given for the system of justice in Quebec differing from that of Three Rivers and Montreal during the military regime does not satisfy me. I may not find the way out, but I am going to do a deal more struggling yet. The passage of time and the halting of my work is beginning to alarm me. I may not be able to do much of the writing here, but may have to content myself with collecting more material to work up after I return. These kinks are most exasperating, especially when they force me to read through countless pages of xviii Century French in mss., as I am doing now.

Burt's industry in these years was laying the foundation for his legendary reputation among his associates, including the staff of the Archives. He is reputed to have read and mastered the contents of the 'Q' series for a sixty-year period – a massive collection running to several hundred volumes. One of his students recalls a facetious story which L.B. Pearson claimed was making the rounds in the Archives, that 'Professor Burt was planning to copy all the National Archives and then set fire to the building, so that he would have a complete monopoly.'[13]

July 2, 1926

...I have been going through records of cases tried in the military courts between 1760 and 1764 to find some gleam of light to lead me out of the darkness. The records are all in French, xviii Century French, and the writing is at times abominable. It has been dreary ploughing – all in vain. It is hard to see ahead in this work of research and it is quite possible that I will spend my time searching and collecting rather than writing. I can do the latter after I have finished here, for it does not have to be in till next February....

The Commons met on 30 June and 1 July, with all of the big guns of the two major parties firing continuous salvos across the floor of the House for hours at a time. The Liberal opposition chose the constitutionality of Meighen's ministry as the main target of their attack. Burt's friend Bury was one of the last speakers on the confidence motion and gave a cogent defence of the Conservative position. But the motion was carried by a one-vote majority at 2 a.m. on 2 July. The Governor General thereupon assented to Meighen's request for a dissolution.

So the political duel has been suddenly ended for the nonce! Everybody here is discussing the action of the Governor General, Liberals condemning him for granting Meighen what he refused King, and the Conservatives replying that King was given his chance and only sought a dissolution to escape the vote of censure that was hanging over his head and finally descended upon it. I have not been up on the Hill since Tuesday, when I heard Drayton make his statement in the house for Meighen. It has been interesting, but I was physically incapable. I have been going off to bed early and lying in as late as I could. ... When I went into the bathroom to shave, I found myself beside Woodsworth, who remarked to me "Well that was the strangest Dominion Day celebration I ever saw," and on my questioning him told me how the government had been defeated early this morning by a majority of one. At noon, feeling better, I went to the house only to hear the announcement of the dissolution....

July 3rd, 1926

Now I am settling down in the Archives – except when I spend the hours chatting with that dearest friend William Smith. I feel very sad to think of his sailing a week from today. When I am his age, I pray you and Heaven may have combined to make me half so sweet in disposition and stimulating in mind. Every day he sends up for me – sometimes several times – to go down for a smoke and a chat, and we discuss everything from the customs probe and the constitutionality of the governor general's action, down to amusing anecdotes and up again to the philosophy of St. Paul or the Roman Church....

July 6, 1926

Bury explained a mystery that had been troubling my mind. Why had the Progressives supported Meighen in two divisions in the house – on matters of policy – later ratted, precipitating the Dissolution? It was incongruous. ... According to Bury, the Progressives were expecting the Conservative government to approach them for a bargain. They were disappointed. Then King approached them, suggesting that Meighen if defeated would be refused a dissolution, which would of course mean that King would come back. Then he promised to form a coalition with the Progressives who would no longer be in the outer chamber of power. It is a scandalous business, for before Byng called upon Meighen to form a government, he was assured by Forke that the Progressives would co-operate to finish the business of the session.[14] Certainly the coming election is going to be a hot fight. The Liberals will try to obscure the issue by talking of constitutional rights – all bosh because King was going to do the very thing Meighen has done had he been given a dissolution. And what is the outcry against Byng for giving Meighen what he refused King? A smoke screen. The Governor General was right. No government has the right to demand a dissolution in order to avoid a vote of censure of parliament. There is the central point upon which the Conservatives will try to focus and from which the Liberals will try to distract them by a smoke screen of voluminous words. For the life of me, I cannot see where there can be any considerable change in the complexion of the house of commons. The Liberals may lose a few seats in Alberta over their bungling of the resources, and there is talk of the Conservatives winning some seats in Quebec now that Patenaude has come under Meighen's umbrella....

...Bury dropped in to see me at the Archives and we had another session in Smith's office. It has been a great pleasure to have Bury here and I was sorry to see him go. Poor Bury! He has had six strenuous months here. Now, instead of a rest, he returns to his law practice and another election fight. He is a poor man, and it is as hard on his purse as it is on his body. I do hope he is returned,[15] for he is a representative to be proud of. He is head and shoulders above most of his fellows....

This afternoon I finished writing an account of the military regime 1759–1764. I am rather pleased with the way it is shaping. But I shall not be satisfied with it until you have combed it over. I have decided to do the final writing in Edmonton. The only other writing I may do here is a little on the Royal Proclamation of October 7, 1763, which laid the basis of civil government in 1764. Then I think I will spend the rest of my time examining the minutes of the Council down to 1791 with a view of writing something on the actual government of the country, pointing out the development toward parliamentary procedure in Canada and the political struggle that went on within the Council. In conversation with such people as Smith and McArthur, I gather that I have some stuff that others have not seen and that I may make some contribution to our history in that other important corner of it.

July 9, 1926

McArthur has been tearing around at a great rate, instructing his research class in their beginnings, and visiting professional and amateur politicians to glean a harvest of information. He confirms what I have heard that Skelton[16] has been advising King very closely in this whole constitutional crisis. I fear he had been a poor friend to King and to himself. He has pushed King into a difficult position and himself into another. It may go hard with him if the Conservatives come back from the country, for he has violated the tradition of the civil service in giving political advice beyond the borders of his official province....

I have plunged into the minutes of the Legislative Council and am working my typewriter like a threshing machine. It is going much faster than when I was here last and I am in hopes of collecting fairly complete reports of its doings and procedure before I depart. With that treasure trove, I hope to produce a good study. In reality it presents a foreshortened picture of parliament. When civil government was set up, the Council began wholesale legislation. Soon experience slowed them down, for they made many mistakes. Then they gradually adopted the parliamentary practice of reading a bill three times and the Governor withdrew from the meetings, except on formal occasions when he gave his assent to the legislation that was passed. There was also the problem of admitting the public to the debates, but the Councillors were opposed successfully. But most interesting to me is the political history which has been quite ignored by writers hitherto – the appearance of parties within the council and the consequent party struggle. To several with whom I have discussed the subject, it has appeared an attractive study which ought to be published.

Today the Archives presents a contrast with what it was five years ago. For some while then I was the only visitor digging in the mine of the manuscript room. Now there are about a dozen. Morton is busy on the North West, gathering some illuminating material. Harvey is continuing his work on P.E.I., hoping to reach confederation, the end of its separate history, before he has to leave later in the month. Pearson is quite intoxicated by his study of the Loyalist settlement in Upper Canada, and is bringing his wife down this evening to introduce her as an assistant in the hunt. She arrived in town only this morning. Underhill comes up in the afternoons – his mornings he spends in the Parliamentary Library. McDougall[17] whom MacGibbon was appointing to Alberta until Toronto snapped him up, is here also. ... There are several others whom I know not – but that is nothing against them.

There is always a knot of us at the University Club, lunching and dining together and sometimes we drag in members of the club to join in a good discussion. One of these is a cousin of Jack Read of Dalhousie. He was a freshman when he [Jack Read] and Harvey were seniors. Another was a year after me in Toronto and is now an official in the Justice Department here ... It is very pleasant because we are welcome guests. In the summer many of the members of the club travel through the Dominion on scientific and other work and the club has hard sledding...

July 11, 1926

...J.S. Ewart K.C.[18] you may remember is the man who wrote the Kingdom Papers which advocated the elevation of Canada into a separate kingdom under the present sovereign. For some time he has been back of the Progressives, perhaps inspiring their wider views – which are a bit narrow.

Conversation here is getting a bit stale on the political issue. But soon the campaigners will whip up the tired jade and make her gallop and froth at the mouth. It will be amusing to see the antics. One most interesting bit which may come out during the fight is that King himself appealed to Byng to consult Downing Street – he appealed himself to the authority he pretends to repudiate.

8

The Flowering of
Canadian History

The mid-1920s saw the first flowering of Canadian history based on scientific methods as modern historians define that term, with its exhaustive search for evidence and critical evaluation of primary sources. It was an exciting period for ambitious young men and others in their prime of life – an intoxicating time of continuous discoveries.

> Attempt the end, and never stand to doubt;
> Nothing's so hard, but search will find it out.[1]

might well have been their motto. Most of the research and writing was designed to improve the accuracy, scope, and depth of the existing accounts of Canadian political and economic development. Burt's work was a notable example of this. There was a strong, almost exclusive emphasis on the pre-Confederation period, on the history of the various regions of Canada, and on the earlier period in imperial and Canadian-American relations. Post-Confederation national development attracted less attention, as did biography and social and intellectual history. The reasons for this preoccupation with the remoter past are not entirely clear, but there were at least three predisposing circumstances: the shallowness of earlier work provoked the younger men to undertake revisionist studies; the historiographically conservative conviction that recent history could not be treated objectively; and finally the inadequacy of source material on the post-Confederation period. The Public Archives had few collections of papers of prime ministers and other leading political figures of the recent past; the holdings of post-Confederation federal departmental records were limited, and complete files of many newspapers were almost inaccessible. Nevertheless, the activities of these archives-oriented pioneers of the 1920s were highly significant, and provided a sound foundation for the treatment of national history in future years.

'It is very interesting to see the actual renaissance of Canadian history in course of preparation,' Burt wrote on 13 July 1926:

In the old building it would have been impossible to accommodate the number of researchers that are now busy here.[2] Beside those I have earlier mentioned, Morton, Harvey, Underhill, Pearson and his wife, there are General Cruickshank,[3] Mackintosh,[4] (Economics at Queen's) Wilson[5] (History at Dalhousie) Armstrong (an old Queen's man teaching in a middle west u.s. college) Fife (who went over in the tanks with me and is now teaching in a Vermont college). Then there is McArthur and his regular class. I forgot to mention Brebner,[6] who appeared today and is already half buried. In addition, I hear that two other members of the Toronto history department are due here this month, as well as Chester Martin from Manitoba.[7] We may foregather at a dinner next week where we may focus some of our separate conversations. There has been considerable talk of coming to some understanding about being here in July as much as possible to get the maximum number here at the same time. Then we would have a sort of clearing house of research information and gain much by mutual criticism and suggestion. Certainly all the professional historians in Canada are turning their eyes on the Archives during the summer and a revolution is bound to come about as the result. It is a great change from five years ago when I came down here with your encouragement to find that I was almost alone. Of course this growing interest will affect the Archives, directing them in the channels where they should seek new material and enabling them to get more money from the government.

These impressions are reinforced by Professor W.M. Whitelaw's recollections of these years. With characteristic vivacity he describes the relationships which developed in the relaxed atmosphere of summer days and evenings in the building on Sussex Street:

I would fain ... recall the long, gaunt figure of General Cruikshank, off in a corner of the student's room at the Archives, pecking out, year by year, with one bony finger on a typewriter almost as worn, but quite as dauntless as himself, the story of the Niagara Frontier: In the center of that same room (itself the center of Canadian Historiography) I can see Mr. Burt, driving home an argument with the small end of his trusty briar....

The Archives, Whitelaw recalled, was 'more than a mere repository and disseminator of information.'

It became the Mecca to which there came an ever increasing number of scholars from an ever widening circle. Here in unhurried and easy intimacy we discussed our mutually interlocking problems, often with considerable heat, but never so far as I can remember, with bitterness. Here was education at its best, international, interprovincial; education without tears, without examinations, without lectures.[8]

On 18 July Burt described a visit with colleagues on the Archives staff which gave him much pleasure:

After a light supper here – for tea and heat reduced our appetites – McArthur and I went out to Marion's[9] where he and Fee[10] were awaiting us. Fee is in charge of the Map Room of the Archives. ... Marion is a French Canadian who took his degree in Paris. For five years he was professor of French at R.M.C. Kingston and now is official translator of the archives. Now you know the four of us who sat down to smoke and talk – first. We kept pretty well within French Canada and all the time were fairly close to Bourassa. Marion has a great admiration for him but can never forgive him for his alliance with the Conservatives against Laurier in 1911. He and the Conservatives in that warm summer campaign certainly sowed the political wild oats that are choking the national field today. Marion says that Bourassa laughs when any Tory accuses him or Quebec of disloyalty and replies "Your money did it." Indeed Atholstan[11] gave him $15000. He refused to take it but A. insisted. Thereupon he said "very good, you do not give this to me but to my cause. You pay for 15,000 subscriptions for my paper, and I will pick out a list of names all over the province to receive it." From Bourassa we passed to Sam Hughes – as he appeared in Quebec. Let us hope for Sam's sake that the doorkeeper above was not from French Canada. Finally we were lifted up by a discussion of Laurier, and we were all of one sweet accord. McArthur told us the story of how he threshed out his contribution of Papineau to Canada and its Provinces in a short series of interviews with Laurier just after his defeat in 1911.

I cannot tell how long we talked. It must have been a long while – judging by the sequel. At last we called a truce on politics and Marion produced three bottles of wine. We had a glass of each and then voted unanimously in favour of no. 3. Then he raided the cellar, in which the bottles were counted by the hundred, and produced several of no. 3. It was a delicious sparkling red wine – home made. We drank each other's healths, pledged France and Canada, and plunged into bridge, – for love....

...Morton, I am getting to know and like better all the time. My first impression of two years ago – that he was tedious – has quite melted away as I have broken through the barrier of his deafness. He is a plain-looking man of fifty or more with iron grey hair, a merry mouth half concealed by a grey moustache, and blue eyes that twinkle most of the time. He is a wide scholar with a rather rich background of Trinidad, Edinburgh, Pine Hill College (Halifax), and Knox College (Toronto). He is an old friend of President Murray and is much consulted by him. He knows the West and its history as few know it, and will some day write something of great value. He has no side – he is all substance – and light withal. You would wonder who were those two old cronies, if you could see us daily walking to and from the archives arm in arm.

Harvey too, I am enjoying very much. ... His volume on P.E.I., which you will find in the study, has been well reviewed – even in the London Times Literary Supplement. Every year we get together the friendship we formed years ago in Oxford grows richer – I suppose because we have certain confidence in each other and know each other pretty well. He has to leave on Friday for P.E.I., where he is to deliver some addresses on Whelan, one of the fathers of Confederation. I shall miss him very much....

I have had several good conversations with McArthur about the period on which I hope to write. A chance remark the other day made me fear that we were far apart on the Quebec Act, and that our chapters might present a clash to the reader. But I seized the bull by the horns and found that it was no bull and had no horns. At 2 a.m. when we parted after two nights' discussion, we discovered that we stood on practically the same ground.

His history of Canada for high schools is coming out and I promised to read all the proofs he has here, the first 32 galleys. I began it last night and have been at it all day except for the pleasant time at Underhill's. I have promised to finish it this weekend while he is in Montreal and Kingston. It is now 10 p.m. and I have still 10 galleys to scour and cut before I retire. His substance is excellent but he needs a wife like you. You have revolutionized my style. His is not so bad as mine was, but I hope to effect some improvement.

July 20, 1926

...Instead of digging into McArthur's proofs, I had him himself. ... We roamed all over from his proofs to the history of Canada and on to educational policy generally. He feels as we do that our chief problem is the student who comes up for the asset of a couple of letters after his name instead of development within....

Yesterday at noon, Harvey, McArthur and I lunched together and got deeply engrossed in a discussion of several problems in Canadian history – how the Englishman writing on colonial affairs knows too little of local conditions, and the Canadian writer is too ignorant of the important background of British politics and government – how the French developed an entirely different empire in

America from what the English built up – and the fallacy that the exclusion of the Huguenot was chiefly responsible, a fallacy born of ignorance of European conditions. Then we drifted off into a discussion of P.E.I., Harvey asking our advice on the work he was doing. Inseparable as yet, we retired to McArthur's and continued for half the afternoon. Here's the great value of foregathering at Ottawa. We who are attempting to do work are scattered. Here we meet in close contact and discuss our problems with each other. It must lead to us submitting our results to others who are competent to judge before we dare forth into print. Harvey had not done this with his volume on the French period, fearing it would be an imposition because he thought few would be interested in it. I am glad that McArthur asked Harvey to send him the ms. of the new book he is preparing and he insisted that it would be to his benefit to submit it to me also. We have all been too much inclined to stick our heads in our own holes, and we have suffered.

Last night at dinner we had a little informal meeting with Morton added to our number. In a general way we laid plans for the dinner which is to be held in the Rideau Club. I am to lead off with a little appreciation of Doughty. Morton is to raise the question of publications, and McArthur is to present the problem of closer co-operation of us professional historians in a group around the Archives. The purpose of the dinner is twofold – to thresh out our own general problems and to strengthen Doughty's hands. All of us who are doing research here and a few others such as Doughty, Skelton, Senator Haydon, and perhaps Sir George Perley or Sir Robert Borden, are to be present....

I came across a very interesting document on Saturday – or rather two of them – by John Gray who died in 1768. He was a trader in Canada and was deeply engaged in the fur trade. In his long account of the conditions of the trade and discussion of the policy which ought to be adopted, I came across a contrast between the personnel of the French and the English traders. There he laid his finger on the cause of much of the trouble after the conquest. The French traders coming from a better social class, were imbued with a sense of honour which the English traders, coming from a lower class, had little of, and thus the English were more unscrupulous in their dealings with the natives.

Burt's letter of 23 July describes the dinner for the Dominion Archivist, Dr Doughty, given by Sir George Perley, former High Commissioner for Canada in London, and Secretary of State in the Meighen ministry formed after King's resignation. It was an appropriate gesture on the minister's part, for Doughty experienced many frustrations in his period of service as Dominion Archivist, and in view of these his achievements were remarkable. Sound principles of archives administration, close working relationships with federal government departments, and spacious physical facilities, now taken for granted by researchers in the Public Archives of Canada, existed only in rudimentary form, or in the mind's eye of the chief archivist.

The principal obstacle to archival progress was government indifference, which was reflected in budgetary and administrative limitations. It was not Doughty's fault that so many post-Confederation departmental records and ministerial papers were not in archival custody. In 1920 he drew Borden's attention to the failure to implement the report of the Royal Commission on Public Records, which in 1912 had proposed that the Archives assume the role of a public records office, having the same function as the British Public Record Office.[12] In the following year he emphasized how far ahead of Canada the United States was in archival activity, and in the resultant quality of historical scholarship and university teaching. 'This will in course of time,' he wrote to Meighen, 'have a very serious effect on Canadian development, and it is certainly worthy of the most earnest and careful consideration by those who are entrusted with the Government of this country.'[13] In subsequent years he renewed his plea for the establishment of a policy regarding the disposal of departmental records.

Despite staff limitations, service to university staff and students, and the general public, was liberally extended, and Doughty was generous with his own time in dealing with requests for assistance – often spending ten to fifteen hours per day at his desk or in the manuscript room. He was a tireless and resourceful collector of private records in Canada and the United Kingdom and was particularly interested in the development of the picture division, for he was convinced that historical works would attract greater public interest if suitably illustrated. He hoped that the universities could be encouraged to assist their professors of Canadian history to prepare collections of documentary sources of the same type which he and his staff were selecting and editing for publication, and pled with Wrong to encourage Toronto staff and students to make more use of the growing collections. 'The digging and delving is a very tedious process,' he wrote, but 'the fact is that there is not a chapter in Canadian History that can be properly written with a knowledge obtained from books.'[14]

George Smith,[15] who is next to Wrong and was one year ahead of me at Oxford, and Glazebrook,[16] a junior member of the history dept. at Toronto, came up specially for the occasion....

The Country Club is a beautiful place up the river a few miles – on the Quebec or club side of the 'great divide.' About 22 sat down to dinner – McArthur's class and all the rest of us that are digging here. I was very delighted over the whole affair because of one thing. Several years ago George Smith was very scornful about my going to the Archives – so much so that I did not care if I ever saw him again. Just before the Hart House dinner this summer, he hailed me for a minute, and was very friendly. Then he sent a still friendlier message after me here and yesterday and today, he impressed us all with his keenness to get to work here and me with his very friendly attitude. I gather that he had a sort of "complex" about the Archives. He has wanted to come but feared to come lest the initiation be humiliating. I think that he was very pleasantly surprised. He is to be back for a real session on August 8.

Well, after the dinner we adjourned to a bright room with easy chairs and talked. I led off with a few words of appreciation directed at Sir George and Dr. Doughty, both of whom replied. Then we got down to discussing our problems generally – cooperation around the archives and the publication of the results of research. This morning, to continue the discussion, McArthur, Smith, Morton and I breakfasted together here and then retired to a quiet room. We decided that a committee should be selected at a dinner to be held after Smith returns next month – when Kennedy will be here also. By the way, Kennedy has suddenly landed back in Canada and he is now a full professor in Toronto with a department all to himself – Constitutional History. The other decision which we reached was that we workers in the Archives should work towards being an interuniversity faculty or rather committee to guide research here in the summer – an extension of the Queen's work. Everyone's of the opinion that we should place ourselves freely at the disposal of advanced students who resort hither.

It was probably as a result of these discussions that, beginning in 1927, the *Canadian Historical Review* commenced publishing an annual list of MA and PH D theses dealing with Canadian history, which had been completed or were in course of preparation. The first list was compiled by George Brown.

July 25, 1926

During the last couple of days I have been helping another novice [Glazebrook] get his feet wet. ... He has begun to dip in the stream at the point where I plunged in. This is merely to assist in a lecture course he has to deliver this year. He hopes to return about the middle of August and may bury himself in the post-Loyalist settlements of Upper Canada, which will dovetail in well with the work Pearson is undertaking. Pearson is a daily joy. Such a contrast to the dejected fellow I met in

Toronto! He has found his feet and is as happy as a lark digging up materials on the Loyalist settlement in Canada. He has to return to Toronto to prepare for next winter's work.

While going through some newly acquired material yesterday I came upon a most touching series of letters – between Pitt and Henry Wolfe. Pitt is consoling the latter, who is heartbroken over the death of his son and is fondly treasuring his box of papers just sent in. I felt as if I were there.

The other evening at dinner Morton told an amusing story about an old elder whom he once knew. This elder, who was on most intimate terms with the Almighty, was called upon to pray at a church meeting. He had suffered heavy business losses during the week. This was known to the community in a general way. During the course of the prayer they learned some of the particulars, until he dismissed the subject by concluding "O, Lord, with all thy faults we love thee still."

July 29, 1926

...My alarm at the mass of stuff still ahead of me has set me typing furiously. I must have taken over 10,000 words of documents today and I will get a few thousand more before I go back to bed....

McArthur is like the flying Dutchman. He is here, there and everywhere all at once. Now he is off to Kingston again, eternally busy over this endowment campaign. He is great company. The night before last Marion asked us out to his house to discuss the Alberta School and Natural Resources question. He is a great worshipper of Bourassa and wanted an opportunity to convert me. But instead of this, he drew a double attack from McA. and myself. The amusing thing is that we all have the same end in view – harmony and equality of French and English in Canada, but temporarily break harmony in discussing the means of establishing it. We played a few rounds of bridge and drank some of his good wine and said that we were going to retire early. That was a rash statement, for when we dropped bridge we fell back into the general discussion of French and English in Canada and talked and talked. It is very good, for Marion is an ardent churchman and also a man who appreciates old France....

It was during this summer of 1926 that Burt met J.S. Ewart, then seventy-seven, the tutor of the Canadian public on constitutional issues, who had been preaching the doctrine of national independence for over twenty years. Ewart believed that it was in the best interests of Canada to extend the powers of self-government, won in domestic affairs during the nineteenth century, to embrace all the powers which a nation-state possessed in a world of independent nation-states. Throughout most of his long career as a propagandist, he favoured a continuing relationship with

Britain and the other dominions only in the form of a common sovereign, defined as a Personal Union with each dominion having the name and status of a kingdom, although for a time during and after the Great War he shifted to the more radical position of proposing that Canada become an independent republic.

July 31, 1926

This afternoon I took off quite unexpectedly. Yesterday Morton fell in with J.S. Ewart and when he told him of the various people working here, Ewart sent a message for me to lunch with him at the Rideau to-day. There I went at 1 p.m. and then, as the day was hot, we motored out to the Royal Ottawa Golf Club to lunch there. We talked and talked of everything from the causes of the great war to the mistakes of King and Meighen and back again to the results of the war. Then he told me of a map of Europe which he had prepared to show in a graphic manner the complicated troubles of the old world. He wanted very much to show it to me, so he ran me back to his house, where we arrived just in time for tea. After that we retired to his study to examine the map and discuss Canadian history. It was nearly six before I could tear myself away and then he insisted on driving me back to the Archives where I salved my conscience by getting in an hour's work.

Ewart is an old man, though he looks little more than sixty. He showed me a photo of the lacrosse team which won the championship of Canada in 1875 – of which celebrated team he was a member.

Though he has many friends – everyone spoke to him at the Golf Club – he seemed to me quite lonely and a little out of touch with life. Years ago he started to dig in the Archives and worked up the materials down to 1818 in about 6 volumes. Then the war interrupted his Canadian historical studies and drew him off into European politics. His recent work on the causes of the European war has been highly reviewed. He has just received a very eulogistic letter from W.H. Dawson,[17] the author of several good books on recent Germany, but cannot read it. Dawson writes an abominable hand, and I spent most of the lunch hour trying to decipher it.

He [Ewart] has been an eminently successful counsel and has had a great influence behind the scenes of politics – though he will line up with neither political party. He agrees that there is little practical difference between the parties though there may be great talking differences, and he places his hopes in the Progressives. There I think he is sound, for the imaginary difference between the two old parties really demands an independent jury to hold the balance between them. Really, I should not be surprised at a larger Progressive contingent this election.

He says that King was quite sound in his remarks about not being in fear of the result of the vote on the customs report. He, Ewart, had some doubts upon that point, and therefore he approached Forke and some of his followers, who confirmed King's statement that he would have pulled through on the vote. Then I asked him why King did not forge ahead to the vote. To this he replied that King was uneasy about the Alberta Resources and really feared a motion on that subject. Whereupon I asked him if King has not erred – that the Alberta Resources would make a better election cry than the customs report. ... He agreed, and said that this was a tremendous error on King's part. Meighen, however, made his mistake, according to Ewart, and I think he's right. He says that Meighen should have refused to assume the reins of government and King would have been forced to the country on the customs probe without any covering mantle of a constitutional issue. Meighen's over-eagerness may be his own undoing.

Ewart was assessing Meighen's decision in the context of purely political considerations, and in this respect his judgment was correct, as the 1926 general election results were to show. Meighen, however, had based his decision to assume office on the constitutional principle that Byng 'had properly declined to follow most improper advice,' and that there was 'no honourable alternative to the acceptance of office.'[18]

I asked Ewart how was a poor independent to vote – who agreed with King on the constitutional issue but believed his government was responsible for corruption on a dangerously large scale. He doubted whether there were any such independent individuals. When I suggested that I thought I knew many, he seemed to catch at this as a substantial hope – that many men were not hide-bound to a party or a formula. I was rather amused at this, for he [Ewart] is generally regarded as a slave to his formula of independence. The refusal of a dissolution by Byng is almost a nightmare to him. We seem plunged back in the medieval days of Canada – when Governors really governed and the people obeyed. He cannot see that there is little difference – we have the election anyway. He quoted Borden's words to support King and I quoted Asquith's[19] to uphold Meighen.

That Burt had little sympathy for the views of the imperialist Tory establishment in Toronto and Montreal is abundantly clear from his next comment on Ewart's ideas:

But underneath it all, he is tremendously sound in his placing Canada first for Canadians and his desire to make them think of Canada as a self-respecting nation. On one point I had misunderstood him and I was glad to be corrected. He is commonly suspected of an anti-British prejudice. It has been said that hatred of

Britain – or mistrust of Britain – is the mainspring of his thought. When I suggested by way of repeating the story of Chancellor Stuart's[20] talk to our British Universities Club, that the champions of Canadian nationalism can win if they pay a generous tribute to England, what she has done and what she stands for, he came through handsomely. Indeed he almost repeated Justice Stuart's phrases.

But all said and done, Ewart is a theorist who impresses me as up in the clouds, his feet hardly touching the ground.

August 2, 1926

I have been in the "slough of Despond" for some days past. The unmastered – ungathered – material is so mountainous, and the open questions so numerous, I despair of approaching a satisfactory study – much less any finality. I shall just have to content myself with gathering what I can and doing the best with it. Yesterday, I spent a number of hours with McArthur going over my rough draught on the military regime. He has "raked it fore and aft" and I am extremely grateful to him. Everytime I discuss Canadian history with him, the more profound is my respect for him. His knowledge is wider and intenser than Smith's. Indeed he is the only one who may be regarded as a sort of master of Canadian history. When I get my chapter written, I am going to send it down to him to criticize and he is going to do the same with his two chapters which follow on mine.[21] It is a great joy to have such a friend. If he passes anything I do, I need not care what anyone else may say. At times there is the reverse of the coin sitting uppermost, and I despair of ever getting to know the elusive history of this country. I am really an ignoramus and wonder if I am any good at all....

Saturday, I think I told you, I had an interesting experience with John S. Ewart. Yesterday afternoon, I had another when McArthur and I called on Sir Robert Borden. There were no other guests for tea and we had a very delightful time. We discussed the European dislike of America, the Mexican situation and the Roman Church, the Maritime probe, the Progressives, and gardens. You see I nearly spelled the last with a capital letter – because the Bordens are such keen gardeners and it is a real subject with them – and I have much enthusiasm though little intelligence. Lady Borden was quite amusing in her denunciation of the Progressives. They upset things so! If they were all straight Liberals, it would not be so bad, for then you could know where you are! Of course I had to draw her on by apologizing for them and their supporters who find no difference between the two historic parties except talk. Very mischievously, but sincerely, I suggested that the coming elections might strengthen the disturbing contingent. I really think that likely, because one of the outstanding lessons of the last session was the power which a balancing third party may exercise. There must be such a party till the average voter can cast an intelligent and honest vote for either of the old parties.

We talked also of the investigations into the condition of the Maritime Provinces.[22] Sir Andrew Race Duncan, the Chairman, is an extremely able man, according to Sir Robert. The two others are a Nova Scotian judge and Cyrus Macmillan. The only opinion about the last which I have heard here is that he is a lightweight. It is expected that the report will be a Duncan report. Sir Robert thinks that the people in the Maritime provinces are themselves to blame for many of their ills. They do not work so hard as men do in other parts of the Dominion – or in the u.s. He [Borden] says that Nova Scotia is preeminently suited to sheep-raising and yet the Nova Scotians have not sufficient enterprise to undertake it. He suggests that they might make a great deal of the tourist traffic if they would only set out to capture it – but they are lazy....

My last days here are apt to be busy and interesting. Kennedy arrives this evening and next Sunday George Smith and George Brown return. Then we are to have more meetings. One thing we are now discussing is a survey of printed sources for Canadian History. Many American state historical societies and other organizations have published large collections of documents as a foundation for their own history. In them is a great deal of most valuable material for Canadian history. The plan is that each man will take a block of this and work through it carefully to index all bearing on Canada. It makes me feel hopelessly ignorant and even helpless – for our poor library has nothing. They have much more in Saskatoon...

Having trod these highways and byways of scholarship and politics, Burt returned to Edmonton in August. As indicated in his letters, he hoped and expected that the Progressives would retain their position of influence in Canadian politics. While he was in Ottawa the Alberta wing of the party, the United Farmers of Alberta, had won a second sweeping victory in the provincial general election of 1926. In the federal election, held at the beginning of the fall term, on 14 September, the voters of Alberta returned eleven UFA members, three Liberals, and one Conservative. Although the popular vote was much closer than these figures indicate, UFA success in federal politics was more decisive than in 1925. However, the national result gave the Liberals their first over-all majority in the House of Commons since 1921.[23]

9

Last Years at Alberta

The 1920s in Alberta was a period of slow and sporadic growth in the provincial economy in contrast to the boom years preceding the war. Farm income fluctuated with varying climatic conditions and market prices. Private capital investment was still chiefly directed to extractive industries such as coal mining, and to disappointingly capricious oil discoveries in Turner Valley, and had not created extensive industrial employment. Throughout the decade the population was predominantly rural – 62 per cent of the 1931 total of 731,000. Although the rate of population increase was larger than in the other two prairie provinces, it lagged behind British Columbia. In general, the buoyance and optimism of the pre-war years had evaporated.

The victory of the United Farmers of Alberta in provincial politics did not revolutionize the economy or the administration of public affairs – the cabinet was cautious and conservative in outlook, and there were more innovators in the Labour and Liberal parties and among the rank and file of the farmers' organization. The most significant development occurred outside the ambit of government initiative – the creation of the Alberta Wheat Pool – and this involved action by the farm movements of the three prairie provinces.

The public debt inherited from the Liberal government was large and provincial finances were chronically precarious. For most of the decade the provincial government pursued a policy of rigid economy in educational expenditures. The annual grants for operating expenses of the University of Alberta increased only slightly, despite a 40 per cent increase in enrolment between 1919 and 1929. Salary scales were lower than those of many universities in Canada. Since public demand stressed the vocational value of a university education, the chief developments in the twenties were the creation of additional professional faculties, and the university made much of its extension services to the rural population and its participation in the activities of the Research Council of Alberta. It was not an encouraging period for scholars in the humanities and social sciences – no new departments were created in the Faculty of Arts and the University library had only about 33,000 volumes by 1930. There was practically no increase in the number of graduates in Arts during these years.

In the department of history, C.S. Burgess continued to provide part-time assistance until 1928 when two young scholars, Miss Jean Murray, MA,[1] and Mr Wallace Sterling, BA,[2] were appointed, the former as an instructor and the latter as a sessional lecturer. But there was no increase in the number of students enrolled in history courses.

During these years Burt continued to accept public speaking engagements and to participate actively in League of Nations Society affairs. In February 1927, he spoke to the Calgary Board of Trade on the 1926 Imperial Conference,[3] whose deliberations, he declared, had produced fewer changes in the imperial relationship than many people believed who were unacquainted with the arrangements arrived at during the previous decade. The most important result of the Conference, he asserted, was that while it had 'given us practically no new liberty ... it had added a mighty responsibility.'

Our international notes will bear no endorsation by the government in Britain. We will have to bear full responsibility for our own signature. We can no longer shut our eyes to the question of defence. ... If we trust to the Monroe Doctrine rather than to ourselves, we are accepting a position of inferiority. We likewise degrade ourselves if we rely on the British navy without doing our utmost to provide for our protection in time of danger. Some think that it is good business to take this advantage of Great Britain and of the United States, but it is not and cannot be good business, for it is bad morals. ... We need to grow up to our voice, and it is not the body but the mind and character that make the man.

It has been claimed that Mackenzie King's creation of an external affairs bureaucracy in Ottawa and a few legations abroad after 1926 was 'a daring innovation ... which would end dependence on British diplomacy and make equality of status something more than a convenient fiction.'[4] But unlike King, Burt could identify the clear implications and responsibilities of dominion status in a world of nation-states in which international anarchy always lurks. A diplomatic service, no matter how well staffed, is impotent unless it is the instrument of realistic international policies. King was quite content with supervising a policy of no commitments to collective security under either Commonwealth or League of Nations auspices. It was the same policy which in other democratic states led to appeasement of Mussolini, Hitler, and Japanese imperialism, with its tragic sequence.

In 1927 Burt spent about six weeks prior to the summer school session at the Archives, in a continuation of his research on the post-Conquest period for the chapter in the *Cambridge History of the British Empire*. D.C. Harvey and Chester Martin were already there, but McArthur was not coming until later in the summer.

June 2, 1927

Tuesday evening in a shower of rain, Martin, Harvey, Spry[5] and myself visited the Merediths'[6] for a good chat and a "snack"....

The more I see of Martin the more I like him. He used to be a terrible stick from what I have heard, but he is obviously mellowing. Somehow I feel terribly tempted to rag him and I frequently yield. Harvey says that he is unused to it but will find it wholesome.

Dear old Mr. Smith was away when I arrived and I was somewhat concerned, for the letter from him, which you forwarded, told me that he had been quite sick most of the time since he returned from the Privy Council hearing...

June 6, 1927

...My machine is going thunderously, reaping a thick harvest and splitting the ends of my fingers. Every now and then relief comes when Smith carries me off below for a cup of tea, a chat and a pipe in his office....

I was discussing the Privy Council decision on the Labrador boundary with him this afternoon and he gave me an interesting insight into why the judgment had gone in favour of Newfoundland. There was not title really to the territory back of the coastline. Canada's claim rested on the fact that the Indians who inhabit those lands have always been looked after by the Canadian government through its posts on the gulf. The Newfoundland people did not know how to combat this argument, but our own counsel saved them. Geffrion, says Smith, would not listen to his exposition of the Indian question and therefore in presenting the Canadian case missed the heart of it. Therefore the Privy Council acted on the old principle that the hinterland should go with the shore line.[7]

A measure of Burt's devotion to his research was the refusal of an invitation by President Arthur Currie of the University of Toronto to join a Canadian delegation to the meeting of the Pan-Pacific Institute of Political Affairs – an all-expense-paid trip to Honolulu!

His letter of 6 June continued:

My social activities have been limited to the personnel in the Archives. Glazebrook and Innis are here from Toronto and have raised our luncheon party to five. ... Harvey, of course I am very fond of, but the most interesting experience is the unfolding of Martin. Harvey says that he never saw him limber up so much and would not have thought it possible in such a stick. Martin and I are usually the last to leave the building at night and we always have a good argument as we walk home under the stars and the glare of the street lights.

June 15, 1927

...I have just lighted upon yards and yards of unbound papers which I was told by various people on the staff had disappeared ages ago. I have therefore had to stop copying and will probably spend the rest of my time exploring and taking notes of documents to have copied and sent to me....

June 18, 1927

Our little society here had suffered from Martin's departure and Kennedy's arrival, for Martin I find a congenial soul and Kennedy the reverse. ... While here I study more than documents – I study human nature and grow daily fonder of Harvey, Glazebrook and Brown. We make a harmonious quartet at meals and rag each other to make a richer harmony. Just at present I am the chief victim because I am cursing a man who is probably in the infernal regions – Edmond Roy. Nearly twenty years ago he broke loose and tore loose an invaluable series of unbound papers, distributing them all over in an arbitrary manner. Every day or so I am discovering another precious section in the miles of mss. shelves.

Last evening I distinctly felt the strain of high pressure work and Harvey came to my rescue at 11 p.m. by insisting that I go for a walk with him and off we went – chiefly around the paths on Parliament Hill whence we had a grand view of the lights of Hull and their reflection in the wrinkled river. He was expounding the thesis of his completed history of P.E.I. most of the time, and I enjoyed it greatly.

It is good that the Archives building lies at the far end of a park for we have to walk through it four times a day, and I take a delight in watching the way the flowers are growing and in the graceful shape of the trees. There are two or three particularly fine ash trees – huge ones – and I wonder if ours will ever grow to be such stately things. And it is good to see the wind playing in the branches.

Yesterday my attention was caught and I was amused for several minutes by a sparrow chasing a big fly – I think it is what they call a herring fly. The insect led the bird a merry chase, glancing hither and thither within twenty feet of the ground and all within a radius of as many yards. It was as exciting to watch as, I imagine, is a bull fight to a Spaniard.

The view from this window is very interesting. The park seems to be the playground of the whole city. Every evening and Saturday afternoon it is crowded with people of various ages engaged in various kinds of games – senior baseball and junior (very junior) baseball – and the same with football, the seniority of the game being marked at a glance by the thickness of the crowd. It is good to see them enjoy themselves.

Every time I come East, I have a curious reaction. At first I feel that I should enjoy living down here with its paved roads and shaded avenues, its older and more settled life. But after a few weeks I recover my Western spirit and am thankful that my lot is cast in larger spaces where the atmosphere seems freer and human nature more genuine.

The next letter alludes to the booklet on the League, which the League of Nations Society had asked him to prepare. This was published in 1927 under the title *A New World or the League of Nations*. The greater part is devoted to an analysis of those episodes in international affairs since 1920 in which the League had played a constructive part in resolving conflicts of interest and preventing resort to force. This was designed to illustrate the thesis that the League was not a 'peace at any price' institution, but an instrument for the attainment of justice 'and, through justice, to establish peace.'[8]

June 21, 1927

This History of the League has taken a lot of my time. A few days ago I had to spend the whole of a morning going over the page proofs and getting the appendices in shape. Thursday, I hope to see the last of it in Ottawa at a meeting of the Education Committee. I have got a little impatient with it, but Harvey sooths my ruffled nerves by assuring me that I will be rewarded for this work at some time in the future – perhaps in heaven if I get there.

You remember, perhaps, my mentioning lists of labourers in Upper Canada at the time of the U.E. Loyalist settlement, on which those who signed for their pay did so only with crosses. Adam Shortt told me of them. Well, I have plunged into them while floundering in the sea of finances, and I am not sure that Shortt is right. They may be disbanded soldiers who assisted in the survey, and not Loyalists at all. I have my eye on another shelf of loose papers where, if I have time, I hope to find some evidence on the subject. This searching is quite an adventurous business, particularly because the papers are so disordered. But, though I curse the utter lack of organizing genius in the archives, I bless the kindness of the whole staff. They do everything to help one that they possibly can. I am going to be saved quite some time by getting some photostat copies which have been promised.

June 23, 1927

This morning I had quite a conversation with Marion. He and Lanctot are at opposite poles, the former being a strong clerical. He denies that the *curés* in 1896 were against the *hierarchy*, but confessed ignorance of the reason for the break in that year. He is a strong disciple of Bourassa and Abbé Groulx[9] whom Lanctot denounces. It is very amusing to hear them – separately. Each denies, without mentioning names, that the other's views have any validity or wide currency. I wish that we had more men like these around the University – it is unfortunate that all our Frenchmen are from France. If we had a representative or two of Quebec we could have some great conversations and imagine, at least, that we have some insight into French Canada.

This afternoon I have to attend the Educational Committee of the L. of N. Society to pass the little volume finally. Several bouquets have been thrown at me and I hope this afternoon will see no bricks.

Not only were no bricks thrown, but the material in the booklet was updated and a second edition published in 1933.

Burt had accepted an invitation from W.J. Gage and Co. of Toronto to write a history of the prairie provinces for school use. This was completed in October, 1929, under the title *The Romance of the Prairie Provinces*. In letters written from Ottawa and Toronto in 1927 and 1928 he alludes to this assignment.

June 24, 1927

During the last few days I have spent a few hours at odd intervals poring over maps and pictures. I am going to get photostat copies of a select few of the former for my volume on the Canadas and a couple of dozen or so of the latter for me to choose as illustrations for the smaller volume on the West. Love[10] took for granted that the book was to be illustrated and that I would pick the pictures. I am going to have them copy some mss. material in the same way – at the request of several people on the staff who wanted to help me in any way they could. Really, the eagerness of the people here is sometimes almost embarrassing....

Ottawa is beginning to don her gala attire for the great celebration. A pavilion has been erected in front of the Parliament Buildings and flags and coats of arms are sprouting everywhere. I have just secured a copy of the official program for July 1st and it is truly splendid – prepared by Dr. Doughty. He has a genius for such things. I believe that the premier's speech is being written by a number of the Archives staff who are trying to keep him to a minimum of purple patches. The most interesting preparation of which I have heard is that of T. Eaton's, who used the resources of the Archives to reproduce exactly the room in which Confederation was agreed on and lifesize models of all the 'fathers.'

At the beginning of the 1927–8 term, in an address to students at the university Sunday service in Convocation Hall, Burt reiterated his convictions on the nature of university life, in terms which have a continuing validity despite their unpopularity in later years.[11] He chose as his text the verse from Ecclesiastes (7:25) 'I applied mine heart to know, and to search, and to seek out wisdom, and the reason of things.'

One prime essential is a good heart. Of the several limitations which hedge about our existence, the most serious is that of self – the ego. Our personalities cramp us all, more or less, and it is most important to break through them, or to expand them – to see through other's eyes and to feel with other's hearts. Some find this harder than others but it is not impossible for anybody. We are all endowed with the means of escape from ourselves – the God-given impulse of sympathy....

Now here is one thing which the university ought to teach – not in any formal instruction, but in the atmosphere which it creates and keeps. It is the richest field of friendships in the world....

The college or university without a strong student life is a poor place to send a young man or woman. There is a wonderful education in merely playing, working, and living together. Such a life trains the individual to adjust himself to his fellows and develops in him a keen sense of loyalty and duty to those around him. This is the very best preparation for public life. Public life! Politics! What have they to do with a Sunday service?

...One of the greatest moral duties of our society is to share as fully as possible in its public life. And one of the best places where this sense of the responsible citizen can be developed is in the universities. Indeed, there is something seriously wrong with the student life of any university where there does not appear a live interest in public questions. If a university graduates men who turn their back upon politics, the government should turn its back upon that university.

A good heart must be balanced by a good head. There is as much wrong done in this world by fault of head as by fault of heart....

Here the university may be of inestimable value. It opens the doors of the world of knowledge. Its function is not to tell you what to think or what to believe. That would lead to mental stagnation. Nor is it to cram your heads with a lot of facts learned by rote. That would lead to mental indigestion. It is rather to help you understand the world in which we live, to help you to think straight and not in circles, to stimulate an inquiring mind ... into your own and the world's business....

By paying only lip service to this concept of university life, many Canadian universities of the mid-twentieth century, the University of Alberta among them, reaped many tares in the harvest. Under the impact of public pressure for so-called 'practical' education, the Arts degree came to be regarded primarily as a business asset. Moreover, the expansion and reorganization of academic life inadvertently but inevitably created impersonal bureaucratic structures and procedures which engendered cynicism, alienation, and apathy. Today, as in Burt's time, socially sensitive faculty and students seek ways of mitigating these evils.

The 1927–8 academic year taxed all of Burt's remarkable energy, with work for the League of Nations Society, the preparation of an address for the Royal Society of Canada for its 1928 meeting in Winnipeg,[12] a notable lecture to the first-year Arts students 'On the Study of History,'[13] and the preparation of an 81-page treatment of the British, Canadian, and Alberta constitutions entitled *High School Civics*, published in 1928.[14] This last was designed to provide a source for the course at the Grade XI level, in an era when the Department of Education required of students a knowledge of the evolution of British parliamentary government and of the rights of the British subject. In 1930 it also appeared in a Manitoba edition entitled *Manitoba High School Civics*. Had Alberta continued to use a well-organized and clearly-written text of this type, there would have been a less uncertain public knowledge of the Canadian constitution, one price of the subsequent adoption of the American-inspired 'social studies' curriculum.

Following the end of the term, Burt taught the spring quarter freshman course on the modern world at the University of Minnesota, on the recommendation of Herbert Heaton, the distinguished authority on economic history.[15] Heaton, a member of the Minnesota history department, had visited Edmonton a few years earlier and was much impressed by Burt's keenness and competence. On the way to Minneapolis, Burt stopped in Winnipeg for consultations with Gage's editor, John C. Saul, who was promoting the forthcoming history of the prairie provinces for school use. 'The bitter memories of the Riel Rebellion,' he wrote Mrs Burt, 'still linger here so that Saul fears the attempt to speak out. Therefore I may have to do a new dance over the two chapters on Riel to avoid breaking any eggs.'[16] The 'Winnipeg establishment' view of Louis Riel, best represented by the Rev. R.G. MacBeth in his *Romance of Western Canada*,[17] published ten years earlier, was one of bitter disapproval, reflecting an Anglo-Saxon ethnocentric viewpoint. Burt's treatment of the two 'rebellions,' as it appeared in the school text, was much more moderate and balanced.

The visit to Minneapolis proved to be both strenuous and stimulating. He had a class of over 350 students, whom he found very responsive: 'they astonished me by bursting into prolonged applause when the time was up,' he wrote after his first lecture.[18] This must have been very satisfying, since Burt's intellectual and emotional resources were always fully engaged in his lectures. Over the years few, if any, of his hearers realized that his forceful, and often dramatic, discourses were often preceded by a sense of nervousness, and his family had been rigidly schooled not to intrude on his meditations in the hour before he met a class. But once 'on stage' he never failed to hold his audience, as one student at Minnesota later recalled:

'In talking to his tiny Canadian history group he sat at his table, chin down touching his chest, and rumbled in a deep bass voice. But put him in Burton Auditorium with a class of about 200, and he walked about the platform almost acting the story he was telling – no need for a mike – and students used to gamble on whether, and when, he would fall off the edge of the platform.[19]

The same student recalls a *bon mot* he used: 'Elizabeth the virgin queen. As a queen she was a great success.' But there was more to Burt's lectures than compelling platform style. In a course like the one on the modern world he could speak to the interests and concerns of the students, as evidenced by the student newspaper's report on one of his last lectures during this initial visit to Minnesota.[20]

Somewhat reluctantly, for he was already homesick, Burt made his way from Minneapolis to Ottawa, with a stopover in Toronto.

Toronto, June 9, 1928

Yesterday morning I called on Kennedy at the University and had a pleasant chat. No other member of the history staff was in, and therefore I spent the time with him. On leaving the building, however, Underhill and George Brown encountered me and held me for a very pleasant little visit in the hall of Baldwin House.

Arriving at the Gage establishment, I learned that my modification and addition, effected in Winnipeg, have disarmed most of the Winnipeg criticism. You may know that Winnipeg is hypersensitive on the whole question of rebellion and the relations between French and English. Saul[21] wants me to add a couple of paragraphs on the life of the people on the Red River, and one or two other paragraphs here and there to fill out the picture. I have to do it in Ottawa, where also I am to pick out illustrations and then the book is to appear in September. Love carried me off to lunch in the Albany Club where I had a pleasant time imagining that I was one of the select circle of Toronto citizens with fat purses. ... When in Gage's I received a telephone message which brought me now to the Ryerson Press. Pierce's[22] secretary was collecting some books for me and was anxious to find me for Sage,[23] who is in town. His message was that he would seek me in the Convocation garden party yesterday afternoon. Leaving Pierce's office I was about to enter the elevator to escape when I heard a familiar voice but saw an unfamiliar face. I accosted the individual & found that he was an old college friend now an official in the Ryerson Press. He carried me off to his office for a good chat. When I had risen to escape from his office, the door opened & let in Dr. Creighton, the editor of the New Outlook, the organ of the United Church. Upon hearing my name, he said "Just the man I am looking for." He has been anxious for some time to get me to write something for his paper. The Press Bulletins were responsible.

While in Toronto he called on the Underhills, George Wrong, and Roland Michener[24] and his family. Michener, a Rhodes Scholar from Alberta in 1919 was one of his former students, then practising law in Toronto. Burt found his father in vigorous health, but his mother's condition was a cause for worry, since her physical and mental vigour had deteriorated.

Ottawa, June 16, 1928

I reached here 8:15 yesterday morning and at once went on the scout for a room. I have a back parlour in an old fashioned house just round the corner from here and much quieter than the Y.M.C.A.

Yesterday I accomplished little at the Archives, except to gather a pile of books on the table which I have appropriated. Of course I called on Doughty first and enjoyed a reception which grows more cordial every year. He had to show me a mass of new stuff which he had just acquired, including some very fine pictures on the West. Then there was everybody else on the staff and endless chats. "Payer de personne" is both pleasant and necessary at the beginning and end of every visit to the Archives....

June 18, 1928

Yesterday afternoon I called on the Bordens and found them at home and delightful as ever. He had put me up in the Rideau Club and also in the Chaudiere Golf Club. Over the latter's course we played this afternoon. ... I was quite amused, when driving out with him, by his suggestion that I would be a proper choice to succeed Dr. Tory!

This morning I was early at the archives, having wakened at 6 a.m. Thus I managed several hours' work during which I think I have pretty well licked into shape the proof of the Romance of the Prairie Provinces. On going to Doughty to get permission to get photos of some Archives pictures for the little book, he took me in hand, ransacking the place for more pictures. During the search. he unearthed a number of excellent pictures which I had not seen and which have never been used. He is more than ever anxious to please.

I have not seen dear old William Smith since our conversation Friday evening, and will greatly miss him this summer, for he is sailing for England this month. He is to edit some Mss. for the Hudson's Bay Company and give them some assistance in organizing their Archives.

June 23, 1928

For the last several days I have been varying my routine by lunching at the Rideau Clu`. Yesterday O.M. Biggar brought two legal friends to the table where I was sitting in splendid isolation, and we had some good conversation lasting for an hour after the meal was over. Biggar is quite impressed with the development of the Prime Minister, and thinks that Bennett may be a real improvement upon Meighen.

During the last few days I renewed my friendship with Whitelaw whom I met here some years ago when he was digging into the Quebec Conference. He is now back in the movement for Maritime union which preceded federation. He is on the staff of Rutgers College at present, but is going off to the Orient for a year's wandering leave of absence after he finishes his thesis this summer....

Yesterday, Sir George Foster, hearing that I was in town, sent for me. I went at once to his house to find Lady Foster away on a few days' visit and him stretched out on a couch, convalescing after a bout of illness. ... He wants me to go to Toronto for him and speak to Ontario teachers in Convocation Hall next month. So do I escape in Edmonton only to be caught down here by the toils of the L. of N. Society.

June 25, 1928

The Assembly of the League of Nations is being enacted here next Friday by the youth of Ottawa, and he [C.P. Meredith] wanted me to be the Secretary General. I returned his compliment by insisting that he must do it because he has been there and I have not, his French would be recognized and mine would not, and because he is Secretary General of the Society while I am nobody.

Coming up here to lunch, I called at the Laurier to see if Dr. Tory had returned that I might convey Sir George Foster's invitation to deliver one of the lectures in Toronto. As I suspected, he cannot attempt it, but I was delighted to hear their impressions of Malcolm,[25] the Minister under whom the Research Council exists. Dr. and Mrs. Tory had just returned from a trip to Washington with Malcolm in the latter's private car and they were enthusiastic.

June 27, 1928

...This morning General Cruickshank appeared beside my chair, suspecting that I was digging in a field near his, and the result was a conversation that lasted half of the morning and an agreement that we should continue it after dinner in his house Friday evening.

You may remember that he was the officer commanding the military district in which Alberta lies when I was in Sarcee Camp. He is now the historian of the Militia Department. He has been a great student of history during his long life of nearly eighty years and has published a great deal of very valuable stuff. His latest was the set of Simcoe Papers, 4 vols., which I picked up in Toronto. He is also editing the Council Minutes of Upper Canada, 1792–96, to appear this summer, which will be a great assistance to me. While in the u.s. I read his little book on Butler's Rangers and the beginning of the Niagara Settlement, published in 1893. He is perhaps the greatest living authority on the War of 1812 on which he has also published many papers.

Monday evening, I had a great surprise on entering the Club for dinner, when Miss Fraser, the secretary, informed me of the presence of a man who had travelled through Italy with me. I dashed into the sitting room to find my old friend Read, Dean of the Dalhousie Law School. After dinner we had a long walk and talk together to make up for the 15 years during which we have not seen each other. He is to be here for a couple of months doing some work for the Department of External Affairs against the Imperial Conference of next year.

Morton arrived this morning and we had a very pleasant chat. He promises many more when he recovers from the fatigue of travelling. McArthur arrives Sunday and is to live in a room upstairs which Read now occupies. When expelled, he is to have the front parlour in the house where I have the back – just around the corner from here. Dear old Smith leaves tomorrow for England, where he will be engaged for several months, and I shall greatly miss his tea and conversation, both of which I have already relished.

Somehow, I seem to have lost my spring and feel that I know nothing and can do nothing. I am pinning my shrinking faith upon having many documents copied for me. It would take endless time to do it myself. Already I am sighing for the good holiday which I must have when I get this volume off my hands next summer. Last fall was the first time when I would have preferred to sit at home rather than go to a lecture, and I have been struggling with an attack of lethargy ever since.

By 1928 the Burts were finding his long summers away from the family an increasingly severe trial to both of them. 'If we are to remain in Edmonton,' he had written, 'I am determined to do much more work with copied material, for I do not think we can continue to stand this business and preserve the freshness of our spirits.'[26] He was delighted when the librarian at the University of Minnesota promised to send him two rare volumes of eighteenth-century travel in Canada, and he hoped to make similar arrangements in Toronto. In this pre-interlibrary loan and pre-union catalogue era, research was difficult and expensive for scholars who did not live close to a major library.

June 30, 1928

Yesterday, the Ottawa branch of the League of Nations Society put on a model Assembly according to the enclosed programme. Invited to be present, I attended for an hour in the beginning and returned to preside at the luncheon. Sir Robert Borden was invited to do it, but he declined and with a laugh "commanded" me to sit and eat in his place. My only function was to call upon a parson to say grace and to introduce a very heavy "uplifty" speaker.

Last night General Cruickshank carried me off to dinner. The only other guest was a man named Sykes who is some responsible official of the Parliamentary Library and a very attractive man. Mrs. Cruickshank has been a great beauty in her youth which she has not left far behind. As we three men were bursting with talk, she knitted. However, she did inform us as we sat down, that it was the General's birthday (75th or 76th), whereupon we drank his health in good wine. I am greatly delighted to have made the acquaintance of the General who has a great fund of scholarship and of humour.

Caught at the Archives in my thin summer suit and new panama, last Thursday evening, by the deluge, I had to taxi here for dinner and carried with me two others who were marooned. One was ... a stranger who had just arrived from the u.s. He retaliated by taking me out to lunch today. As we left the Archives, he pulled out his tobacco pouch to fill his pipe and I caught sight of a colored crest on the pouch. It looked familiar. Mine host was one of the very first brew of American Rhodes Scholars [L.H. Gipson] and is now professor of history in Lehigh College,

Penn.,[27] a small but wealthy institution. He is spending his lifetime working up the period from 1748 to 1775 in American history, concentrating on the frontier and its repercussion upon institutions. You will not be surprised when I tell you that we spent two hours over our meal.

July 15, 1928

Friday, Morton asked me to be sure to lunch at the same time with him, for "Big Bear" Cameron was coming along. Needless to say I delivered in person the enthusiastic message which a letter might have cramped. He was in good form and told us several fine stories – one of which I have shortened for Forrie's benefit.

Another which he told was very beautiful. It was of a man named Schultz[28] who married a Piegan woman and lived many years with the Indians. Schultz has written a full account of his experiences in a book published some time ago and from this Cameron gathered the tale.

W.B. Cameron (1862–1951) was an Ontarian who had migrated to western Canada as a young man. He was a clerk in the Hudson's Bay Company's store at Frog Lake, and was the only male survivor of the massacre of 2 April 1885. He later practised journalism in Fort Frances, Ontario, New York, and Vermilion, Alberta. His *War Trial of Big Bear*, published in 1926, is a standard reference on the massacre and is sympathetic to the great Cree chief. He later edited Sir Cecil Denny's *The Law Marches West* (1939). Following the meeting described here he was a guest of Burt in Edmonton.

July 15, 1928

...I have gone through the state papers on Lower Canada to 1810 and hope soon to plough through the war. Then I pick up Upper Canada in 1796 and come down to the same time. This will be a shorter job, judging from the reconnaissance that I have made in the calendars. I am still hoping to finish this by the end of the month. Instead of stopping to copy documents I am writing short notes in my printed calendar and making a long list of documents to be copied and sent me.

Pritchett,[29] lecturer at Queen's and researcher in the history of the West, has read the proof of the Romance to the end of the 1869–70 rebellion and caught only a few mistakes where I have followed blindly in the wake of tradition. He is kind enough to say that it gives a new interpretation and will have a great success.

July 19, 1928

Since my last letter, I have taken no time off except for sleeping and eating and have come across some interesting documents. One was quite a revelation to me.

You may recall that I have long been puzzled over why Britain should agree in 1783 to a boundary that excluded the great territory that is now the Northern Middle States but was until then part of the colony. The negotiations were largely in the hands of a man named Oswald, who, I have just discovered, was quite ignorant of the location of Michilimackinac and Detroit and did not realize what he was doing when he agreed to the stipulated line. When a group of London merchants, hearing of what was happening, interviewed him on the point, he confessed his ignorance and burst into tears as he informed them that it was too late to do anything.

I also encountered some amusing descriptions of political conditions in Lower Canada early in the last century. Apparently it was not unusual, in heated altercations, for members of the Assembly to chase each other round the table. On one occasion a fight broke out and the French Canadian speaker was rescued by one of the English Canadian members "tucking him under his arm" and running out with him.

Every day as I pass the disappearing Russell House,[30] I imagine how the children would enjoy watching the workmen tear down that old building. A fire last winter and the wreckers this summer make it appear a most picturesque ruins. Portions of the walls are pulled down by means of ropes and then the materials are picked up, sorted out and packed on drays which are weighed before they are driven off. This work is part of a grand plan for beautifying the city. The park along the canal is to be continued right up to the government buildings and already many old structures have disappeared.

July 22, 1928

Last evening, Morton and I left the Archives just before 9 p.m. and made for the apartment of Graham Spry. There we met the general secretary of the Canadian League, Brooke Claxton.[31] He was at McGill when the war broke and finished afterwards in law. He struck me as quite an able fellow. We talked about the possible ways of amending the Canadian constitution, about the St. Lawrence deep waterways, and about immigration. Read, who was also along, was particularly good on the whole constitutional field.

Beside the mental aliment, Spry served up good physical food – biscuits and cheese and beer. For this I blessed him then and more now, because I had the best night's sleep for some time and threw off a tired feeling that was oppressing me all yesterday.

When the academic year 1928–9 began, the University of Alberta had a new president, Dr R.C. Wallace, formerly head of the Department of Geology at the University of Manitoba. After twenty years' service with the University of Alberta, Tory had resigned on 1 June to become president of the National Research Council, with which he had been associated since 1923 but which now was being reorganized and expanded, with research laboratories in Ottawa. Although Burt was pleased with Dr Wallace's appointment,[32] he must have regretted the departure of a man with whom he had such close and friendly associations for fifteen years. Tory 'was one of the greatest men Canada has produced,' 'a rare combination of the visionary and the man of action,' he later declared.[33] Burt did not visit the Archives in 1929 or 1930, devoting his time outside the classroom to further work on the manuscript for *The Old Province of Quebec*, using the photostat copies of documents which he had purchased from the Archives. In 1930 his *Romance of the Prairie Provinces* was issued, as well as *Lord Dorchester*, a booklet in the Ryerson Canadian History Readers series, and an article on Carleton and Lord George Germain in the *Canadian Historical Review*.[34] His chapter in Volume vi of the *Cambridge History of the British Empire* also appeared this year.

The Romance of the Prairie Provinces, the 'opuscule' to which he referred in his letters of 1927 and 1928, was in fact his first major literary effort since the appearance of *Imperial Architects*. The two works were completely different in purpose and style: the latter was a scholarly monograph whereas the former was designed for young people in the schools of the prairie provinces. The art of writing history books for young people requires special talents: simplicity and clarity of language, orderly composition, a swift-flowing narrative of significant circumstances and events, and an infectious admiration for the human beings whose achievements and difficulties comprise the substance of the story. Above all there must be no shadow of condescension – the reader, though young, must be treated as a reasonable and thoughtful being, capable of responding rationally to the inevitable dilemmas and controversies which are a feature of human affairs. In all of these respects Burt's text was a notably successful treatment of the period prior to 1905. It will be recalled that the Public Archives provided him with reproductions from the picture collection, since numerous illustrations and maps were a distinguishing feature of Gage's texts. The book was reprinted many times without revision, and was used for supplementary reading in British Columbia, Alberta, Saskatchewan, and Ontario.

During the same year (1930) *The Press Bulletin* published an address which Burt had delivered before various audiences in the province, entitled 'Our Dynamic Society.'[35] This foreshadowed three articles which appeared some years later dealing with the applicability to Canadian history of Frederick Jackson Turner's famous 'frontier thesis.' This American historian had propounded the theory that the frontier experience had imparted a unique quality to the history and society of the United States. The heart of his argument was that the European immigrants arriving in the wilderness of North America had been forced, due to relative isolation, to abandon or at least greatly modify, their ancestral attitudes, customs, and life-style in order to survive in the primitive conditions of the New World. Building a new society from the ground up, they had created a civilization bearing the indelible imprint of this experience, and distinguished by individualism, pragmatism, acquisitiveness, optimism, restless mobility, idealism, and social and political equality. 'Frontier individualism has from the beginning promoted democracy,' Turner declared. A brilliant teacher at the University of Wisconsin and at Harvard, Turner had profoundly influenced a whole generation of historians by his interpretation of American history. Burt, with his keen interest in interpretive history, was naturally intrigued by the question of the applicability of this analysis to Canadian history. Moreover he had developed, as we have seen from one of his letters, an intuitive appreciation of western Canadian society, thankful that his lot was 'cast in larger spaces where the atmosphere seems freer and human nature more genuine.'[36] The Ontarian had become a Westerner by adoption.

In general, 'Our Dynamic Society' is a sympathetic exposition of Turner's arguments, which were applicable, with some exceptions, Burt believed, to much of Canadian experience. It is clear that his research and reflections had led to the conclusion that Canada was, in its essential character, a North American society; this, despite the fact that the impact of the frontier had been interrupted from time to time, for example by the boundary settlement of 1783 which produced an energy and brain drain to the mid-West United States.

Life in the West had given him an understanding of, and general sympathy for, western political behaviour:

At first they [the pioneers] were inclined to revolt against the restraints of government imposed by the east and were inspired by a strong individualism. But as time passed they felt the pressure of economic problems too big for them to handle, such as transportation, distant marketing, and irrigation. Then the westerners developed a marked genius for co-operation and a growing desire for government interference to conquer their difficulties. The west has always tended to produce a type of thinking which we know as pioneer radicalism, and which has alarmed the more conservative east. Third parties, born of this political insurgence, have forever been springing up, but their existence has been ephemeral. The older parties sooner or later bid against each other for the support of the growing west, and in this bidding they have taken over the sound and dropped the unsound ideas to which the west has given birth.

This shrewd comment was justified by the appearance on the Canadian prairies of the Patrons of Industry (in the 1890s), the Non-Partisan League (during the First World War), and the even more influential Progressive party of the 1920s. Burt's assessment of the impact of the Progressives anticipated one of the conclusions of W.L. Morton's definitive history of the party;[37] it was also pertinent to the subsequent experience and influence of the Cooperative Commonwealth Federation, which had its major power base in western Canada. The distinctiveness and vigor of western political life was a consequence of the fact that 'the bulk of any eastern community has known no life outside itself, whereas a western community experiences the stimulating cross-fertilization of ideas produced by people brought together from widely different sources.'

The historian concerned with the impact of forces and movements in human affairs sees history as a continuum. As Burt had written from London a decade earlier, 'the present is only a little point in the continuous stream of time.'[38] Hence the frontier process would in due course give way to new forces. So he ended his discourse with unanswered questions:

May not our buoyant spirit flag when its primal cause has been removed? ... Will not our [western] society be composed of those who have grown up here and are ignorant of life elsewhere? What effect will this have upon our national outlook and our tendency to sectional and provincial feeling? ... Will it not incline in spirit to be like European democracy, and may not our politics tend to a division between the "haves" and the "have nots"? And as our society loses its plastic character and hardens down, will we have a leisured class and the culture usually associated with it? Or can we keep such a class in this climate?...

10

First Years at Minnesota

Burt's move to the University of Minnesota in 1930 was promoted by several influences. Although by now a mature scholar of forty-two, he was still receptive to the challenge of a new environment and new opportunities. Nor is it uncommon for a man at midpoint in his career to take stock of his achievements and future prospects; the result may be removal to a new scene of activity or a reorientation of energies and objectives. A feeling that the University of Alberta was in a quiescent, if not a stagnant condition, may well have affected him. The Minnesota history department offered the opportunity for intimate contact with distinguished authorities in the fields of European, American, and British history, and was a large department by contemporary Canadian standards. Yet despite its size 'there is an attractive informality about the place,' he wrote to Mrs Burt during his visit in 1928. 'Everybody speaks to everybody.'[1] On this occasion, dining with colleagues at the faculty club, or in their homes, he enjoyed regular contacts with scholars in other disciplines – the word 'interdisciplinary' had not yet been coined – and with interesting visitors. Burt was impressed by the amount of noteworthy research in which the members of the department were engaged, in addition to their teaching commitments. The department offered a well-established graduate program at both the MA and PHD levels, and its undergraduate courses were healthy and growing.

The university library was another attraction. 'You never saw anything like the number of books there are here,' he noted in a letter to his wife.[2]

The Canadian section was weak, but there were funds to build it up and Burt was asked to advise on purchases.

Minnesota was a wealthy and progressive state, comparable to Ontario, with a cosmopolitan population of New England, Nova Scotian, Irish, German, and Scandinavian origin. There was a vigorous non-partisan, independent political tradition, with significant voting strength. There was also a good school system, and the state university, chartered in 1851 and organized for instruction in 1869, had acquired an excellent reputation. The Twin Cities possessed many cultural amentities not available in Edmonton, including a fine symphony orchestra and first-rate art galleries. The local press, the Minneapolis *Star-Journal*, was intelligently edited and international in orientation as compared with the xenophobic isolationism of much of the mid-West American press.

Burt's performance as a visiting teacher in 1928 was so successful that in 1930 he was offered a full professorship with special responsibility for a sophomore course in English history previously taught by Dean Guy Stanton Ford (1873–1962), who had headed the Graduate School since 1913. Ford was a distinguished scholar and successful administrator – so successful that he had become involved in many aspects of university affairs, including the strengthening of the library and the launching of the University of Minnesota Press. By shrewd recruitment he had created a strong history department, but increasing involvement in university administration forced him to relinquish his teaching responsibilities. In Ford's definition of the goals of higher education we can find the same ideas which Burt had proclaimed at Alberta:

....There must be for anyone who gets full value out of a college or professional training a curriculum beyond books and assignments and comprehensive examinations. It is outlined in no catalog and tested only by living. Its invisible lessons are legible to all men as you reveal that character in everything you do....

The privilege of scholarship and your disciplined power to increase knowledge, make you the trustee of your fellow men. The measure with which you discharge that trust will be the measure of the success of this university in training you to live by some other ideal of success than your own advantage and material gain.[3]

Burt accepted the offer, but not without hestation, for he found the decision to leave Alberta a difficult one. It was 'with very mixed feelings that I now look forward to leaving this institution to which I have become more and more attached since I came to it 17 years ago and in which I have never been happier than during the past year,' he wrote to President Wallace in his letter of resignation.[4] Wallace held Burt's position open for a year in the hope that he might decide to return, but the latter felt he should hold to his decision. 'I was much touched [he wrote Wallace] by your hesitation to fill my old position on the chance that I might be another prodigal son. Though we would all be happier and more comfortable back in Edmonton with you and so many other dear friends, and though I have had many moments of longing to retrace my steps, yet I have decided that I ought not to go back.'[5] Burt was not unaffected by national sentiment, and had a congenial position in Canada become available, he would have returned; he postponed the purchase of a house for a number of years for this reason.

One must recall that many Canadian intellectuals of the period regarded the United States as a country where liberal values were esteemed and were the currency of all major political transactions. The failure to join the League of Nations could be regarded as an unfortunate accident, and a reversal of isolationist policy was to be anticipated. The Quaker president, Herbert Hoover, was famed for his administration of a vast famine relief program in Europe in the immediate post-war years, and had been a strong supporter of Wilson's plan for a League of Nations. Migration to the United States did not require of politically-conscious Canadians the abandonment of cherished values. Moreover Burt the historian regarded the two countries as essentially North American communities in character; both had experienced the impact of the frontier way of life. And there had been a continuous interchange of migration. United States influence on Canadian life since the Revolution he regarded as a basic datum of Canadian history. Now the two nations were permanently wedded by bonds of economic interest. One of Burt's well-known witticisms illustrated this relationship:

It's like the long wed couple. Asked if she ever thought of divorce the wife said, horrified, Divorce? No, never, but I've often contemplated murder!

Like many others who found employment in the United States before World War II, Burt discovered that Americans welcomed Canadians warmly, recognized their abilities, and provided them with substantial material rewards. His strong sense of civic responsibility and desire to participate fully in the life of his adopted country finally led to his decision in 1941 to take out his first papers, and in 1944 he became an American citizen – 'For the first time in my life, I appeared in court,' he wrote his father.[6]

last December I submitted to an examination with two of my colleagues, White and Shippee, as witnesses to my character. It was rather amusing, for I had to satisfy the examiner that I was familiar with the American form of government, which I first began to study thirty-five years ago when I was a student at Toronto. Apparently the examiner also thought it was a joke, for yesterday, as I was leaving court he sent a clerk after me to know if I had yet been caught on a question about government, and then the three of us had a good laugh over it. There was quite a crowd of new citizens – about 75 – mostly from continental Europe – and the judge made an address that commanded my admiration.

Nevertheless, there were those among his former students who regretted his decision to move to the United States. A decade of productive effort had identified him as a distinguished Canadian historian, and this decision seemed to be a betrayal. But it is equally difficult to understand why a congenial position was not offered to him by one of the universities in Ontario, which would have facilitated his research at the Public Archives. One consideration in the painful uprooting was Burt's concern for promoting the cause of Canadian-American understanding. Americans, he was convinced, needed to know much more about Canadian history and the Canadian outlook, particularly that aspect which was rooted in British traditions.

Burt was not a continentalist in the sense that he favoured the ultimate political amalgamation of Canada and the United States. Nor did he believe in the superiority of American liberal political ideals and culture, as did Frank H. Underhill. Although he recognized the importance of the frontier experience in the history of the two countries, they were essentially two different societies. His admiration for British political traditions pointed in the direction of the North Atlantic Triangle concept. Like J.B. Brebner he saw Canadian nationality as an essential constituent in a trans-Atlantic community. His commitment was not to the ideology of either nationalism or continentalism, but to the pragmatic value of a closer association of the English-speaking peoples.

There appears to have been no prior departmental commitment to teach Canadian history at Minnesota when Burt was appointed. But from the start he was encouraged to offer a senior course in Canadian history. This was never a large class, for the number of undergraduates who were interested in Canadian affairs was small – a typical reaction which Canadians have never been able to understand in view of the role of their country as the United States' largest trading partner. In anticipation of a growing but as yet limited interest in the subject, Burt built up the Canadian section of the library to significant proportions.

Burt's reputation as a Canadian specialist soon resulted in the arrival of his first PH D student, Miss Hilda Neatby, a brilliant graduate of the University of Saskatchewan. In the following years he supervised the work of eleven other doctoral candidates who completed their studies at Minnesota, four Canadians, five Americans, and two from the United Kingdom. Their dissertation topics spanned a wide range of Canadian history from the Conquest to the twentieth century, as well as Anglo-American relations. Most of their studies were subsequently published either in book form or incorporated in expanded works. Although not completing his dissertation under Burt's supervision, Dr Wilfred Smith, the present Dominion Archivist, worked closely with him during his graduate years at Minnesota.

Burt made his widest contact with students in his large sophomore class in English history, often about two hundred in number. He taught it for twenty-four years, right up to retirement. It was a popular course, for Burt had mastered the subject and spoke without notes, often in dramatic and stirring cadences.

Shortly after his arrival in Minnesota, his colleague Herbert Heaton taught him to drive a car, a somewhat traumatic experience for both, Professor Heaton recalls.[7] A used seven-seater Buick was purchased, and Burt became a good driver, subsequently transporting the family to Vancouver for a summer school session at the University of British Columbia, and later, to the delight of the children, back across the continent to Toronto for a visit with their grandparents. One practical advantage of the move to Minnesota was the easier access to Ottawa by highway travel, which led first in 1932 to the rental of a cottage, and later to the purchase of a summer home on the Gatineau River at Larrimac. This permitted the family to accompany him on his annual pilgrimages to the Archives, and removed the tension between his role as husband and father and his scholarly ambitions, which had so distressed him during the 1920s. Except for a period during the war years, and for his one and only sabbatical leave spent in England in 1947–8, the late spring and summer days found him reading, writing, golfing, and watching his children grow. Old friendships with such cottagers as the Jennesses and Lanctots were cultivated, and in later years his graduate students at the Archives were always invited for meals and an evening of conversation. Thus as time passed the circle of the Burts' friendships with students and their own children's companions grew, compensating to some extent for the death in the 1930s of his mother, and of older friends such as Sir Robert Borden. As always, Mrs Burt was the soul of the household; her hospitality and affectionate interest made a visit to the summer home a memorable occasion.

In 1933 the work on which Burt had been chiefly engaged for more than a decade finally appeared – *The Old Province of Quebec*. This 551-page work was published by the University of Minnesota Press and distributed in Canada by the Ryerson Press of Toronto, and was dedicated 'to my former colleagues and students in the University of Alberta.' The reception which this first thorough treatment of a formative period in Canadian history received was uniformly favourable in scholarly journals on both sides of the Atlantic, and on both sides of the border; the reviewers had only a few minor substantive criticisms to advance. As for style, Gustave Lanctot wrote in the *Canadian Historical Review* that it was 'lucid and stimulating – capable, according to occasion, of vigour, humour, or emotion.'[8] The author must have been pleased by the congratulations in letters from friends in Canada. Professor Wrong wrote that it was 'a thoroughly sound piece of work based on a wide range of research.'[9] Appreciative comments were also forthcoming from Mackenzie King, Borden, and Armand Lavergne. Reginald Coupland, who had succeeded Egerton as Beit Professor of History of the British Empire at Oxford, wrote three years later that he had re-read the book for a new course he was preparing, and that his opinion of Carleton had been modified: 'I felt compelled to write and say how very good I think it is. It is not only a masterly disposition of a mass of learning but so finely impartial and objective.'[10] That *The Old Province of Quebec* remains a standard reference in Canadian historiography is attested by its reprinting intact in a two-volume paperback edition in 1968, thirty-five years after its first appearance.

Even his severest critic, Michel Brunet of the University of Montreal, paid him a graceful and perceptive tribute in 1969 in his *Les Canadiens après la Conquête*:

...Je désire rendre un hommage tout particulier à l'éminent historien A.L. Burt qui a consacré plusieurs années de sa féconde carrière à la préparation de son livre magistral, *The Old Province of Quebec* (Toronto, 1933). Quelques-uns de ses plus importants articles complètent son étude sur la période. Ce chercheur patient et méthodique conserve le mérite d'avoir mis à jour les principaux événements qui se sont déroulés après la Conquête. Son interprétation des faits marquait un progrès sensible sur celle de ses prédécesseurs et a ouvert la voie à un renouvellement de l'historiographie consacrée à ces années cruciales de l'histoire du Canada.[11]

One result of the appearance of *The Old Province of Quebec* was that Burt was invited by Canadian-born James T. Shotwell, Director of the Division of Economics and History of the Carnegie Endowment for International Peace, to prepare one of the twenty-five volumes of the Canadian-American Relations series – a series which was to be a landmark in Canadian historiography. Burt's assignment covered the period 1783 to 1818, and involved him during the next few years in the most intensive and extensive research of his lifetime as a scholar. Foreshadowing this work were two papers read at meetings of the Canadian Historical Association in 1931 and 1935. The first was a revisionist interpretation of the issues involved in the boundary settlement of 1783 and the retention of the western posts. The primary motive for the British delay in surrendering the posts, Burt showed, was the prevention of a general Indian uprising, but this motive became entangled with another, the vision of 'a British commercial empire over the heart of the continent' – an early articulation of this interpretation of Canadian history. In the 1935 paper he returned to a familiar theme – his reinterpretation of Carleton's personality and the controversial aspects of his career.

During these and succeeding years Burt was often invited to submit book reviews for the *Canadian Historical Review*, the *American Historical Review*, and *Minnesota History*. These dealt with a wide variety of works on Canadian history, the late colonial period of American history, and Anglo-American diplomatic history. Over fifty reviews were published during the next thirty years. The last, which appeared following his retirement, was of a work by his old friend of Oxford and Public Archives days, Gustave Lanctot, who was completing his well-researched *Histoire du Canada*.[12]

The work of the reviewer in a professional journal is a mystery to most laymen, who commonly read newspaper reviews designed to promote book sales, and are unaware of the value of a dispassionate and critical analysis of the contribution of a work to the progress of historical scholarship. Always aware of the importance of style in historical presentation, Burt was also happy to recognize it in his assessments. His comments on Samuel Flagg Bemis' *The Diplomacy of the American Revolution*,[13] illustrates both this interest and his own gift for vivid characterization:

His scholarship is impressive without being in the least oppressive. To produce this work, he has consumed a mountain of books in English, French, German, Spanish, and Dutch, and he has eaten his way through the archives of the old world as well as the new. Fortunately, the strength of his appetite is matched by the power of his digestion, or we would have been lost in a bewildering maze....

Burt was also versatile and wide-ranging in his capacity to detect errors in detail. And for authors writing for the layman, he applied scholarly standards, while being appreciative of their objective. Bruce Hutchinson's *The Incredible Canadian* was 'a fascinating, informative, and misleading book on an important subject.' Hutchinson was 'incapable of turning out a dull paragraph, for he wields the magic pen of a fine literary artist...'[14]

This study is constructed after the fashion of a symphony, to produce a desired effect. But the movements are not all well balanced, and several themes have got out of hand. One is chance. Though Mackenzie King had the good fortune to face a succession of Conservative leaders every one of whom played into his hands, his luck resembles that of Napoleon on the battlefield in that he possessed an uncanny ability to make the most of his opponents' mistakes. They deserved to lose, he to win; and to say that he slit their throats, as Hutchinson repeatedly does, is less like poetic license than licentious journalism.

Of Douglas MacKay's *The Honourable Company*, a popular work, Burt wrote 'the general reader will find it both interesting and profitable.'[15] Generous in his tributes to conscientious scholarship displayed by fellow professionals, he could also be blistering in his assessments, as in the case of Ferns' and Ostry's *The Age of Mackenzie King*.[16] In sum, he was a judicious and penetrating critic.

Meanwhile in the middle thirties Gage and Company induced Burt to write a high school history, which appeared in 1937 under the title *The Romance of Canada*. Authorized as a textbook in British Columbia and the Protestant schools of Quebec, and as a reference book in Alberta, it probably produced larger royalties than any other of his publications. Possessing a strong narrative line, not over-weighted with detail, it was frankly explanatory and interpretive. Canadian development emerges as a dynamic process. As such, it differed from those detailed, duller texts whose authors do not seem enthusiastic about any of the themes they are presenting. Its chief limitation was that only one-third of the account was reserved for the Confederation movement and national history. Its distinguishing characteristics were the emphasis on personalities, the perceptive treatment of French-Canadian questions, and the inclusion of the western farmers' movement. The emphasis was on the growth of a national spirit. In its most recent manifestations, this spirit was strengthened, he wrote, by the study of history:

Of all the ways in which the national spirit has expressed itself, none is more remarkable than the awakening interest in our own history ... The more we study the history of Canada, the more will we think and feel as one Canadian people, and only thus may we become a greater people.

This textbook was, with a minor revision, in use for nearly fifteen years following its first publication.

Following the completion of *The Romance of Canada*, Burt reported to his father:

...I plunge into the task that will absorb me for many months to come – writing the history of the early relations between Canada and the United States. I find it very interesting, particularly as my work in Ottawa has led me to conclusions quite different from those which have been accepted for some years now.[17]

This was the Carnegie series volume, which appeared in 1940 under the title *The United States, Great Britain and British North America from the Revolution to the Establishment of Peace After the War of 1812*.

The Old Province of Quebec had focussed on internal developments in Britain's most important colony, but external relations had not been neglected. This second major work, on which Burt's international reputation as a scholar was based, continued this latter theme. The period is the most complex in the long history of Canada's relations with the United States. Like its predecessor, this book dealt with a subject which had been investigated by other scholars, in this case chiefly by Americans, but Burt's treatment was notable for its continuous narrative over a long time span (1775–1818), for its examination of British, American, and Canadian primary sources which other writers had passed over lightly, and for its new interpretations of controversial issues. Stylistically, it owes much to Mrs Burt, 'the best critic I have ever known,' her husband wrote in the preface, '[who] has delayed the completion by making me improve at least one passage in almost every paragraph.'

The United States, Great Britain and British North America was widely reviewed in historical journals. The reviewers were all impressed by its importance as a contribution to the historiography of the United States and Canada. Burt's enthusiasm for grappling with controversial questions, and for stating his own opinions with vigour and cogency, was noted.

The work began with a discussion of the Revolutionary War and the peace settlement which followed it. Sir Guy Carleton is held responsible for the British defeat. More controversial was his discussion of the British retention of the western fur posts south of the new international boundary. Burt believed that this breach of the treaty obligation was designed to ensure the confidence of the Indians and reconcile them with the United States in anticipation of the time when the posts would have to be surrendered. This was a major reversal, reviewers noted, of the traditional view that the retention of the posts was a result of the influence of the Montreal traders. A major section of the work consisted of what all the reviewers agreed was a brilliant treatment of the War of 1812. The author took issue with Julius W. Pratt's thesis that the chief cause of the war was the political influence of the western expansionists. After a review of a large mass of evidence, Burt upheld the traditional emphasis on Anglo-American disputes over impressment and maritime rights. So far as the internal development of Canada was concerned, he stressed the significance of the war in checking the northward movement of American settlers and the resulting ideological, religious, and social influences emanating from the United States. 'The American declaration of war in 1812 severed the growing connection between the United States and Upper Canada as if with a knife.'[18] The effectiveness of the treatment of the strategy and operations of the war was noted by a number of the reviewers. Equally satisfactory was the discussion of the negotiations during the four years which followed the Treaty of Ghent, featuring the Rush-Bagot Agreement and the Convention of 1818.

It is interesting to note that Professor Pratt, whose views on the causes of the war of 1812 Burt had disputed, wrote in the *American Historical Review* as follows:

Professor Burt has written the most thorough and detailed summary which has yet appeared of the whole course of Canadian-American relations, and of Anglo-American relations so far as they affected these, from the beginning of the Revolution to the partial settlement of the boundary and fisheries questions in the Convention of 1818. He has not only covered the ground minutely; he has offered quite definite answers to a number of controversial questions and has made or suggested important revisions of generally accepted views on a number of points.[19]

Naturally some of Burt's arguments were contested, since final conclusions are seldom arrived at in historical study. The general consensus, however, was that the work was a *tour de force* in terms of the period covered and its attention to those internal developments on both sides of the boundary which explained the complex diplomatic relations of Britain and the United States. '[With] impartial mind it explores the causes of events in the terms in which they were presented to the actors themselves [Shotwell wrote in his introduction]. Its judgments are not misplaced wishful thinking in the light of the world today but the full statement of how things happened in their own time, when men had other interests to keep in mind than those which seem so important to us now.' Burt's study continues to be an authoritative interpretation, and is represented in anthologies on the causes of the war published over twenty years later.[20]

It is not surprising that Burt's scholarly interests, his lifelong commitment to an activist role in influencing public opinion, and his decision to become an American citizen would involve him in enterprises to improve Canadian-American relations. In 'The American Key,' an article published in 1942 in the *Revue de l'Université d'Ottawa*, he demonstrated the influence which the Revolution of 1776 and the subsequent emergence of the American nation had had on British imperial policy and on the struggle for responsible government; this 'has been too much ignored' he claimed. Another argument was that within the Empire 'in times of peace imperial sentiment and national sentiment always worked at crossed purposes, except in Canada.' 'There they frequently cooperated. They have been natural allies in the recurrent suppression of annexationism.' But despite the threat to their national identity, Canadians should recognize the constructive character of many American influences on their constitutional development, Burt asserted.

In the same year (1942) there appeared *A Short History of Canada for Americans*, which the University of Minnesota Press had requested Burt to write to permit the citizens of the republic to understand better their largely unknown northern neighbour and ally. The book derives some of its content and viewpoint from his *Romance of Canada*, but these are developed for the benefit of the more mature student and general reader. Since it is the fullest expression of his view of Canadian history, its distinguishing features should be noted. The objective of the book is achieved by treating the similarities and contrasts with American experience at appropriate points in the narrative; only the brief first chapter, 'Comparisons and Contrasts,' is topical in character. The impact of the frontier on New France and New England and the contrast between the English and French attitude toward the Indians are described. The effects of the Loyalist migration, the War of 1812, and American expansionism on the emergence of a Canadian national spirit are explained. The value of American constitutional experience in framing the British North America Act is a prominent feature of the chapter 'How Canada is Governed.'

The *Short History* had another distinguishing feature. 'It has long been my ambition to contribute to Canadian national unity by moderating the natural antagonism between French Canada and English Canada,' Burt had declared in a letter written in 1942.[21] He shared this commitment with his 'dear friend' Abbé Maheux.[22] Since Americans had been influenced by Francis Parkman's critical view of the society of New France, readers on both sides of the border would profit from his message, he hoped. From Laval to Laurier the exertions of French Canadians are described, particularly during the colonial period. But he was not uncritical: 'His words and his actions strongly suggested that he was a fascist,' he wrote of Duplessis. The life of the habitant and the voyageur, and the dilemmas of the French in the century and a half of Anglo-Saxon dominance, including the conscription crisis of 1917, are sympathetically presented. In this connection, he appears to be the first author of a general history of Canada to draw attention to the fears of French Canadians expressed in the 1865 debates and vote on the Seventy-Two Resolutions in the legislature of the province of Canada.

It is clear from this and other writings and addresses that Burt, while proud of the Anglo-Saxon cultural tradition in which he was reared, rejected the shibboleth of 'national unity' as a subtle form of cultural assimilation for the French, and stressed instead the concept of a state founded on the principle of cultural dualism. His education may also have been a factor, since the historian can hardly fail to understand how civilizations develop as a consequence of the cross-fertilization of cultures.

Burt is notably successful in handling one of the basic problems of Canadian historiography – the presentation of developments in the major regions of the country while retaining an emphasis on the theme of national evolution. As might be expected from his background, the book excels in its discussion of the significance of events in western Canada. While not slighting the importance of central Canada, Burt avoided the preoccupation of his professional colleagues with affairs in that self-centred, self-interested region.

In his interpretation of Canadian history he implicitly rejected economic determinism. The frank discussion of motivation includes the factors of national origin, religious concerns, and political ideals, as well as economic self-interest, and is uninhibited in its admiration of heroism, adventurous impulses, and constructive achievements. Although not a socialist, Burt asserted that 'There has been much nonsense talked about the Canadian National Railway, particularly in the United States.'[23]

Stylistically, the *Short History* is a clear, fast-moving narrative which, despite its title, was well suited to the Canadian reader. Burt expected, however, that the work would be largely ignored in Canada,[24] as it was, but its reception in the United States by reviewers in both non-professional and scholarly periodicals was flattering. A second edition, up-dated and with an expanded treatment of the period after the out-break of World War I, was issued two years later. H.H. Love, the president of W.J. Gage and Company, which published the book in Canada, was enthusiastic, and sent fifty copies to prominent politicians 'believing that it would induce in them a more understanding attitude toward the problem of French-English relations.'[25] There was a cordial response from Prime Minister King, who referred to the value of the book in improving Canadian-American and English-French relations: 'the volume is one certain to prove of real help to the public men of Canada and the United States.'[26]

11

Internationalist

Although Burt's removal to Minnesota did not terminate his productivity in the field of Canadian history, he became more and more concerned with developments in international affairs and Canadian-American relations. Indeed, he identified himself as a specialist in international relations in the biographical entry supplied to the *Directory of American Scholars*. From the early 1930s he was increasingly concerned with the growing world anarchy, and played an active role in the only way open to him – by informing and influencing public opinion through lectures in the Twin Cities and elsewhere in the state. One lecture, reprinted in full in the *St Paul Pioneer Press*,[1] warned of the danger of 'a narrow and blind nationalism':

Each nation does what is right in its own eyes, and of course is blind to any evil effects elsewhere. It seemed right for the Senate in Washington to reject the Treaty of Versailles. How many people in this country cared what that action would do to the rest of the world?

He criticized the preaching of such unrealistic panaceas as pacifism, the imposition of American-style democracy, disarmament, and the eradication of nationalism. None of these responses would save modern civilization, which was in real danger of extinction:

It is high presumption on our part to imagine, as we so commonly do, that our civilization will last permanently, that it is the final goal of human progress.

Progress is only an optimistic name for change, and the very conception of progress is of most recent origin. Progress may be down as well as up. In some respects we are better than the people of by-gone ages. In other respects we are worse. ... But we do know that through the long yesterday of the human race there have been many great changes for the worse. Mighty states have fallen, one after another; and whole civilizations have passed away....

Our civilization will go too, and it may be nearer the end than we think. ... Powerful states and whole civilizations have perished because their people failed to grapple successfully with the fundamental problems which faced them. The one gigantic problem which threatens to drag us down is the problem of establishing justice and order in place of the chaos which reigns in the world of international affairs....

...Nationalism itself cannot be destroyed, and it does not need to be destroyed. Without patriotism, where would be that sense of public service and citizenship without which self-government is impossible? It is not necessary for a man to spurn his wife in order to love his country. No more is it necessary for a man to spurn his country in order to seek the interest of the civilized world. The finest patriot is the man who is ever on guard against the mob impulse that sets nation against nation, the man who sees that there is right on the other side as well as on his own, the man who seeks to harmonize his country with the rest of the world.

In a letter to his daughter Forrest, then studying at McGill, he expressed his disquiet in specific terms:

October 21, 1936

Have you been following the international situation? On the whole, it seems to me to be worse than it was in 1914. Anything may happen at any time. If, as seems most likely, the Fascists win in Spain, what will France do, almost surrounded by dictators? Will not Germany then be sitting on the top of Europe? The moment Russia becomes engaged at one end of her huge territory she will be embroiled at the other end, and the war of one continent will flash into a war of two continents. It is hard to surmise when things will reach this crisis. If the present visit of Ciano to Hitler ends the uncertainty about Italy's position by tying that country to Germany, then look out for trouble soon. Many people in this country think they have learned wisdom and will never again be drawn out of their neutrality as they were in 1917, but I am strongly of the opinion that the only way for the United States to stay out of war is to cooperate with the rest of the world to prevent war. That of course is not a practical political question. Indeed I sometimes wonder if the world is not going through the process that individual countries passed – England a thousand years ago, and most others later. They fought out the problem of unity. Even as we may be obliged to fight and fight because we will not willingly surrender the sovereignty of the state for the sake of peace. Most people who cry out for peace give me a pain. They do not know the price of what they demand, if they knew it they would not pay it.

On 8 February 1938, he wrote, obviously unimpressed with the Munich Agreement: 'Of course war is never inevitable, but I have growing fears that it is not far off.'[2] A month later Hitler absorbed Czechoslovakia in the Third Reich.

If Burt anticipated that his views on international affairs would be acceptable in Minnesota, he was not mistaken, for he was in constant demand as a speaker on this subject before a wide variety of groups. Writing to his father on 14 February 1937, he reported:

Thursday afternoon I went with Dorrie to the University Club in St. Paul to address the Thursday Club, a society of ladies who seek to combine entertainment with self-improvement. I addressed them on the European situation, which is so bad that I could not give them any entertainment....

Next month I have to pose as an Italian in a debate against an Englishman before the St. Paul Foreign Policy Association. It ought to be good fun, particularly if, as I am told, this Englishman is very imperialist. Later in the month I have to travel 200 miles to address the Women's University Club in Wausau, Wisconsin, on the Far Eastern Crisis....

There were also addresses on international affairs during the 1930s and the war years to the Hennepin County Historical Association, the Minneapolis *Star-Journal* North West Women's Conference, the Minnesota Unitarian Association, the district Federation of Women's Clubs, the State Teachers' College at River Falls (Wisconsin), Hamline University (St Paul), and Augustana College (Rock Island, Illinois). The last was enthusiastically received, he reported. 'I was talking about international relations and what we will have to do if we really want permanent peace – my favorite topic.'[3]

Addresses on Canadian-American relations, and on French-English relations in Canada, were solicited by the Minneapolis Women's Club, the local business and professional men's club, the Twin Cities History Teachers' Association, a joint organization gathering at Red Wing, and Carleton College (Northfield). In 1932, in an address for the annual meeting of the Minnesota Historical Society, he returned to the theme of 'Our Dynamic Society' by briefly restating the frontier thesis, but balanc-

ing it with an extended discussion of the rise of urban, industrial civilization in the United States, and its impact on the character and quality of
American life.

Burt was also generous with his time in meetings of students' organizations, such as the Cosmopolitan Club, in which his children took an active
interest. His last formal connection with the League of Nations Society in
Canada took the form of a revision of his booklet on the League, reprinted by the Society in 1933.

The results of over twenty years of constant study, discussion, and
reflection on the problems of international relations were focussed in a
forceful, plainly worded speech on 'A World Gone Mad' delivered at
Rochester, Minnesota, at the beginning of March 1938.[4]

Since 1931 [he declared] there has been a progressive disintegration of world
order under the pressure of three great powers, Japan, Germany, and Italy. The
other powers have retreated before them, and we have seen international affairs
take on a new and at the same time an old form. The world has tended to split into
two groups of states which someone has recently characterized as the lunatics and
the paralytics.

Japan's aggression, he demonstrated, originated in the failure of the
world to cope with Manchurian anarchy, the intrusion of westerners into
the Far East 'making China weak and Japan strong,' the problems of
population pressure, and the exclusion of Japanese products from many
markets. Russia, Britain, and the United States could have blocked her
resort to a forcible solution to her problem, but 'they were hopelessly
divided,' and could not respond individually.

Nazi Germany's posture was a direct consequence of the vengeance
exacted by the Treaty of Versailles which, it will be recalled, Burt had
condemned in 1919. With the occupation of the Ruhr, 'the iron entered
into Germany's soul,' and Germany concluded that she 'would never be
treated as an equal until she was an equal – in strength.' Hitler's opportunity had come, and he seized it. His ambitions were clear to anyone who
would read *Mein Kampf*.

Italy's position was the most precarious and frustrating: surrounded
by British sea power, militarily weak, with few outlets for population
pressure, and with Italian products excluded by a world 'going mad in the
pursuit of economic nationalism.' Mussolini's defiance of the League 'may
come to be regarded as a great turning point in the world's history.' 'A
solid League led by Britain and supported by the cooperation of the

United States in imposing sanctions might have restrained Italy and that check might have given Germany pause.' Burt asked,

Where will it all end?
...So long as we cling to the doctrine of the sovereignty of the state we are bound to live in international anarchy.
...It all resolves itself into the problem of an international morality based on a far-seeing view of the coincidence of national interest and the welfare of the world as a whole.

The outbreak of war in 1939 and the involvement of the United States in 1941 came as no surprise to Burt. His public addresses during this period had all contained the warning that with the spread of international anarchy no nation, even a great power like the United States, could remain unaffected. He was now widely known, not only as an author of historical works on the interrelations of Britain, Canada, and the United States, but also as a committed internationalist. His *Short History of Canada for Americans* was scarcely off the press when professors Allan Nevins and Louis M. Hacker of Columbia University invited him, and his colleague Professor Heaton, to join eleven other nationally known scholars in preparing a textbook entitled *The United States and Its Place in World Affairs, 1918–1943*, to be used in teaching the thousands of armed services personnel who were to be stationed at various campuses during the summer. It was a congenial assignment, for the editors announced that the authors were expected 'to set down what seem to them the unescapable lessons of the period to the United States.'

They have not hesitated to assert that "the United States could live at peace only in a world that was ready to come to grips realistically with its fundamental economic, political, and military problems"; and that far from making its due contribution to this realistic effort, the United States "hung suspended between two worlds, so that we were incapable of facing in mature fashion all the requirements of a purely nationalist policy on the one hand, or one based wholly on international collaboration on the other.'[5]

The deadline (1943) required Burt to write quickly, and the nine chapters from his pen illustrate his mastery of forceful and readable exposition. The fact that he had been following the course of international affairs so closely since his first participation in the League of Nations Society's activities in Canada meant that he had the facts at his finger-tips, although as with all his writing he was forever revising his drafts: 'I am so critical that it is very hard to please myself.'[6] The chapters dealt with international affairs in Europe and the Orient and the American response to them from the beginning of Hoover's presidency to Pearl Harbor. He had never been diffident in expressing his convictions; soon to become an American citizen, he could write without reserve, as in the following passage:

In the general rush for cover, we were determined not to be behind; but the sort of cover we sought left us behind. We increased our naval and military appropriations, but not as much as we should have done had we not trusted the oceans that separated us from the dangerous aggressors. Safety for us seemed to lie in tight isolation. The administration did not think so, and a minority in the nation agreed with the administration. To them isolation was both futile and immoral, for it would encourage aggression, make war more certain, and allow it to spread until it engulfed us in the end. But those who held such views were then helpless. The mere suggestion of co-operation with other Powers to maintain the peace was enough to frighten the isolationists and harden their determination to get a foolproof permanent neutrality law.[7]

'As I read his account,' Professor Heaton remarks. 'I was amazed by his industry; and he and I felt he had done a grand job for the students in arms who came to the Minnesota campus to be prepared in knowledge for the task of occupying when victory was attained.'[8]

The need for some form of international government provided the thesis which Burt developed for the Armstrong Lectures delivered at his *alma mater*, Victoria College, in January 1945, and bearing the title 'The Tug of War and Peace.'[9] The lectures, given by distinguished scholars, had been endowed by G.H. Armstrong of Toronto, a public school inspector, 'to be used in the field of religion and education.' Burt discussed the problems which were derived from the pursuit of uninhibited national self-interest; he pointed to the emergence of international arrangements such as the Danube Riparian Comission, the Universal Postal Union, and the International Sanitary Convention, which restricted sovereignty to achieve the objectives of enlightened self-interest. In this context, he extolled the virtues of free trade and condemned the excesses of nationalism. Nationalism in its earlier manifestations had identified itself with democracy, liberalism, humanitarianism, and a flowering of cultural expression. But this coincidence was a historical circumstance and had been largely displaced by ugly manifestations. Still, he concluded, nationalism was a fact of life, and men could only escape from continuous international anarchy by recognizing and using to the utmost the coincidence of national self-interest and the general welfare.

Burt repeated the same analysis and argument in 1946 in an address 'The Problem of Nationalism' delivered to the Seventh Conference on Science, Philosophy, and Religion at the University of Chicago, concluding in the following words:

Now that the splitting of the atom has produced a bomb that may destroy our civilization, physical scientists say there is no defence against this bomb; and therefore, they are becoming political scientists, impatient to get such a world organization as will make war impossible. We may have peace in our time as the result of exhaustion, but whether we can use this respite to erect such an organization depends on whether we can split something that appears to be more difficult than the atom. It is nationalism, whose good influence in binding the brotherhood of the nation has been inseparable from its evil influence in perpetuating international anarchy by blinding men's minds to the fundamental community of interests between nations. Here is the problem of nationalism. How can we solve it?[10]

It was in this context that he interested himself in the improvement of understanding between Canada and the United States. His *Short History* had this as its stated objective, but his activities soon ranged farther afield. In 1942 he participated in planning for consultation between scholars interested in research and teaching relating to the development of the interior of the continent. The project was sponsored by the Rockefeller Foundation, and resulted in interdisciplinary meetings held in Lincoln, Nebraska, and Saskatoon, Saskatchewan, dealing with the northern Great Plains.[11] A study guide for adult education groups was produced, and there is some evidence that the perspectives of the participating researchers and university teachers were broadened by these conferences. Burt was more directly involved, however, in the activities of the Canada-United States Committee on Education, which was organized in 1944 as a voluntary organization of educators devoted to the improvement of the knowledge and understanding of each country in the other, particularly among students in the senior high schools.[12] Financed largely by the Carnegie Corporation, it organized teachers' workshops and exchanges, promoted the transfer of educational broadcasts and films, and published articles and surveys of textbooks used in the two countries. In addition to participating in the deliberations of the Committee, Burt acted as the educational collaborator for *Canada's History: Colony to Commonwealth*, produced in Chicago by Coronet Instructional Films.

We have already seen something of Burt's apprehension that a second world war was drawing near, and of his efforts to combat isolationist thinking. He accepted as his special contribution to the war effort a commitment during 1943 and 1945 to teach large classes in the Army Special Training Program. The men enrolled in these classes were those who would be involved in the administration of occupied territory. The course was modern history and Burt was free to determine the content. He discovered to his joy that many of the students were graduates of American and European universities – in effect graduate level men. He organized the course topically, including a treatment of such movements as imperialism, socialism, communism, and humanitarianism, in the context of an evolving internationalism. The students were alert and interested, and he found this the most satisfying experience of his teaching career. His daughter Joan recalls his comment that all of his previous reflection and research seemed to have come to full fruition in this assignment.

During the winter of 1944–5 he prepared a 58-page pamphlet *Canada: Our Oldest Good Neighbor*, which was published in the *GI Round Table* series by the US Government Printing Office. The purpose of the series was to provide materials for group discussions on a wide variety of topics of contemporary interest, led by education officers in camps in the United States and overseas. Burt's contribution outlined simply and clearly the current aspects of certain issues of long standing in Canada's domestic concerns and in its relations with the United States.

During the summer of 1945 Burt participated in the summer conference of the University of Michigan on The United States and the Postwar World, delivering an address entitled 'American Cooperation with Britain, and the Canadian-American Marriage.'[13] Within a few weeks the atomic bomb would be dropped on Japan, and already it appeared that of the Great Powers only the Soviet Union, the United States, and Great Britain would be in a position to shape the course of post-war international relations. 'If they fall out,' Burt declared, 'the world will fall apart, peace will vanish, and with it the chance of laying the foundations for any stable international order that would be acceptable to us.'

We simply have to cooperate with the British and the Russians, despite the perverse preaching of some of our big newspapermen and a few of our little politicians who apparently believe – they can hardly be said to think – that our proper policy is to bait the bear and twist the lion's tail.

The potential power of the Soviet Union was greater than that of the other two powers, and a counterpoise of Anglo-American co-operation would be necessary – but this would have to be managed without a breach with the Russians. The war years had demonstrated, Burt argued at a later point in the address, that Britain and the United States were interdependent, but American relations with Canada could not be regarded as a real test of these relations: 'our relations with Canada are *sui generis.*'

Canadians, he stated, are more like Americans than any other people, but there were also differences in the quality of life which explained their apprehension of being absorbed by the United States. This apprehension was not felt in the other countries of the Commonwealth, but at the same time Canadians had 'steadily and successfully resisted pressure from Britain and from other dominions to establish in London any new form of imperial government in which they would all share.' 'Canada is really more closely tied to the United States than to Britain,' and World War II had intertwined their interests still further. It was unrealistic for Canadians to think that they were 'the interpreter and link between the two great powers.'

In the last analysis, however, Canada's relations with the two powers depend on how they get along with each other; and this is the most important consideration of all – for all three. Indeed, the British people the world over realize how much they depend on the United States. If the American people realize how much they depend on the British Commonwealth to build the world we want, World War II may be the last world war.

Viewing other prospects of the post-war years, Burt commented in a letter to his father early in 1944:

The great power of the future promises to be not the United States or Great Britain, but Russia; and the problem of the future is how to live with her on the best terms.[14]

Two years later he took a coolly dispassionate view of the Gouzenko spy revelations. The West would be similarly tempted if our ally had discovered radar and the atom bomb and kept the secrets herself, he thought. The wartime alliance should be preserved 'for almost invariably, after every war, the allies who have gained the victory then fall out among themselves'; and he believed that Russian memories of the effort to overthrow the Soviet régime should not be ignored by the Western allies.[15]

In 1946 the Royal Society of Canada awarded Burt its Tyrrell Gold Medal for outstanding work in connection with the history of Canada. The presentation was made by D.C. Harvey, whose citation read in part:

I am presenting to you a man who, though still not old, has long been known to many generations of students in Canada and the United States as a gifted, enthusiastic teacher of history and to the reading public as a versatile writer on historical subjects and contemporary problems. ...

Though all these ... volumes give evidence of laborious days spent in dry-as-dust research, the dry bones are so covered with flesh and blood and the theses are elaborated with such enthusiasm that the reader imbibes old ideas without dust and accepts new ideas without pain; for Professor Burt is a historian who works hard but sings at his work.[16]

The 1947–8 term was spent on sabbatical leave at Oxford – his first return visit in thirty years. It was a thoroughly enjoyable sojourn for Mrs Burt as well as 'A.L.'.[17] The experiences of the year included a lecture for a course at Cambridge on Anglo-American relations, for which his book was prescribed reading, and a visit to Paris where he represented the American Historical Association at the International Committee on Histor..al Sciences. No doubt the relief from teaching duties provided time to work on his last major publication, a textbook of nearly a thousand pages entitled *The Evolution of the British Empire and Commonwealth from the American Revolution*. A book on this subject had been commissioned by a New York publisher as early as 1943, but while Burt was working on the early chapters the management changed their plans. Subsequently D.C. Heath and Company of Boston invited him to prepare a longer work on the same subject, which was several years in preparation.

In 1949 Burt was elected President of the Canadian Historical Association, and in his presidential address in 1950, entitled 'Broad Horizons,' he expressed some of the basic ideas which formed the guidelines of the forthcoming book. Although Canadian historiography, he remarked, had not been free of nationalistic bias, 'Canadian historians have had to take a wider view simply because Canada was the child of France and Great Britain, because it grew up within the British imperial fold, and because it has been indissolubly married to the American giant.' Yet the study of imperial history had been too much neglected, despite the fact that 'Canadian history, when examined in the light of the history of the Empire, gains much in perspective and depth of meaning.' Burt devoted the remainder of his address to the troubles and problems associated with the attainment of self-government in the West Indies, Australia, and

Ireland, and compared these to the movement in Canada, which was uniquely influenced by the American presence.

Although Burt was contending that imperial history had a special meaning for teachers of Canadian history, there was another motive in preparing a work on this subject for American students – 'to undermine the latent American prejudice against Britain.'[18] *The Evolution of the British Empire and Commonwealth* is Burt's longest work, and displays his characteristically effective narrative style, in this case applied to the presentation of a great mass of factual detail. The manuscript evoked an enthusiastic comment from the head of Heath's College Department: 'Your manuscript is certainly a pleasure; we seldom have this kind of writing and it is very welcome indeed.'[19] The special character of the book is not its exclusive use of primary sources, for it is based on thorough consultation of reliable secondary works, but in its selection, balance, and emphasis on the treatment of the many themes involved in such a wide-ranging subject. 'Personalities, however interesting in themselves, have been kept to a minimum; and so also have the details of internal history of each part of the empire,' Burt wrote in the foreword. The one exception to this statement is the prominent position which he gave to political, economic, and humanitarian movements in Great Britain, which were formative influences on imperial policy-making.

The author's object was to present the evolution of the Empire 'as an organic whole,' and in this he was certainly successful. In the works of some authors the relationship with Ireland is ignored, but not so in Burt's study. The 'dominant ideas and forces' with which he was concerned throughout the narrative were superlatively illustrated in the account of the emergence of the commonwealth after World War I. In this connection, the United States' new position as a world power with the potential capacity to preserve world peace in association with the Empire, 'league or no league,' was 'what really undermined the Round Table movement and all other efforts to achieve imperial reintegration,' he wrote. Professor D.J. McDougall of the University of Toronto, in his assessment in the *Canadian Historical Review*,[20] was critical of some particulars, as any specialist in the field would be, but was generally favourable: 'for its purpose it is a successful book, and is almost certain to gain a wide popularity.' Charles Mowat, the brilliant son of Burt's tutor at Oxford, a Minnesota PH D, and Professor at the University of Chicago commented,

Here, as so often, I think your combination of experience and insight – British, Canadian, American – enables you to see truths and connections which escape most people. And you have triumphantly solved the problem that defeated poor Knaplund – of combining the treatment of topics with a chronological narrative that preserves the sense of movement which is of the very essence of history.[21]

McDougall's prediction of the popularity of *The Evolution of the British Empire and Commonwealth* was borne out by its adoption within a year by over forty universities in the United States. This was partly the result of the sweep and range of the work, for this last of his major publications was the type of historical exposition which he had so admired in Sorel in 1919:

He takes long views of history and connects up distant but similar effects by unearthing deep and permanent causes. That grander style of history appeals to me more and more.[22]

Burt's career at the University of Minnesota ended with his retirement in 1957. Professor Heaton, then chairman of the department, recalls that he cited Burt and E.S. Osgood, who retired the same year, as up-daters of the Turner thesis – men who had begun life as easterners who had moved to the far west, subsequently turning back as far as the Midwest – 'living examples of the Turnaround Theory.'[23]

Burt's retirement did not terminate his scholarly activities; during the following academic year he was visiting professor at Carleton University, Ottawa, which had been founded by Dr Tory fifteen years earlier. In addition to his university duties, he delivered a series of six public lectures in Ottawa on the Commonwealth, sponsored by the English-Speaking Union. In 1958–9 he was visiting professor at the University of Chicago. In 1960–1, at the age of seventy-two, he taught at the University of Manitoba. Professor Carl Berger recalls the course which Burt offered that year, in which he displayed the same stamina in a three- or four-hour seminar which Professor Lillian Cobb had noticed 43 years before in Edmonton. And his characteristic emphasis on clarity in composition as the essence of the historian's craft continued undiminished. 'He was the first teacher I ever had,' Professor Berger claims, 'who went through an essay word by word, line by line, paragraph by paragraph to show me exactly how it could have been put together more effectively and like everybody else who came into contact with him I have never forgotten that experience.'[24]

After the end of the term Burt suffered a stroke, which limited his capacities, despite a gradual recovery in subsequent years. In 1963 he wrote a preface for the Carleton Library's edition of Professor Aileen

Dunham's *Political Unrest in Upper Canada 1815–1836*. The reprinting of this work after the lapse of nearly forty years was a signal recognition of the scholarship of one of his first honours students at Alberta, and his participation in its reissuance was a happy epilogue to his long teaching career.

The late sixties were a quiet time spent happily in Minneapolis, with regular summer sojourns at Kirk's Ferry (Larrimac) on the Gatineau. In 1966 he returned to Edmonton to receive the University's honorary degree of Doctor of Laws, and to renew acquaintance with many distinguished Albertans who, as senior members of the History Club, organized a banquet and presentation in honour of the Burts. During the following year the Minneapolis home was sold to permit a move to Wellesley, Massachusetts, where Arthur and his wife were anxious to have his parents nearby. Unfortunately this arrangement was to benefit A.L. only, for Mrs Burt died rather unexpectedly in 1967. This blow he accepted with sorrowful resignation. Dorothy Burt, in addition to the contribution she had made to A.L.'s literary endeavours, had been an affectionate wife and mother, a generous hostess, and an active community worker, particularly in the affairs of the local Anglican (in the United States, Episcopal) congregation. Her wisdom and tact were decisive elements in fifty-two years of married life, while endearing her to friends young and old.

Fully alert in his mental faculties, though handicapped in his ability to communicate, Burt's last years were spent tranquilly in Wellesley, and with his other children. His music record collection remained a solace to the end, which came quietly on 21 June 1971. Those who had known him were reminded of the last words of Bunyan's Mr Valiant-for-truth:

My sword I give to him that shall succeed me in my pilgrimage, and my courage and skill to him that can get it. My marks and scars I carry with me, to be a witness for me. ... So he passed over, and all the trumpets sounded for him on the other side.

[John Bunyan, *The Pilgrim's Progress. The Second Part*]

12

Committed Scholar and
Dedicated Teacher

There can be no disputing that A.L. Burt was one of the leaders of the group of historians who revitalized Canadian history in the 1920s and 1930s by establishing it on a firm basis of exhaustive documentary research. Younger scholars in the years since World War II have inaugurated important work in new directions – social, economic, and intellectual history, as well as political – which were ignored or passed over lightly by these pioneers. Yet it is noteworthy that revisionism has not seriously modified the contributions to the discipline made by Burt and his contemporaries. Their concentration of effort was both necessary and, in its end products, creative.

In assessing Burt's role in the intellectual life of his time, it is essential in the first place to refer to his role as a teacher. His effectiveness on the rostrum in front of a large class has been noted previously. His object was to arouse the interest of the students, to convey to them something of his own love and enthusiasm for the subject. He succeeded because he was a bit of an actor, and by gesture, declamation, and embellishment of phrase clothed the abstractions of historical fact with a rich texture of realism. To prepare for these appearances he insisted on an uninterrupted hour before class time. His lecturing technique involved a close observation of the reactions of his class. If he sensed that they were not getting the point, he tackled it again from a different angle; conversely, if they had grasped the point quickly, he cut short his illustrations and explanations.

In contrast to these undergraduate lectures, Burt's seminars on Canadian history were informal and intimate, as he discussed the implications of a particular document, or the students' interpretations of some episode of the period under consideration. On one principle only he was authoritarian: 'Reserve judgment till you can get all the evidence – get to the source.'[1]

Without exception, his graduate students found him 'a very warm man, generous, friendly, even fatherly,' as one of them has described him.[2] 'More than one hungry young man was fed at Mrs Burt's table, and benefited by Mr Burt's conversation and sage advice,' recalls Miss Louise Olsen, an MA in history, the omnicompetent and perceptive departmental secretary. 'Some of the graduate students simply gorged themselves with both food and drink.'[3]

On one occasion I was able to accept Mrs. Burt's invitation to Thanksgiving dinner, when the board was loaded with all kinds of good food. We stood while Mr. Burt said grace (in Latin, and wearing his Oxford jacket). We were a large group of family and graduate teaching assistants. Mr. Burt carved the turkey, while Arthur cut slices from a slab of roast bacon.[4]

Burt's conversations with his graduate students extended beyond the realm of mutual professional interest, notably in the field of music. Visitors at his home soon became aware of his competence at the keyboard of the family piano, and his infectious enthusiasm for the orchestral works of the classical composers was one of their enduring memories of his friendship.

Although his own research was concentrated on political, constitutional, and diplomatic history, Burt welcomed scholarly contributions in other fields of historical study, as his book reviews testify. Strongly convinced of the social function of history, he stressed the importance of literary style in establishing communication with the reader. He applied the same standard to his own work: 'I fill my scrap basket several times with discarded drafts before I can complete a chapter. It is like sweating blood....'[5]

The thrust of his thinking exhibited a consistently liberal bias – for he was an ideologue of neither the right nor the left. He can best be described as a pragmatic democrat, with a basic sympathy for the economically weak and underprivileged. Nationalism, imperialism, *laissez-faire* capitalism, socialism, and communism were human concerns, deserving of analysis and understanding in their historical context, but he was committed to none of them. However, his dislike of authoritarianism and blind prejudice is abundantly clear in his books and public addresses. This was a corollary of his oft repeated dictum that a democratic society could survive only if it possesses an informed public opinion.

His democratic and humanitarian instincts, which were so clearly evident during his sojourn in London, coupled with his experience of life in the Canadian West, are vigorously expressed in an analysis of the Social Credit victory in Alberta and of the origins of the Union Nationale in Quebec, which he published in the New York monthly, *Events*, in 1937.

Premier Aberhart of Alberta has done more for Canada than for his own province. This wild man of the West has taught the wise men of the East a much needed lesson. The economic collapse gave fantastic proportions to the debt structure of the Canadian West, making readjustment imperative, but the financiers of the East were blindly stubborn until the Premier of Alberta shook them. He did it because they made him. As eager lenders, they shared with the equally eager borrowers the responsibility for the "extravagance" of the West, but they were so determined to make the West pay the whole bill that they contributed more than a little to the political victory of the Social Credit party in Alberta. ...

Burt was undoubtedly correct in claiming that 'If the legislature were dissolved today for another election, his party would win again, for he has given the people something and there is no alternative government visible.' Turning to Quebec, he wrote:

Down East, French Canadian nationalism is insurgent once more and, incidentally, has given another shock to the financial interests already hit by the rise of Aberhart in the West. Whether Liberals or Conservatives were in office in Quebec, there was little doubt that the seat of power was St. James Street, Montreal, the Wall Street of Canada. But the election last August [1936] saw a great upheaval. Liberals, Conservatives and St. James Street were all routed at the polls by a racial movement organized under the name *Union Nationale*. ...

Instead of reacting against the economic system, French Canadians have reacted against the unquestionable economic domination of the British, and thus the radicalism born of hard times has in French Canada taken on a distinct racial and political form. They will be masters in their own house. Some of them have been talking and more have been dreaming of a day when they will form a French and Roman Catholic republic on the shores of the St. Lawrence.[6]

A few months later in an article in the same periodical, 'Stress and Strain in Canada,' he wrote

Another feature of this ... movement has been the failure of the traditional parties, seated in the East, to understand the new society growing in the West, and here lies what may be a valuable lesson. For the present predicament of Alberta, the historic political parties are much to blame. Liberals and Conservatives alike, and even the United Farmers who held office for fourteen years, have been too absorbed in playing the game of politics to have much concern for the political education of the electorate. ...[7]

As an Ontarian who had lived in western Canada during a period of rapid cultural change, Burt was interested in the applicability of Turner's thesis as an explanation of what had been distinctive qualities of Western life. As we have noted in a previous chapter, he explored this theme in a general way in a public address in 1930. Other Canadian historians, particularly A.R.M. Lower and Frank Underhill, were finding the thesis applicable to some strictly circumscribed developments in Canada, while Walter N. Sage had delivered a general endorsement in 1928. Burt's approach was both subtle and selective. In the region west of the Great Lakes he stressed the impact of frontier conditions on a population who 'were not an average representative of the society which they left behind.'

They were a picked lot, selected by conditions. They were the poor who had a hope of becoming richer and [with] the ability and the energy to realize their hope if it was at all possible.[8]

Like the more perceptive British travellers who published their impressions of the western mentality before World War I, Burt stressed the distinctive qualities of responses which are convincing to anyone who has lived in the West:

The new life which they created was crude and material. Conditions made it so. But it was redeemed by a peculiar idealism – an intense belief in what man can do and a tremendous faith in the future. It was free of the feeling of restraint which the growing past throws over a man. It was emancipated; it was creative. ...

Thus we have had in North America, in Canada as well as in the United States, a life with little leisure or culture, a life that is intensely practical and concerned with material things, a life in which emphasis is laid on growth and quantity, and on the future instead of the past.[9]

'But all this is a tale of yesterday,' Burt observed, turning to an elucidation of the new conditions which had transformed Western society – the mechanization of agriculture, the declining size of the farming population, the influence of machine-made, mass-produced goods, the growth of an urban industrial society.

Reverting to the past again, it is interesting to note that in his 1932 address to the Minnesota Historical Society Burt first propounded what became one of his settled convictions, although it was not one which went unchallenged by some of his colleagues in later years: that Turner's hypothesis was confirmed by the history of New France.

Feudalism lost all its strength on being transplanted into Canada; and the government of the colony, though autocratic according to the letter of the law, was very far from autocratic in practice. The eyes, the ears, and the mouth of the government in every parish were those of the local militia captain; and he, though formally appointed by the governor, was substantially the elected leader of the people. From the earliest days of New France, the breath of liberty entered into the lives of the French Canadians to a degree which has been little appreciated except by themselves. ... It was physically impossible to hold down the habitant as the peasant was held down in old France. America emancipated him. The woods were at his very door and liberty was forever beckoning him through the trees. ...

This thesis Burt developed more fully in a paper read in 1940 at the annual meeting of the Canadian Historical Association. He repeated it in 1957 in a chapter entitled 'If Turner had Looked at Canada, Australia, and New Zealand When He Wrote about the West,' in the book *The Frontier in Perspective*. Australia on the other hand, he observed, exhibited a sharp contrast in development as compared with North America; on that continent the small independent farmer was almost non-existent, and hence of little influence in shaping politics and society; in New Zealand the farmer or rancher emerged only after fifty years of subservience to a pastoral oligarchy of large estate owners.

Turner's and his disciples' failure to discover that the frontier was not peculiar to the United States, Burt concluded, was the most serious criticism which could be leveled at their work.

They have studied and written as national historians without realizing that the besetting sin of national history, in this as in every other country, is too exclusive a concern with what has happened within its own borders. To avoid this insidious snare is not easy, for nationalism by its very nature is introspective and given to self-glorification. If Frederick Jackson Turner and his followers fell into this sin, they are not alone. They have plenty of company.

Burt's views on French-English relations in Canada have been frequently referred to elsewhere in this work, and it remains to note his attitude to the Francophone historiographical tradition. His closest French-Canadian friends were Gustave Lanctot and the Abbé Arthur Maheux, who in the 1970s would be labelled federalists. There is no evidence of any contact with the Abbé Groulx, whose uncompromising nationalism and hostility to British influence in Canada were being transmitted to successive generations of college students during his long career as a teacher and prolific writer. As a moderate critic of the ideology of nationalism, there was no possibility of a productive dialogue; avoiding direct confrontation, Burt confined himself to lamenting the tendency of those French-Canadian historians and writers who sought 'to preserve their national integrity by withdrawing within themselves, indulging in self-pity over their hard lot, and nursing their prejudices.' He approved Maheux's use of history 'pour inspirer à la jeunesse la très positive notion d'égalité entre les deux groupes du Canada.'[10]

As a professional, Burt gained the respect of other professional historians. He was tireless in the search for facts in the documentary sources, discriminating in weighing them as evidence, acute in his conclusions and generalizations, and tireless in striving for effective literary expression. His major works were in the mainstream of contemporary historiography. Like other historians whom Professor Arthur Marwick has labelled the 'straight line professionals of the inter-war years,' his two major works were concerned with 'the obvious centrality of institutions and political activity.'[11] Considering these skills and interests, one must ask why his productivity was relatively limited. The answer is to be found in Burt's concept of the range of his commitments.

Reviewing his career as a whole, it is obvious that Burt sought continuously to relate his professional labours to the needs and concerns of contemporary society as he saw them. Serious-minded from his earliest years, he did not take his responsibilities as a citizen lightly. War service, activities for the League of Nations Society, participation in the Canada-United States Committee on Education, and the Canadian Institute of International Affairs, were time-consuming. Above all, his ready acceptance of numerous speaking engagements in Alberta and Minnesota to advance the cause of international understanding were an expression of his conviction that the scholar in a democratic society has an obligation to share his insights and knowledge with the public.

The same motive was involved in the time he devoted to popular articles and to writing books for school and college students. In these works, his knowledge of history was explicitly used as an instrument to advance such causes as a better understanding of Canada's dual nationality, improvements in Canadian-American relations and, above all, the construction of a peaceful world order. From first to last, by perceptive assessments of individual and group character, he combatted irrational fears and prejudices. In these writings he did not shun moralizing.

Like other historians, Burt must be judged in the light of the fact that 'each age writes its own history,' each age has its evaluations of what is significant in its past, and 'will tend to see the past in the light of its own preoccupations.'[12] World War I had a profound influence on his thinking, and the prevention of a similar catastrophe was his chief imperative – indeed it almost became an obsession. The mobilizing of public opinion in support of the League of Nations concept was a 'tremendous moral responsibility.' 'If we fail to shoulder this great responsibility, we will stumble along the same old way which we all know leads to disaster,' he had declared.[13]

Had he eschewed what for him was the scholar's responsibility as an activist, and the obligation to communicate, Burt would undoubtedly have produced a larger corpus of original contributions to historical knowledge, but this was the price he was ready and willing to pay for a conscience which, had he overruled it, would have left him restless and unsatisfied – a hollow man.

Men exist for the sake of one another. Teach them then or bear with them.
[*The Thoughts of Marcus Aurelius*, Book VIII, No. 59]

APPENDICES

1 'On the Study of History'

Extracts from two lectures
delivered to the students in the first year of
the Faculty of Arts and Sciences,
University of Alberta, October 1927

Before discussing the value of studying history, I wish to protect you and me from a possible misunderstanding. I have not the slightest wish or intention to decry any other subject. Some people have the notion that every professor thinks his own subject the only one worth while. Personally, I doubt the existence of such bespectacled mental monstrosities, but I quite understand how a man who sets out to spend the most of his life in delving deeper into one particular subject may sometimes leave such a false impression. I hope that I will not. I merely want to give you a peep into the reasons why we study history.

It often happens that we attempt to explain what we take for granted, that we find a most inadequate justification. We take life for granted. Who of us could sit down and write out a convincing argument to prove that life is worth living? Most of us would make a sorry mess of it. ... As a student of history speaking to other students of history, I feel that I am very likely to advance reasons for the study of history which may seem hopelessly inadequate or even trivial. If you condemn me for this, I will agree with you most heartily, for I have never yet been able to find a fully satisfactory explanation of why I have undertaken to spend my life in the study of history. I fear that I will never find it, but I am confident that I will be able to analyse the inner urge a little better as life goes on. As I see it now, the value of the study of history is both practical and ideal. Let us concentrate first on the practical value, on the study as a means to an end in our everyday life.

It provides us with a stock of knowledge which is necessary to intelligent reading and conversation. Surely it is of some real practical value to know what other people are speaking and thinking about, for otherwise we would be cut off from our fellows. Somebody mentions Sir John A. Macdonald and some political trick which he played, or perhaps the great part he took in making this fair country of ours. He might as well have spoken in Chinese, if we have no knowledge of the history of Macdonald and his time. We read some reference to Abraham Lincoln, but it means nothing to us if we are ignorant of the history of the United States at one of its supreme crises. Someone talks of Oliver Cromwell, but we must be dumb if we have never read or heard of that great man who ruled over the destinies of Great Britain when they were trembling in the balance. ... Someone may speak of the religious difficulties faced by King Feisal today in Mesopotamia, but the meaning of what he says is locked up in the history of over a thousand years ago when the Moslem world split. We may hear that England by her conquest of India was threatened with the fate of Rome. But what does that mean unless we recall how Rome's military conquests reacted to injure Roman character? ... Almost all intelligent conversation and thinking is coloured by the past, and unless we are tolerably familiar with it, we are perpetually at a loss.

Other subjects are equally valuable as a sort of stock in trade of educated conversation, but history is as important and as necessary as any of them. A knowledge of history is one of the marks of an educated man whatever be his profession or business. ... There are other and more compelling reasons for turning our eyes backwards – without running any danger of imitating Lot's wife.

It is impossible to turn our back upon the past without coming to grief. There are some who purposely shut their eyes upon the past as all bad and useless – something to be discarded. Let us see what happens to those who trust to their own blind wisdom. After the 'wisest fool of Christendom' came down from Scotland to rule England, he did not make the success of it that other Scots have done. The times grew more and more out of joint, till at last the Great Rebellion broke forth, and England was torn by civil war. The Roundheads won on the battlefield and then they tried to set matters right so that they would never go wrong again, and they did it thoroughly. They cut off the head of the king, they abolished the church of Archbishop Laud, they swept away the old House of Lords, and they radically remodelled what they had left of the ancient institution of parliament. By these simple operations, they sought to make a new and a better England, and indeed they foreshadowed many of the great reforms of the nineteenth century. But did they succeed then in doing what they were trying to do? No! They found that Charles I when dead was a more powerful enemy than he had been when alive. ... And the result? Only a few months after Cromwell was laid in his grave, the king came back in the person of Charles II, the House of Lords returned, and the established church was restored – and all with such wild enthusiasm that the naive Charles II observed that it must have been his own fault that he had stayed out of his own realm so long.

Another example occurred a century and a half later. When the French Revolution broke out, men were carried away by their hatred of the past. They destroyed their old institutions in a night, and they tried to create a new heaven and a new earth in a day. But they could not, for they were not Gods but only men. What happened? The Revolution turned and devoured her own children. Then came Napoleon, a more tyrannous master than any king had been, and at last the French restored the monarchy which they had guillotined. And the Church which they had thought they abolished came back too. They could not help it.

Very recently, the Russians have also tried the glorious experiment of taking the Golden Jerusalem by storm. The Bolsheviks abolished almost everything but themselves, and they even made a beginning at that. But what have they done? The Czar is dead, but tyranny is not.

Of course later generations have benefitted from the English Civil War and the French Revolution, and, very possibly, Russia may be a better country in the future for the events of the last years. But the significant fact is that the revolutionaries all failed for the most part in what they were trying to do at that time. They were baffled by some unseen power that held them in its mysterious grasp. What was it? It was the past which rose up against them and defeated them. No individual at any moment of his existence can cut loose from his past, for that is himself. So it is with any people. It cannot shut the door upon the past, and cut itself off from its history, for that is its essence.

...Here lies a grave danger, for every so-called reform or 'step in advance' will be in vain and may very probably bring trouble unless the past is taken into account....

At present there is a good deal of discontent and unrest with parliamentary government as it exists, not only in Italy but in many parts of the world as well. Again I would suggest that a sense of the past is indispensable. Parliamentary government has been working best in that country where the history of that institution is best known – in England. It is only by a study of the past that we can see that our laws and our parliaments are not dead but living things which are changing all the time....

But while we are learning the nature of the present by a study of the past, at the same time we develop our mental faculties, we develop our judgment. The study of history is much more than learning a story or a lot of events. That is the 'A.B.C.' of history. It is the attempt to find a connection, a cause for things. Why did the Reformation in England come under Henry VIII? Why was America discovered when it was? Why did the Crusades come when they did? Why were they a failure, and why did the movement die out in the 13th century? Why did Rome conquer Carthage? Why did that home of individual liberty, Greece, become enslaved? Why did civilization arise in the Nile valley? Sometimes we find the answer easily, even though it very seldom lies on the surface....

Sometimes the answer long eludes our prying search. Not until about 30 years ago did we really understand why Carthage fell. Sometimes we never find the answer. But we hope to do so some day. Meanwhile, the inquiry into the working of cause and effect in human affairs, whether it leads to a definite conclusion or not, is extremely valuable to our minds. We are developing judgment. Here the study of history is of great practical value. Our judgment upon present day problems is keener and sounder in proportion as we exercise it upon the problems of the past....

History is not a simple science; it is a most complicated business. But how can it be applied if there is no certainty to it? Our judgment is aided by some particular qualities of mind and by several general conclusions which we may deduce from the past.

One quality of mind which is sadly needed today is imagination. The absence of this has been one of the greatest causes of wars. People in one country cannot understand the people of another. They live their daily lives largely in ignorance of them, until suddenly they are confronted by some serious clash of feeling and interest, and then, on the spur of the moment, they condemn the other people as wrong and bad, simply because they think and feel in a different way. They give full vent to their tempers, and think that they are doing the work of God. If only we had more imagination, to project ourselves into the lives of people different from ourselves, to think their thoughts, to experience their feelings, to peer out upon the world through their eyes, how much more tolerant, how much more peaceful would we be! Here is one of the greatest uses of the study of history, the study of the life of other peoples, of other conditions of living, of other ages. It is more than just reading about them, it is living with them. There is no better way to train this imagination which is necessary if we are going to live in any harmony with other people both beyond and within our own borders.

Closely linked with imagination are other mental qualities which are necessary for the welfare of our society and which may be greatly developed by the study of history. One of the commonest sins of youth, and even of maturer age, is the forming of hard uncompromising opinions. Even when we do not form them ourselves, we catch them from others. For this prevalent disease, the best antidote by far is the study of history, which ever inculcates a largeness rather than a narrowness of view. Another valuable mental quality which it gives is a sense of proportion. Two illustrations of this will suffice. Almost every people, at one time or another, has thought that it was the chosen of Heaven. If this continent understood a little more history, we would hear less about God's country, and the biggest talkers in the world would tell us less about all the biggest things in the world, including themselves. We would also have a sounder sense of proportion about the age in which we live. It is only a moment of time in the life of mankind, and we should not be impatient because we cannot do in a few years more than has been done in centuries in the past.

From the past, also, we may draw some very practical general conclusions. In this, however, we must be most careful, for history, like the Bible, can be made to teach anything which people want it to teach. For the most part, the lessons of the past are very broad, and are forced home time after time without any possibility of mistaking. Incidentally, we have already discovered one of the most important of these – that we cannot cut ourselves off from the past, for if we try it will rise up against us. But while there is this law of permanence, there is also the law of change. One of the first things to strike the student of history is the successive fall of empires. ... Each was great in its age, because it was adapted to existing conditions. But they could not stand still and the times changed. Then each in turn lost the faculty of clinging to life by a new adaptation to the world around us. Whose turn is next?

These are not the only lessons which the past holds in store for us. There is the law of interdependence. This operates in many ways. One of the simplest is the reaction of the conquered upon the conqueror. ... Still another lesson is the value of individual initiative. People are like children. They are much better when they do things for themselves.

And so we might go on, but let us look back to see what all this practical value of history means. Our greatest heritage today, is not the wealth of our natural resources. It is our past, the experience of generation after generation, without which these resources would be of no more value than nature is to the utter savage.

In the present state of our civilization, there is a greater need to delve into this wonderful storehouse of the experience of mankind than has ever existed before. We often flatter ourselves because we live in the most democratic age that the world has seen. Indeed we have raised democracy up into a sort of dogma or religion. Now there lies a very grave danger right here. As never before we have given the power of government into the hands of the people, but are the people able to shoulder this mighty responsibility? No answer to this question can yet be given, for our democracy is very young. It has developed within the last hundred years. We are in the midst of a great experiment, upon which the fate of our society rests. Whether this fate will be further human development, or the doom of our society, will depend in large part upon how far our masters, the people, will take to heart the experience of the past. The future will be dark without a much wider study of history than there has ever yet been.

Apart from this practical purpose, there is another great reason for the study of history. It is an end in itself. If properly approached, it becomes an ever-growing joy, for it enlarges our being. ... There are some people whose lives are bound about closely by time and place, the twin tyrants of mankind. But we may burst through their close restraints, and the process of expansion is one of the greatest and finest joys that we can win. We may grow until our lives reach out over time past, and even penetrate somewhat into the future, and though our bodies may be in one little place, our minds may rove over space. The curiosity with which nature has endowed us all, is the magic charm which may set us free. We want to know the why of everything, and so we pursue many studies. But of them all none is more fascinating, more noble than history – the growth of mankind. But of this I will say no more. For if you have this great vision of the study of history as an end in itself, my words would be stale and unprofitable; and if you have it not, they would be unavailing, for this is a vision that is caught only by trying to penetrate into the wonderful mystery of the world of man.

2 A.L. Burt: A Bibliography

Abbreviation UAED, University of Alberta Extension Department

1913

Imperial Architects: Being an Account of Proposals in the Direction of a Closer Imperial Union Made Previous to the Opening of the First Colonial Conference of 1887 (Oxford: B.H. Blackwell)

'The Relation of Music to the Other Arts,' *The Pelican Record* (Corpus Christi College), XI, 5 (March 1913) 153–63

1917

'Is Life Worth Living?' *The Gateway* (University of Alberta Students' Union), (May 1917) 17–19

1921

'Thoughts on the Russian Revolution,' *The Gateway* (March 1921) 8–12

1922

'The Mystery of Walker's Ear,' *Canadian Historical Review* III, 233–55

1923

'Sir Guy Carleton and His First Council,' *Canadian Historical Review*, IV, 321–2

'The League of Nations. I: Its Organization,' *The Press Bulletin*, UAED, VIII, 10 (19 January 1923) 1–4

'The League of Nations. II: Its Working,' *The Press Bulletin*, UAED, VIII, 11 (26 January 1923) 1–4

'The Need for a Wider Study of Canadian History,' *The Press Bulletin*, UAED, IX, 5 (23 November 1923) 1–4

'The Horoscope of Mars,' *Queen's Quarterly*, XXX, 3 (January–March 1923) 273–96

1924

A Short History of the League of Nations: Its Origin, Organization and Problems (Edmonton, UAED)

'The Tragedy of Chief Justice Livius,' *Canadian Historical Review*, V, 196–212

'Canada's Dual Nationality,' *The Press Bulletin*, UAED, IX, 9 (15 February 1924) 1–4

'Le Dualisme canadien,' L'Echo du Collège d'Edmonton, II, 7 (25 mars 1924) 1–7

'The Stumbling Block of Europe – Reparations,' *The Press Bulletin*, UAED, X, 1 (3 October 1924), 1–6

'Disarmament and the Fifth Assembly,' *The Press Bulletin*, UAED, X, 4 (24 October 1924) 1–4

1925

'Shall Canada Accept the Protocol?', *The Press Bulletin*, UAED, X, 11 (26 February 1925) 1–4

1926

Introduction and appendices to A.G. Bradley's *Lord Dorchester*, and J.N. McIlwraith's *Sir Frederick Haldimand*, The Makers of Canada Series, anniversary edition (London and Toronto: Oxford University Press)

'Peace in the Heart of Europe,' *The Press Bulletin*, UAED, XI (22 January 1926) 1–4

'What is Canada?' *The Press Bulletin*, UAED, XI, 4 (8 February 1926) 1–4

'The Policeman: A Story for Young People,' *The Bulletin of the League of Nations Society in Canada*, IV, 6 (December 1926) 8–10

1927

'Who was the "Com[man]d[ant] de la Troupe dans chaque coste"?,' *Canadian Historical Review*, VII, 227–30

'The Imperial Conference,' *The Press Bulletin*, UAED, XII, 7 (25 March 1927) 1–4

A New World or the League of Nations (Ottawa: League of Nations Society in Canada)

1928

High School Civics: A Brief Treatment of the Civics Section of History 3. (Edmonton: School-Book Branch, Department of Education)

'Governor Murray and the British Government,' *Transactions of the Royal Society of Canada*, 3rd series, XXII, sect. ii, 49–56

'On the Study of History,' *The Press Bulletin*, UAED, XIII, 3 (14 March 1928) 1–4

1930

The Romance of the Prairie Provinces (Toronto: W.J. Gage and Co. Ltd.)

Manitoba High School Civics (Toronto: Educational Book Co. Ltd)

'The Problem of Government, 1760–1774,' in *The Cambridge History of the British Empire* (Cambridge: Cambridge University Press) 146–72 (chapter 6)

Lord Dorchester. Ryerson Canadian History Readers (Toronto: Ryerson Press)

'The Quarrel between Germain and Carleton: An Inverted Story,' *Canadian Historical Review*, XI, 202–22

'Our Dynamic Society,' *The Press Bulletin*, UAED, XVI, 3 (12 December 1930) 1–4

1931

'Guy Carleton, First Baron Dorchester (1724–1808),' *Encyclopaedia of the Social Sciences* III (New York: The Macmillan Company) 227–8

'A New Approach to the Problem of the Western Posts,' *Canadian Historical Association Annual Report* 61–75

1932

'Our Dynamic Society,' *Minnesota History*, XIII, 1, pp 3–23

1933

A New World or the League of Nations, revised edition (Ottawa: League of Nations Society in Canada)

The Old Province of Quebec (Minneapolis and Toronto: The University of Minnesota Press and Ryerson Press)

1935

'Guy Carleton, Lord Dorchester: An Estimate,' *Canadian Historical Association Annual Report* 76–87

1937
The Romance of Canada (Toronto: W.J. Gage and Co. Ltd)
'Canadian Cross Currents,' *Events* (New York) I (February 1937) 131–4
'Stress and Strain in Canada,' *Events* (New York) II (July 1937) 69–73

1940
The United States, Great Britain and British North America from the Revolution to the Establishment of Peace after the War of 1812. In the series The Relations of Canada and the United States (New Haven, Toronto, and London: Yale University Press, The Ryerson Press, Oxford University Press)
'The Frontier and the History of New France,' *Canadian Historical Association Annual Report* 93–9

1942
A Short History of Canada for Americans (Minneapolis and Toronto: the University of Minnesota Press, The Educational Book Company of Toronto, Ltd)
'The American Key,' *Revue de l'Université d'Ottawa*, XII, 153–66
'The United States from the Depression to the Second World War' (Part VII), and America's Involvement in the War (Part IX): nine chapters in Allan Nevins and Louis M. Hacker, eds., *The United States and Its Place in World Affairs, 1918–1943* (Boston: D.C. Heath and Company)

1944
A Short History of Canada for Americans, revised and enlarged edition (Minneapolis and Toronto: The University of Minnesota Press, The Educational Book Company of Toronto, Ltd)

1946
Canada: Our Oldest Good Neighbor, EM47, GI Round Table (Washington: US Government Printing Office)

1947
'American Cooperation with Britain and the Canadian-American Marriage,' *The United States in the Postwar World*, addresses given at the 1945 Summer Conference of the University of Michigan (Ann Arbor) 81–94

1950
'Broad Horizons,' *Canadian Historical Association Annual Report* 1–10

1955

Guy Carleton, Lord Dorchester, 1724–1808, revised version, Canadian Historical Association Booklets, No. 5 (Ottawa: Canadian Historical Association)

1956

The Evolution of the British Empire and Commonwealth from the American Revolution (Boston: D.C. Heath and Company)

1957

'If Turner had Looked at Canada, Australia, and New Zealand When He Wrote about the West," in W.D. Wyman and C.B. Kroeber, eds., *The Frontier in Perspective* (Madison: The University of Wisconsin Press) 59–77

1961

'Peter Mitchell on John A. Macdonald,' *Canadian Historical Review*, XLII, 3, pp 209–27
'British America,' in American Historical Association, *Guide to Historical Literature* (New York: Macmillan and Company) 697–708

1964

'The Problem of Nationalism,' in L. Bryson, L. Finkelstein, and R.M. MacIver, eds., *Conflicts of Power in Modern Culture* (New York: Cooper Square Publishers Inc.) 590–6

3 A.L. Burt's PhD Students

1934 Hilda Neatby, 'The Administration of Justice under the Quebec Act'

1947 Gerald M. Craig, 'The Influence of the American Background on the Struggle for Self-Government in Upper Canada'

1947 Paul F. Sharp, 'The American Revolt in Western Canada: A Comparative Study Showing American Parallels'

1948 Gerald S. Brown, 'The Policy of Lord George Germain toward the American Revolution, 1775–1778'

1953 Alvin C. Gluek, Jr, 'The Struggle for the British Northwest: A Study in Canadian-American Relations'

1953 Lewis H. Thomas, 'The Struggle for Responsible Government in the North-West Territories, 1870–1897

1954 P.C.T. White, 'Anglo-American Relations from 1803 to 1815'

1957 Galen Broeker, 'The Problem of Law and Order in Ireland, 1812–1836'

1957 Roy C. Dalton, 'The Jesuit Estates Act (Quebec)'

1957 G.G. Hatheway, 'The Indian Neutral Barrier States'

1957 Leslie L.F. Upton, 'William Smith: Chief Justice of New York and Quebec'

1960 Alan H. Lawrence, 'The Influence of British Ideas in the British North American Revolution'

1968 Wilfred I. Smith, 'Canadian Representation Abroad to 1896'

Notes

CHAPTER 1 FAMILY ROOTS AND EDUCATIONAL EXPERIENCE

1 J.B. Bickersteth, *The Land of Open Doors: Being Letters from Western Canada* (London 1914) 105, 106
2 *Canadian Annual Review* (1913) 702
3 *Review of Historical Publications Relating to Canada*, XVIII (1913) 16. The work was also praised as 'a timely and valuable contribution to a subject that is becoming increasingly important,' in a long review by 'H.P.' in the *Oxford Times* 28 June 1913, and was also favourably reviewed in *The Spectator* and *The Scotsman*.
4 See review of *The Romance of the Prairie Provinces*, *The Mail and Empire* (Toronto) 26 April 1930, by William Arthur Deacon.
5 *The Sudbury Journal* 9 June 1910
6 G.R. Parkin, *The Rhodes Scholarship* (Toronto, etc. 1912) 91
7 See Carl Berger, *The Sense of Power: Studies in the Ideas of Canadian Imperialism, 1867–1914* (Toronto 1970).
8 A.L. Burt, 'Broad Horizons,' Presidential Address, *Canadian Historical Association Annual Report, 1950* 1
9 D.C. Harvey (1886–1966), after his studies at Oxford, taught at McGill and the universities of Manitoba and British Columbia. In 1931 he was appointed Archivist of Nova Scotia, and retired in 1956.
10 J.E. Read to John Arthur Burt, 2 July 1971

11 *The Pelican Record* XI, 5 (March 1913). Reprinted in *The Gateway*, 27 November 1923, University of Alberta Archives, hereinafter cited as UAA

12 F.J. Wylie in Parkin, *The Rhodes Scholarship* 175–6

13 The Head Registry Clerk, Oxford University, to the author, 19 March 1971

14 *Imperial Architects: Being an Account of Proposals in the Direction of a Closer Imperial Union Made Previous to the Opening of the First Colonial Conference of 1887* (Oxford 1913) 225

15 *The Evolution of the British Empire and Commonwealth from the American Revolution* (Boston 1956), foreword

16 Burt to Tory, 4 February 1913, H.M. Tory Papers, Academic Appointments File, UAA

17 Tory autobiography, unpublished, 'Going West,' 9, H.M. Tory Papers, XXIX, Public Archives of Canada, hereinafter cited as PAC

18 For an account of Tory's career, see E.A. Corbett, *Henry Marshall Tory, Beloved Canadian* (Toronto 1954).

19 H.M. Tory to W.H. Alexander, 21 July 1934, Wallace Papers, UAA

20 Quoted in Corbett, *Henry Marshall Tory, Beloved Canadian* 100

21 W.H. Alexander notes (undated), Wallace Papers, UAA

22 *Ibid.*

23 Professor Lillian Cobb to the author, 5 February 1971

24 Professor Aileen Dunham to the author, 2 February 1971

25 *The Gateway* (May 1917) 17–19

CHAPTER 2   THE TANK BATTALION

1 See *Report of the Ministry, Overseas Military Forces of Canada 1918* (London, nd) 377. 'The 1st Tank Battalion was authorized by General Order 64 of 1 May 1918. ... The unit remained there [in England] until its return to Canada on 18 May 1919 and was subsequently disbanded' – Director, Directorate of History, Department of National Defence, to author, 5 April 1971

2 See University of Alberta Soldiers Comforts Club, *Weekly News Letter*, 20 April 1918, UAA

3 H.M. Fife, a private in the University of Alberta contingent

4 The Rev. Tom Marsden was a Cambridge graduate who had come to Edmonton as an Anglican missionary in 1915. He lectured in history and English in the 1917–18 term, and remained in England after the war.

5 A.L. Burt to Mrs Dorothy Burt, 29 June 1918

6 *Ibid.*

7 *Ibid.*, 9 July 1918

8 *Ibid.*, 17 July 1918
9 *Ibid.*, 18 September 1918
10 *Ibid.*, 20 July 1918
11 *Ibid.*, 25 September 1918
12 *Ibid.*, 6 October 1918
13 *Ibid.*, 17 November 1918
14 See below, p 171n9.
15 Miss Roberta MacAdams, a nursing sister who had been active in Women's Institute work in Alberta, was one of the two members of the Assembly elected by the overseas service voters in 1917. See L.G. Thomas *The Liberal Party in Alberta: A History of Politics in the Province of Alberta 1905–1921* (Toronto 1959) 166, 179.

CHAPTER 3   THE KHAKI UNIVERSITY

1 See *Report of the Ministry, Overseas Military Forces of Canada 1918* (London, nd) 472–82; H.M. Tory Papers, VI, PAC.
2 Frank Underhill (1889–1971), was on the teaching staff of the Khaki University. A graduate of Toronto and Oxford, he taught history and political science at the University of Saskatchewan from 1914 to 1927, when he moved to the University of Toronto, retiring as professor of history in 1955.
3 Sir Charles Lucas (1853–1931), civil servant and historian. Lucas, a graduate of Oxford, produced several works on the history of the Empire following his retirement in 1911 as first head of the Dominions Department of the Colonial Office.
4 F.D. Adams (1859–1942) was Dean of the Faculty of Applied Science, McGill University.
5 C.M. MacInnes (1891–1971) was born in Calgary and educated at Dalhousie and Oxford universities. He did not secure a post in Canada; but was appointed to the staff of the University of Bristol in 1919, and became Professor of Imperial History there in 1943. He was the author of several works on the history of the Empire and on the history of Bristol. In 1930 he published *In the Shadow of the Rockies*, the first scholarly treatment of the history of the western plains region of Canada, which remains a standard reference.
6 Ernest Barker (1874–1960), at this time Fellow and Tutor of New College, Oxford, author of standard works on the political thought of the classical world, with a world-wide reputation
7 Hugh J. McLaughlin (1892–1972) of Toronto subsequently became a prominent barrister and Queen's Counsel, and was a Bencher of the Law Society of Upper Canada.

8 Tory Papers, VI, PAC, 'Instructions,' 9 December 1918

9 S.D. Killam (1888–1923) was Assistant Professor and later Professor of Mathematics at the University of Alberta.

10 D.A. MacGibbon (1882–1969), a graduate of McMaster and Chicago, was Professor of Economics at the University of Alberta from 1919 to 1929.

11 J.L.W. Gill (1871–1939) was Professor of Engineering at Queen's University.

12 A.L. Burt to Mrs Dorothy Burt, 6 April 1919

13 See 'Khaki University,' *Encyclopedia Canadiana* v (Ottawa 1958) 400–1; E.A. Corbett, *Henry Marshall Tory, Beloved Canadian* (Toronto 1954) ch. 13

CHAPTER 4   LONDON DAYS

1 See M.P. Follett, *The New State: Group Organization the Solution of Popular Government* (New York and London 1918); on Henry Wise Wood's view of group government, see W.L. Morton, 'Social Philosophy of Henry Wise Wood, the Canadian Agrarian Leader,' *Journal of Agricultural History* XXII (1948) 114–22. The clearest presentation of group government theory was provided by William Irvine in *Co-operative Government* (Ottawa 1929).

2 See A.J.P. Taylor, *English History 1914–1945* (Oxford 1965) 187

3 A.L. Burt to Mrs Dorothy Burt, 28 May 1919

4 *Ibid.*, 30 March 1919. William Temple (1881–1944) became Archbishop of York in 1929 and Archbishop of Canterbury in 1942. As a church leader and writer, he identified himself with the Labour party and was an inflential champion of social justice, church union, and of a reasoned exposition of the Christian faith.

5 Malcolm Muggeridge, *Jesus Rediscovered* (London 1969) 180–1

6 See report in the *New York Times*, 5 July 1918

7 A.L. Burt to Mrs Dorothy Burt, 20 April 1919

8 *Ibid.*, 20 April 1919

9 *Ibid.*, 29 June 1919

10 He was also completing his collection of nineteenth-century political biographies.

11 A.L. Burt to Mrs Dorothy Burt, 19 January 1919. Succeding comments on French historians are taken from letters in April, May, and June.

12 *Ibid.*, 12 May 1919

13 *Ibid.*, 22 May 1919

14 Sir George R. Parkin (1846–1922), the leading Canadian advocate of imperial federation and organizer of the Rhodes Scholarship administration. Author of *The Rhodes Scholarships* (Toronto, etc. 1912)

15 A.L. Burt to Mrs Dorothy Burt, 2 June 1919

CHAPTER 5 SCHOLAR AND COMMENTATOR

1 Morden H. Long (1886–1965). Long was promoted to Professor of History in 1935 and headed the department from 1946 to 1952.
2 *The Gateway* (March 1921) 8–12
3 *Sup.*, 46
4 Foreword, *The Old Province of Quebec* (Minneapolis and Toronto 1933)
5 *Ibid.*
6 Norah Story, 'Sir Arthur George Doughty,' *The Oxford Companion to Canadian History and Literature* (Toronto, etc. 1967) 220
7 Professor D.G. Creighton's experiences a decade later were similar to Burt's: see his 'The Decline and Fall of the Empire of the St Lawrence,' *Canadian Historical Association Annual Report, 1969* 14–16.
8 Gustave Lanctot was educated at the University of Montreal and at Oxford. He joined the staff of the Public Archives of Canada in 1912. He succeeded Sir Arthur Doughty as Dominion Archivist in 1937, retiring in 1948.
9 D.E. Cameron (1879–1946) was a graduate of the University of Edinburgh, and studied theology at New College, Edinburgh, and at Gottingen. A chaplain in World War I, he was on the staff of the Khaki University. He was chief librarian at the university from 1921 to 1945. Miss Calhoun was also a member of the library staff.
10 Chester New (1882–1960) was a Professor of History at McMaster University from 1920 to 1951. His biography of Lord Durham appeared in 1929.
11 The Archives was then housed in a substantial stone structure on Sussex Street, next to the Mint. It was subsequently enlarged in 1926.
12 See H.M. Tory Papers, League of Nations Committee, UAA
13 *The Gateway* (14 November 1922 and 21 April 1923)
14 *The Press Bulletin*, UAED, VIII, nos. 10 and 11 (19 and 26 January 1923)
15 Borden to Burt, 17 June 1924, Sir Robert Borden Papers, PAC

CHAPTER 6 THE OLD PROVINCE OF QUEBEC

1 Hilda Neatby, introduction, Carleton Library reprint of *The Old Province of Quebec* I (Toronto 1968) x. Dr Neatby was Burt's first PH D student (1934). From 1936 to 1944 she taught at Regina College, and subsequently at the University of Saskatchewan where she was head of the Department of History from 1958 until her retirement in 1969.
2 Foreword, *The Old Province of Quebec*
3 J.L. Morison (1875–1952) was born in Scotland and educated at Edinburgh and Glasgow universities. He was Professor of History at Queen's from 1907 to 1922 and at King's College, Newcastle on Tyne, from 1922 to 1940.

4 G.W. Brown (1894–1963) graduated from the universities of Toronto and Chicago, and was appointed to the history staff of Toronto in 1925.

5 Harold A. Innis (1894–1952) graduated from McMaster and the University of Chicago, and in 1920 was appointed to the Department of Political Economy at the University of Toronto.

6 J.A.T. Chapais (1858–1946) was active in law, politics, and journalism, and as professor of history at Laval. In addition to his eight-volume history of Canada he produced biographies of Talon and Montcalm. He was appointed to the Senate in 1919.

7 E.C. Drury was a leader of the United Farmers of Ontario and was premier of Ontario from 1919–23 heading a government supported by farmer, labour, and independent members.

8 For a concise description of Levy's difficulties see *The Old Province of Quebec* 109n.

9 H.P. Biggar (1872–1938) was educated at the universities of Toronto and Oxford. From 1905 to 1938 he was chief archivist for Canada in Europe. He edited several documentary publications of the Public Archives and also the Champlain Society's six-volume work on Champlain. His brother, O.M. Biggar, had practised law in Edmonton, see *inf.* 113.

10 Antoine Gérin-Lajoie (1824–82), lawyer, journalist, librarian, and historian. The book Burt was reading was *Dix Ans au Canada, de 1840 à 1850*, an impartial account of the movement for responsible government.

11 W.P.M. Kennedy (1881–1963) was at this time a member of the Department of History at the University of Toronto, and had published *Documents of the Canadian Constitution: 1759–1915* (1918) and a textbook, *The Constitution of Canada: An Introduction to Its Development and Law* (1922).

12 W.S. Wallace was educated at the universities of Toronto and Oxford. He taught history at the universities of Western Ontario, McMaster, and Toronto and was librarian of the University of Toronto from 1923 to 1954. He edited the *Canadian Historical Review* from 1920 to 1929.

13 L.J. Burpee (1873–1946) was appointed to the federal civil service in 1890 and was secretary of the International Joint Commission, 1912–46. He was a prolific writer of well-researched works on Canadian subjects, particularly the history of exploration. He was the first president of the Canadian Historical Association.

14 *Canadian Historical Association Annual Report, 1922* 8

15 F.R. Latchford (1854–1938) at this time resided in Toronto, but was educated in Ottawa and practised law there before his career in politics and on the bench. He became judge in 1908 and was appointed Chief Justice in appeal, Supreme Court of Ontario in 1923.

16 W.D. Le Sueur (1840–1917) was a civil servant, journalist, and author. His biography, *Count Frontenac*, was published in The Makers of Canada Series, 1906.

17 *A Short History of Canada for Americans*, 2nd ed. (Minneapolis 1944) 249

18 Stanford White (1853–1906), American architect and designer of several important buildings including Madison Square Garden, where he was murdered by Harry K. Thaw.

19 The Shelburne (Lansdowne) Papers were purchased by Wm. L. Clements from Sotheby and Co. in 1921, and subsequently presented to the library of the University of Michigan.

20 Smith to Burt, 18 August 1925, RG 37, PAC

21 Carl P. Russell (1894–1967) received his PH D in history from the University of Michigan and became a member of the staff of the US National Parks Service.

22 C.H. Van Tyne (1896–1930) taught at the University of Michigan from 1903 until his death. An influential teacher, he was the author of many important works on United States history.

23 *The Press Bulletin*, UAED, IX, No. 5 (23 November 1923)

24 *Ibid.*, IX, No. 9 (15 February 1924)

25 *L'Echo du Collège d'Edmonton*, II, No. 7 (25 mars 1924)

26 Lavergne to Burt, 10 April 1924, Burt Papers, PAC

27 Burt to Tory, 12 December 1927, Tory Papers, UAA

28 In 1966 the University of Toronto Press reprinted one of these volumes with Burt's notes, under the title *Sir Guy Carleton*.

29 William R. Watson, *My Desire* (Toronto 1935) 40

30 *The Press Bulletin*, UAED, XI, No. 4 (8 January 1926)

31 *Ibid.*, XI, No. 4 (8 January 1926)

CHAPTER 7 CONSTITUTIONAL ISSUES OLD AND NEW

1 *Cambridge History of the British Empire* VI (Cambridge 1930) ch. 6, 'The Problem of Government, 1760–1774'

2 A.S. Morton (1870–1945) was educated at the University of Edinburgh and in Berlin. He was head of the Department of History at the University of Saskatchewan from 1914 to 1940.

3 A.U.G. Bury (1869–1951) was educated at Trinity College and King's Inn, Dublin, and practised law in Edmonton. He was Member of Parliament for Edmonton East 1925–6 and 1930–5, and mayor of Edmonton 1927–9.

4 L.B. Pearson, Prime Minister of Canada 1963–8. Pearson was educated at the universities of Toronto and Oxford, and taught history at the University of Toronto, 1924–8.

5 D. Donaghy, Liberal member for Vancouver North

6 Collins was the Conservative candidate in the Peace River riding in the election of 1925 and was defeated by a narrow margin. With the support of the Conservative opposition, he petitioned the House of Commons to set aside the result because of proven irregularities in the conduct of the election, but no action was taken prior to the dissolution of the House. See *House of Commons Debates, 1926*, 'Peace River Election.'

7 Burt's information was incorrect insofar as Macdonald was concerned, but two other Liberal appointments to the Senate were made: see *House of Commons Debates, 1926* 5098.

8 S.F. Tolmie (1867–1937), Member of Parliament for Victoria, BC, federal Minister of Agriculture, 1919–21, and subsequently premier of British Columbia, 1928–33

9 See W.R. Graham, *Arthur Meighen* II (Toronto 1963) 419–23, and E. Forsey, *The Royal Power of Dissolution in the British Commonwealth*, 2nd impression (Toronto 1968), chs. 5 and 6, and pp xix–xxiv.

10 The King ministry and the Alberta government had negotiated an agreement for the transfer of the natural resources to the province, but when King subsequently succumbed to pressure by Bourassa to include a proviso that the Roman Catholic minority be given specific guarantees of a share of the proceeds from the sale of school lands, the Alberta government demurred and the agreement was not ratified.

11 Walter Duncan, a confidential inspector in the Department of Finance

12 Woodsworth, however, continued to vote with the Liberals.

13 J.J. Saucier to L. Ogden, 29 June 1969, History Club Records, UAA

14 Bury was in error so far as the time of Lord Byng's interview with Forke is concerned – it was after Meighen had agreed to form a government.

15 Bury was defeated in the 1926 general election by a narrow margin.

16 O.D. Skelton (1878–1941) was educated at Queen's University and the University of Chicago. He was Professor of Political Science at Queen's from 1908 to 1925, and Under-Secretary of State for External Affairs from 1925 to 1941.

17 J.L. McDougall was educated at the University of Toronto, the London School of Economics, and Harvard. He was an instructor in economics at Toronto in 1926–7, and taught at Queen's from 1932 to 1966.

18 J.S. Ewart (1849–1933) practised law in Toronto, Winnipeg, and (after 1904) Ottawa. An advocate of Canadian independence, he wrote a number of books and articles, including *The Kingdom Papers* and *The Independent Papers*. He was also the author of *The Roots and Causes of the War 1914–1918*. For a discussion of his ideas, see F.H. Underhill, 'The Political Ideas of John S. Ewart,' Canadian Historical Association, *Annual Report* (1933) 23–32.

CHAPTER 8   THE FLOWERING OF CANADIAN HISTORY

1 Robert Herrick, *Seek and Find*
2 The new wing of the Public Archives building was opened in 1926.
3 E.A. Cruikshank (1853–1939) was educated at Upper Canada College and began his military career in 1877. After overseas service in World War I, he was appointed director of the historical section of the general staff. He was the author of numerous historical studies and was also the first Chairman of the Historic Sites and Monuments Board of Canada.
4 W.A. Mackintosh was educated at Toronto, Queen's, and Harvard universities. He was Professor of Economics at Queen's, 1925–7, and Principal, 1951–61.
5 G.E. Wilson was educated at Queen's and Harvard universities and was Professor of History at Dalhousie 1919–69, an unequalled period of service in a Canadian Department of History. He is the author of a biography of Robert Baldwin.
6 J.B. Brebner (1895–1957) was educated at Toronto and Oxford universities, and taught at Toronto from 1921–5, and at Columbia University, 1925–57. He was the author of several significant studies on the colonial history of Nova Scotia and on the exploration of North America. *The North Atlantic Triangle* is his most important work.
7 Chester Martin (1882–1958) was educated at the University of New Brunswick and was the first North American Rhodes Scholar at Oxford. He taught at the University of Manitoba for twenty years, and was head of the Department of History at Toronto from 1929 to 1952, succeeding George M. Wrong. His publications include several pioneer studies (the earliest appearing in 1914) on the history of the Canadian West.
8 W.M. Whitelaw, 'Canadian History in Retrospect,' *Canadian Historical Association Annual Report, 1956* 38, 40. Whitelaw was born in 1890 and was a graduate of the University of Toronto, Union Theological Seminary, and Columbia University. He had a peripatetic university teaching career, and was the author of the brilliant and original work *The Maritimes and Canada Before Confederation*, published in 1934.
9 Séraphin Marion was educated at the University of Ottawa and the Sorbonne. He was the French editor in the Archives. Mr Norman Fee informed the author that the visit referred to here was in the home of Marion's father, who was an employee of the architect's branch of the Department of Public Works.
10 Norman Fee joined the staff of the Public Archives in 1907. He served in various capacities until 1929, when he became Director of the Map and Picture divisions. From 1938 to 1956 he was Assistant to the Dominion Archivist, and acting Dominion Archivist in 1948. He retired in 1957.

11 Sir Hugh Graham, Baron Atholstan (1848–1938), founder and publisher of the *Daily Star*, the *Family Herald* and *Weekly Star*, and the *Montreal Standard*, and prominent member of the Conservative party

12 Doughty to Borden, 30 November 1920, RG 37, PAC

13 Doughty to Meighen, 28 April 1921, RG 37, PAC

14 Doughty to G.M. Wrong, 13 May 1921, RG 37, PAC

15 G.M. Smith (1888–1947) was educated at Toronto and Oxford universities. He was a specialist in modern European history and international relations. He came to Edmonton in 1931 as Burt's successor as head of the department, and continued in this position until 1946.

16 G.P. de T. Glazebrook was educated at Toronto and Oxford and taught history at the University of Toronto from 1925 to 1941 and subsequently. He was on the staff of the Department of External Affairs, 1949–56.

17 W.H. Dawson (1860–1948), British author of numerous works on the history of Germany

18 W.R. Graham, *Arthur Meighen*: Vol. II *And Fortune Fled* (Toronto 1963) 420.

19 This was probably a quotation from the former prime minister's speech to the National Liberal Club in the United Kingdom on 18 December 1923, which is referred to in Forsey, *The Royal Power of Dissolution of Parliament in the British Commonwealth* (Toronto 1968) 89.

20 Mr Justice C.A. Stuart, Chancellor of the University of Alberta, 1908–26

21 McArthur wrote Chapters 7, 8, and 9 of the *Cambridge History of the British Empire*, VI.

22 On 7 April 1926, Prime Minister King announced the appointment of a royal commission to investigate the 'Maritime Rights' question, composed of Sir Andrew Duncan, Hon. W.B. Wallace, and Professor Cyrus Macmillan of McGill University.

23 In the general election held in September the Conservative strength declined from 116 to 91. The results were Liberals 128, Conservatives 91, Progressives 20, Others 6. Mackenzie King again became Prime Minister.

CHAPTER 9 LAST YEARS AT ALBERTA

1 Miss Jean Murray subsequently received her PH D from the University of Chicago, and taught at the University of Saskatchewan from 1931 to 1968.

2 J.E.W. Sterling was a graduate of the University of Toronto who received his MA degree in history from the University of Alberta in 1930, and his PH D from Stanford. He has had a notable academic career in the United States, and was President of Stanford University, 1949–68, and on his retirement was appointed Chancellor of that university.

3 'The Imperial Conference,' *The Press Bulletin*, UAED, XII, No. 7 (25 March 1927)
 1–4
4 H.B. Neatby, *William Lyon Mackenzie King, 1924–1932: The Lonely Heights*
 (Toronto 1963) 195
5 Graham Spry was a Rhodes Scholar from Manitoba in 1921, and has had a long
 and distinguished career in business and government administration and as a
 writer on political and economic subjects. From 1927 to 1932 he was living in
 Ottawa as national secretary of the Association of Canadian Clubs and was a
 member of the national executive of the League of Nations Society.
6 C.P. Meredith was General Secretary of the League of Nations Society in
 Canada.
7 The Judicial Committee of the Privy Council gave its decision on the respective
 claims of Canada and Newfoundland on 1 March 1927. The Canadian government had argued for a boundary which would have confined Labrador to a
 narrow strip one mile inland from the high-water mark on the sea coast.
 Newfoundland's claim, with some minor modification, was accepted by the
 Privy Council.
8 *A New World or the League of Nations* (Ottawa 1927) 12
9 Lionel Groulx (1878–1967), cleric and historian, with a long and productive
 career as a teacher and author; founder (1947) of *Revue d'Histoire de l'Amérique
 française* and the author of many works on French-Canadian history and
 contemporary affairs. A vigorous defender of the nationalist cause in Quebec,
 Groulx had a profound influence on several generations of students.
10 H.H. Love, president of W.J. Gage and Co. from 1919 until his retirement in
 the 1940s, was responsible for Gage's specialization in school textbook publishing.
11 A.L. Burt Papers, PAC
12 The Royal Society met for the first time in western Canada at Winnipeg in May
 1928. Burt's paper, 'Governor Murray and the British Government,' was
 presented by Chester Martin, a Fellow of the Society. See *Transactions of the
 Royal Society of Canada*, 3rd series, XXII, section ii (1928) 49–56.
13 *The Press Bulletin*, UAED, XIII, No. 3 (14 March 1928) 1–4. Selections from
 this apologia are reproduced as Appendix 1 of this work.
14 A.L. Burt, *High School Civics: A Brief Treatment of the Civics Section of History* 3
 (Edmonton 1928) 81 pp. Authorized for use in the schools of Alberta by the
 Honourable Perren Baker, Minister of Education
15 Herbert Heaton (1890–1973) was born in England and educated at the universities of Leeds and Birmingham, and the London School of Economics. He
 taught in Australia, 1914–25, at Queen's University, 1925–7, and was professor of economic history at the University of Minnesota, 1927–58.
16 A.L. Burt to Mrs Dorothy Burt, 22 April 1928

17 R.G. MacBeth, *The Romance of Western Canada* (Toronto 1918)

18 A.L. Burt to Mrs Dorothy Burt, 27 April 1928

19 Herbert Heaton to the author, 24 March 1971, describing the observations of his daughter who took courses from Burt

20 A.L. Burt to Mrs Dorothy Burt, 2 June 1928

21 J.C. Saul was editor-in-chief of W.J. Gage and Co. from 1919 to 1939.

22 Lorne Pierce, editor of the Ryerson Press, 1920–60

23 W.N. Sage (1888–1963) was educated at the universities of Toronto and Oxford and taught history at the University of British Columbia from 1918 to 1954, and was head of the department, 1932–53.

24 D.R. Michener was born in Lacombe, Alberta, and was selected as Rhodes Scholar from the University of Alberta in 1919. He practised law in Toronto, 1927–57 and was elected to the Ontario legislature and later to the House of Commons, where he served as speaker. He was appointed Governor General of Canada in 1967 and retired from that post in 1973.

25 James Malcolm (1880–1935) was Minister of Trade and Commerce from 1926–1930.

26 A.L. Burt to Mrs Dorthy Burt, 3 May 1928, a letter written from Minneapolis

27 L.H. Gipson (1880–1970), was Professor and Head of the Department of Government and History, 1924–46. He is the author of the monumental 14-volume work *The British Empire before the American Revolution*.

28 J.W. Schulz (1859–1947), author of *My Life as an Indian, The Story of a Red Woman and a White Man in the Lodges of the Blackfeet* (New York 1907) and numerous other works on western Indian life in the United States

29 J.P. Pritchett was educated at Stanford and Queen's universities. He subsequently taught at Queen's, the University of North Dakota, and, from 1938 to 1950, at Queen's College of the City University of New York.

30 The Russell, at the corner of Sparks and Elgin streets, was the chief Ottawa hotel from the earliest days of the capital until the turn of the century. It was destroyed by fire in 1927, and the property was expropriated by the government.

31 B. Claxton (1898–1960), was educated at McGill and practised law in Montreal and taught commercial law at McGill. Liberal member of Parliament, 1940–54, and a prominent member of the federal cabinet 1944–54

32 A.L. Burt to Mrs Dorothy Burt, 19 July 1928

33 Review of Corbett, *Henry Marshall Tory, Beloved Canadian*, *Canadian Historical Review*, xxxv (1954) 348–9

34 'The Quarrel Between Germain and Carleton: An Inverted Story,' *CHR*, xi (1930) 202–22

35 *The Press Bulletin*, uaed, xvi, No. 3 (12 December 1930) 1–4

36 See above, 107
37 W.L. Morton, *The Progressive Party in Canada* (Toronto 1950) 267
38 See above, 38, A.L. Burt to Mrs Dorothy Burt, 9 March 1919

CHAPTER 10   FIRST YEARS AT MINNESOTA

1 A.L. Burt to Mrs Dorothy Burt, 27 April 1928
2 *Ibid.*, 29 April 1928
3 'For Guy Stanton Ford, A Debt Only History Can Pay,' *Minnesota Alumni News* (February 1963) 10
4 A.L. Burt to R.C. Wallace, 24 April 1930, Wallace Papers, UAA
5 Burt to Wallace, 2 April 1931, *loc. cit.*
6 A.L. Burt to C.K. Burt, 27 January 1944, Burt Papers, PAC. Subsequent references to Burt's letters to his father are all from this collection.
7 Professor H. Heaton to the author, 24 March 1971
8 *Canadian Historical Review* XV (1934) 196
9 G.M. Wrong to A.L. Burt, 4 January 1934, Burt Papers, *loc. cit.*
10 R. Coupland to A.L. Burt, 10 November 1937, Burt Papers
11 Michel Brunet, *Les Canadiens après la Conquête, 1759–1775* (Montreal 1969) 18
12 *Canadian Historical Review* XLI (1960) 330–1
13 *Canadian Historical Review* XVII (1936) 74–6
14 *American Historical Review* LVIII (1952–3) 961
15 *Minnesota History* XVIII (1937) 83
16 *Canadian Historical Review* XXXVII (1956) 177–8
17 A.L. Burt to C.K. Burt, 11 October 1936
18 *The United States, Great Britain and British North America* 184
19 *American Historical Review* XLVII (1941–2) 87
20 See, for example, B. Perkins, ed., *The Causes of the War of 1812: National Honour or National Interest?* (New York 1962); G.R. Taylor, ed., *The War of 1812: Past Justifications and Present Interpretations* (Boston 1963).
21 A.L. Burt to C.K. Burt, 11 October 1942
22 See A.L. Burt to C.K. Burt, 31 May 1945. Abbé J.T.A. Maheux (1884–1967) was educated at Laval University and Paris. He taught at Laval for over thirty years, and in 1938 was appointed archivist of the Quebec Seminary. He was a strong advocate of a better understanding between French-speaking and English-speaking in Canada.
23 *A Short History of Canada for Americans* (Minneapolis 1942) 250
24 A.L. Burt to C.K. Burt, 19 March 1942

25 A.L. Burt to C.K. Burt, 11 October 1942
26 W.L. Mackenzie King to H.H. Love, 12 December 1942, Burt Papers, *loc. cit.*

CHAPTER 11 INTERNATIONALIST

1 Undated offprint, *St Paul Sunday Pioneer Press*, 'Can Modern Civilization Be Saved?'
2 A.L. Burt to Forrest Burt, 8 February 1938, Burt Papers, *loc. cit.*
3 A.L. Burt to C.K. Burt, 8 April 1944
4 Burt Papers, *loc. cit.*
5 Allan Nevins and Louis M. Hacker, eds., *The United States and Its Place in World Affairs, 1918–1943* (New York 1943) vi
6 A.L. Burt to C.K. Burt, 13 February 1943.
7 Nevins and Hacker, *The United States and Its Place in World Affairs, 1918–1943* 392–3
8 Herbert Heaton to the author, 26 May 1972
9 Burt Papers, *loc. cit.*
10 L. Bryson, L. Finkelstein, and R.M. MacIver, eds., *Conflicts of Power in Modern Culture* (New York 1964) 596
11 See A.L. Burt to C.K. Burt, 12 April 1942 and preface to C.F. Kraenzel *et al.*, *The Northern Plains in a World of Change* (Canadian Association for Adult Education 1942).
12 See brochure of the Canada-United States Committee on Education, October 1951, Burt Papers, *loc. cit.*
13 See offprint from *The United States in the Postwar World: Addresses Given at the 1945 Summer Conference of the University of Michigan* (np 1947).
14 A.L. Burt to C.K. Burt, 27 April 1944
15 A.L. Burt to C.K. Burt, 21 February 1946 *et passim*
16 *Transactions of the Royal Society of Canada, 1946*, Proceedings 51
17 See letters to Miss Louise Olsen, secretary of the Department of History, copies in the possession of the author.
18 A.L. Burt to C.K. Burt, 29 July 1943
19 J.A. Walden (D.C. Heath and Co.) to A.L. Burt, 19 February 1943, Burt Papers
20 *Canadian Historical Review* xxxviii (1957) 62–4
21 Charles Mowat to A.L. Burt, 19 September 1956, Burt Papers, *loc. cit.*
22 See above, p 45
23 Professor Herbert Heaton to the author, 24 March 1971
24 Professor Carl Berger to the author, 24 July 1973

CHAPTER 12 COMMITTED SCHOLAR AND DEDICATED TEACHER

1 *Ottawa Journal*, 28 September 1957, 'Carleton's Burt Rewrites History'
2 Alvin C. Gluek, Jr to John Arthur Burt, 7 July 1971, Burt Papers, *loc. cit.*
3 Louise P. Olsen to the author, 4 January 1971
4 'Unpublished Reminiscences' of Louise P. Olsen: selection of material on A.L. Burt and Mrs Burt supplied to the author
5 A.L. Burt to C.K. Burt, 15 November 1945
6 *Events* (February 1937) 131–2, 133–4
7 *Ibid.* (July 1937) 70
8 *The Press Bulletin*, UAED, 12 December 1930, 'Our Dynamic Society'
9 'Our Dynamic Society,' *Minnesota History* XIII (1) 6
10 *Canadian Historical Review* XXII, p 437
11 Arthur Marwick, *The Nature of History* (London 1970) 180
12 *Ibid.* 19
13 See above, p 56

Index